✔ KU-731-142

Social Science Library
Oxford University Library Services
Manor Road
Oxford OX1 3UQ
WITHDRAWN

9 MAR 1992

TJ
163
.15
.ENE

WITHDRAWN

3 0587 69/

WITHDRAWN

WITHDRAWN

Energy for Rural Development

EDITED AND INTRODUCED BY
M. R. BHAGAVAN & STEPHEN KAREKEZI

Proceedings of the United Nations Group of Experts on the Role of New
and Renewable Sources of Energy in Integrated Rural Development,
organized by the New and Renewable Sources of Energy Section,
Department of International Economic and Social Affairs (DIESA),
United Nations, at Stockholm, Sweden, 22–26 January 1990.

ZED BOOKS LTD
LONDON AND NEW JERSEY

Energy for Rural Development was first published by
Zed Books Ltd., 57 Caledonian Road, London N1 9BU, UK and
165 First Avenue, Atlantic Highlands, New Jersey 07716
for and on behalf of the United Nations in 1992.

Copyright © The United Nations, 1992

Cover design by Sophie Buchet
Typeset by Opus 43, Cumbria
Printed and bound in the United Kingdom
by Biddles Ltd., Guildford and King's Lynn

All rights reserved

A catalogue record is available from the British Library
US CIP is available from the Library of Congress

ISBN 1 85649 037 8

The views and opinions expressed in the specific papers are those of the authors and
do not necessarily reflect those of the United Nations.

Published with the support of the Swedish Agency for Research Cooperation with
Developing Countries (SAREC)

Contents

Abbreviations

ABE	Advisory Board on Energy
AED	Alternative Energy Development
AFREPREN	African Energy Policy Research Network
AGA	Assistant Government Agent
AT	Appropriate Technology
BGT	Biogas Technology
BTC	Botswana Technology Centre
C	Centigrade
CDRE	Centre for the Development of Renewable Energy
CEB	Ceylon Electricity Board
CEMAT	Centro Mesoamericano de Estudios sobre Tecnologia Apropiada
CERER	Centre d'Études et de Recherches sur les Energies Renouvelables
CISIR	Ceylon Institute of Scientific and Industrial Research
CNEEMA	Centre d'Études et d'Experimentation du Machinisme Agricole Tropical
CRES	Centre Regional sur l'Energie Solaire
CSC	Commonwealth Science Council
DPW	Department of Public Works
ECOWAS	Economic Community of West African States
ECUP	Extended Coal Utilization Project
ENDA	Environnement et Developpement du Tiers-Monde
EOES	End-Use Oriented Energy Strategy
ERC	Energy Research Council
ERL	Energy Resources Limited
ESCAP	Economic and Social Commission for Asia and the Pacific
ESCWA	Economic and Social Commission for Western Asia
ESMAP	Energy Sector Management Assistance Programme
ETC	ETC (Foundation, Leusden, The Netherlands)
FAO	Food and Agriculture Organization
FWD	Foundation for Woodstove Dissemination
GJ	gigajoules
GRES	Groupe Energies Renouvelables
GRET	Groupe de Recherches et d'Echanges Technologiques
GS	Gramasevaka
ha	hectares
IDB	Industrial Development Board
IDRC	International Development Research Centre
IDS	Institute of Development Studies
IFC	International Finance Corporation
IFIAS	International Federation for the Institutes of Advanced Study
IIED	International Institute for Environment and Development
ILO	International Labour Organization
IRDP	Integrated Rural Development Project
IREDP	Integrated Rural Energy Development Plan
IT Pubs	Intermediate Technology Publications
ITDG	Intermediate Technology Development Group
kcal	kilocalories
kg	kilogrammes

KJ	kilojoules
KW	kilowatts
KWh	kilowatt hours
LESO	Laboratoire sur l'Energie Solaire (Mali)
LESO	Laboratoire Solaire (Togo)
LNG	Liquefied natural gas
LPG	Liquefied petroleum gas
m	metres
MHD	Macro-Hydro Dynamics
MJ	megajoules
MRWA	Ministry of Mineral Resources and Water Affairs
mt	metric tonnes
mtce	million tonnes of coal equivalent
mtoe	million tonnes of oil equivalent
MW	megawatts
NCR	National Council for Research
NCRD	Non-Conventional Resources Division
NDP VI	Sixth National Development Plan (Botswana)
NERD	National Engineering Research and Development
NIR	National Institute of Development Research and Documentation
NORAD	Norwegian Agency for International Development
NRE	New and Renewable Energy Authority of Egypt
NRECA	National Rural Electric Cooperative Association
NRET	New and Renewable Energy Technology
NRSE	New and Renewable Sources of Energy
OAPEC	Organization of Arab Petroleum Exporting Countries
OAU	Organization of African Unity
ODA	Overseas Development Administration
ONERSOL	Office de l'Energie Solaire
P	Pula
PDRY	People's Democratic Republic of the Yemen
PV	photovoltaics
R	Rupee
RAPA	Regional Office for Asia and the Pacific
RF	Revolving Fund
RIIC	Rural Industries Innovation Centre
RRA	Rapid Rural Appraisal
RREDS	Regional Renewable Energy Development Service
s	seconds
SADCC	Southern African Development Coordination Conference
SAREC	Swedish Agency for Research Cooperation with Developing Countries
SERI	Solar Energy Research Institute
SHP	Small Hydro-Power
SIDA	Swedish International Development Agency
SSA	Specified Supply Areas
toe	tons of oil equivalent
UNCTAD	United Nations Conference on Trade and Development
UNDIESA	United Nations Department of International Economic and Social Affairs
UNDP	United Nations Development Programme
UNEP	United Nations Environment Programme
UNICEF	United Nations Children's Fund
UNIDO	United Nations Industrial Development Organization
UNIFEM	United Nations Development Fund for Women
UNITAR	United Nations Institute for Training and Research
UNU	United Nations University
USDA	United States Department of Agriculture

Preface[*]

GÖRAN OHLIN
ASSISTANT SECRETARY-GENERAL,
DEPARTMENT OF INTERNATIONAL ECONOMIC &
SOCIAL AFFAIRS, UN/DIESA

I need not remind this audience how essential energy is to the development process. In a sense, economic development is essentially the mobilization of various forms of energy, partly to replace human or animal work, partly for totally new uses. Energy is not just another element in the production process. In a broad sense, it is the lifeblood of the biosphere itself. The brief and dramatic explosion of industrial production in the last two hundred years has been based on the consumption of fossil fuels formed millions of years ago.

It took a long time for Member States to agree to discuss energy in the United Nations, but, in 1981, the Nairobi Programme of Action for the Development and Utilization of New and Renewable Sources of Energy recognized that, in rural development, energy was a priority.

Ever since then, this issue has been on the agenda of the UN, both in the General Assembly and in the Committee on the Development and Utilization of New and Renewable Sources of Energy. The Committee first met in 1983. It has hammered away on the need for more attention to energy planning, both in a broad sense and in the context of rural development. In the spring of 1988, at the fourth session of the committee, it decided to put the contribution of new and renewable sources of energy to rural development on the agenda of the fifth meeting, for detailed consideration.

What are the issues? Rural areas need energy for rather obvious purposes: in the household they need it for cooking, lighting and water supply, and they need it for the modernization of agricultural cultivation and for rural industry. But in developing countries most of the energy in rural areas comes from traditional and non-commercial sources such as fuelwood, crop residues, and dung. Commercial sources such as coal, oil and gas do not account for more than 10 to 20 per cent.

But population is growing fast in urban areas and the pressure on traditional sources of energy, such as fuelwood, is already quite excessive and environmentally destructive in many parts of the world. And this pressure is not going to recede in the foreseeable future, in spite of the great migration to urban parts that is taking place.

[*] Based on the opening statement made at the Group of Experts Meeting.

Today, some two-thirds of the people in developing countries, or 2.7 billion, live in rural areas, and by the year 2000 it is expected to be 3 billion, with over 2.3 billion in Asia, half a billion in Africa, and about 120 million in Latin America.

How will their energy needs be met? At the time of the UN Conference on New and Renewable Sources of Energy in 1981 it was widely expected that the price of oil, which was then about US $34 per barrel, would continue to rise. This generated increased interest in new and renewable sources of energy and both governments and private corporations initiated ambitious programmes in many areas in an attempt to harness these non-conventional resources. At the same time, both bilateral and multilateral aid organizations expanded their activities in the field.

Following the sharp drop in oil prices after 1986, interest in new and renewable sources of energy has waned. There have been major cutbacks in the funding and related activities. The cutbacks have perhaps been more severe than would be justified by a realistic and up-to-date evaluation of future energy trends. Lower oil prices have provided a breathing space for oil importing developing countries. Future energy prices are obviously uncertain, but they may well be significantly higher than now; even without this incentive, the search for new and more rational energy systems in rural areas has already been given considerable momentum.

So far, it is true that renewable sources of energy have failed to meet their promise in rural areas. Many factors have contributed to this. Many new and renewable sources of energy technologies have not yet become economically competitive with those alternative energy sources. There has been a lack of policy support, in many instances arising from general neglect of the rural sector; this has contributed to the paucity of investment in new and renewable sources of energy projects in rural areas. There is a resistance to the new technologies. Rural poverty, which largely rules out commercial energy sources, may also make it difficult to undertake even very modest investments in renewable energy, especially in the absence of governing interest.

Obviously, it would not make sense to advise new technologies that would make energy for rural development more expensive than greater reliance on commercial sources such as oil. But a number of NRSE technologies have been quite successful. Examples include small-scale hydro plants for electricity generation, wind pumps, biogas plants for cooking and lighting and photovoltaic units for lighting and refrigeration. According to recent estimates, the worldwide contribution of new and renewable sources of energy, including traditional sources, is more than 1 billion metric tons of oil equivalent annually. This is slightly over 13% of total energy supplies, a little less than natural gas, and more than three times as much as nuclear energy.

In the developing countries, new and renewable sources of energy provide an average of 30% of consumed energy. In Africa it is as high as 57%, in Latin America 33% and in the Asia and Pacific region 22%. These results are most encouraging. Considering that the technologies we are talking about are still in their infancy, the future potential seems very great. But many things will have to be done to exploit this potential. There has to be greater participation of the users, more information about new technologies, and above all there has to be investment.

New and renewable sources of energy still have not found their rightful place in national energy plans and strategies. Energy supplies must be ahead of the rest of development, as the power shortages in many developing countries remind us, and rural energy needs are even more vital. Paper plans will not help. Governments have an essential role in charting future needs and the ways to meet them, and they should explore all channels, private and public.

Introduction

M. R. BHAGAVAN AND S. KAREKEZI

This publication brings together nineteen papers which were presented at a meeting of energy experts from both developed and developing countries held in Stockholm in January 1990. The meeting was sponsored by the Swedish Agency for Research Cooperation with Developing Countries (SAREC) and organized by the United Nations Department of International Economic and Social Affairs (UNDIESA) and the Food and Agriculture Organization of the United Nations (FAO). The experts adopted a report which was presented to the Committee on the Development and Utilization of New and Renewable Sources of Energy at its fifth session, 26 March–4 April 1990. The report highlights energy consumption and supply; technological options; social, cultural and political aspects; environmental aspects; energy investment and pricing; and proposals for further action. The participants are listed at the end of this book.

While the theme of the meeting was the use of new and renewable sources of energy in integrated rural development, some of the authors range beyond this somewhat restricted brief to include an examination of the role of conventional non-renewable modern energy forms such as fossil fuels.

One reason for the limited success of renewable energy programmes in promoting rural development is that they rarely have been applied to improving productivity and income in the agricultural and non-agricultural sectors. Their role hitherto has been limited to meeting subsistence energy needs (cooking and heating) in the households. Agriculture accounts for the bulk of the workforce and the national income in developing countries, but for only one-tenth of the consumption of modern forms of energy such as electricity and fossil fuels. The paper by Gustavo Best, which opens the volume, stresses the importance of a mix of energy resources and technologies, including conventional non-renewables, in raising productivity and income in rural areas.

National energy policies and plans rarely focus on the rural sector. Gustavo Best points out that institutional and operational mechanisms for promoting energy programmes are thin on the ground in the countryside. This has led to lack of guidance for energy interventions in the rural areas, compounded by low levels of energy allocation and investment. He goes on to argue that while a number of proven renewable energy technologies already exist in some fields, others need to be developed further and tested in the rural context, with particular attention to the economics of the technology. The complexity of rural energy problems and the number of possible solutions necessitate a coordinated approach by users, technicians, planners and authorities. One can learn much from the relatively successful methodologies and programmes of energy assessment, planning and implementation carried out in developing countries such as Brazil, China, Colombia, India and Indonesia.

In the formulation and implementation of energy programmes, a mix of centralized ('top-down') and decentralized ('bottom-up') approaches are required, with local structures, relations and institutions being given due consideration. Gustavo Best underlines the need of local groups for the training and tools with which to design and implement their own programmes. The local private sector and grassroots organizations have important roles to play in the manufacture and marketing of renewable technologies. The financing of these activities will call for innovations in institutional and credit arrangements.

It is not unusual to find explanations of the rural energy and environmental crises that 'blame the victim'. Rural people are often painted as the (unwitting) agents of land degradation and deforestation. Such approaches avoid examining the role of the dominant political and economic forces, both internal and external, that oblige rural people to adopt self-destructive short-term solutions to their problems. Irene Tinker challenges these 'blame the victim' attitudes. She argues that the strategy of 'identifying the wrong problem' is not conducive to the design of programmes that are supposed to ameliorate the energy crisis of the rural poor. She examines the social, cultural and economic factors that affect the implanting of renewable technologies among rural communities. By skilfully weaving real-life experiences from various countries, she demonstrates that local participation, particularly by women, is central for success in planning and implementing energy programmes. She sees skewed development strategies, pricing policies, rapid urbanization and population growth as the critical issues.

The dissemination and implementation of proven renewable energy technologies have run into difficulties because of the unexpected complexity of the challenges involved. Stephen Karekezi explores several dimensions of this complexity. Dealing with the economic and social aspects of the strategies required he emphasizes, like Gustavo Best and Irene Tinker, the active involvement of rural communities in shaping their own energy futures. That said, several areas remain which can only be addressed effectively on a wider national basis. Of these, Karekezi pinpoints four.

The first is the availability of technical and techno-economic information. Decision makers at both the policy and field levels are often severely handicapped by inadequate access to relevant data on resources as well as technologies. This results in continued reliance on foreign technical assistance, stifling domestic initiative.

Judgements based on the performance of 'stand-alone' energy devices are not enough. They have to be matched by knowledge of how technologies function as parts of a system in the rural environment. This second area includes the need to train local people in the repair and maintenance of devices and systems.

The central role of entrepreneurs in the manufacture, marketing and servicing of equipment is the third area, while the fourth raises the question of unexploited opportunities for saving energy in agriculture, rural transportation and agro-processing industries. Many of the measures required for energy conservation and efficiency require an in-depth understanding of local and national patterns of energy use and resource availability.

The high expectations that prevailed in the 1970s about the breakthroughs in the use of renewable energy sometimes led to over-ambitious projects which failed because of undue haste in planning and design. 'Overselling' of the potential of renewables, both by equipment suppliers and well-meaning enthusiasts, without due warning of technical and organizational hurdles to be crossed, led in the end to a loss of credibility in some developing countries. A classic example was the project to build a wood-fired thermal power plant of 200 MW capacity in the Philippines in the late 1970s, requiring over 70,000 hectares of tree farms spread over more than 60 sites. Ernesto Terrado analyses the failure of this project and of several other renewable programmes in other parts of the developing world. But he also points to notable successes, concluding that renewable projects should identify the niches they can fill, plan carefully, and be realistic in their objectives.

The need for careful planning in renewable energy development in the rural areas is reiterated by Dominic Mbewe who reveals the complexity involved in this sector and underscores the necessity for user needs assessments prior to the dissemination of renewable energy technologies.

J. Massaquoi rounds off the assessment of key issues in Part I with a comprehensive presentation of the potential of agricultural residues as an energy source, demonstrating convincingly that they can make a profound contribution if properly utilized.

Part II focuses on the rural energy experience in sub-Saharan Africa. Michael Bassey reviews rural energy research and development activities in Central and West Africa and identifies the major obstacles. Using detailed data from Botswana, John Diphaha illustrates how rural energy development can prove to be more viable if environmental costing is taken into account. Diphaha demonstrates that the adverse cost of deforestation can be used to justify rural electrification programmes and the development of other suitable energy options. The section ends with a paper by Wardi Hassan that outlines the main renewable energy activities in the Sudan, where commercialization is the framework within which most rural energy initiatives have taken place so far.

The papers by Anhar Hegazi and Mahmoud Saleh provide accounts of rural energy activities in North Africa and the Middle East, which form the subject of Part III. Hegazi concentrates on North Africa and systematically outlines the main renewable energy activities in Egypt, Libya, Algeria, Tunisia and Morocco. Saleh presents a long-term biogas energy programme in the Democratic Republic of Yemen that has successfully involved local artisans and women in the dissemination and use of biogas technology.

Part IV examines the rural energy experience in Asia. As expected, the scale and range of rural energy programmes in China and India are impressive. Da Xiong Qui and Maheshwar Dayal provide comprehensive reviews of rural energy activities in China and India, respectively. Their papers show that although renewables have become integral and established components of national energy development programmes in these countries, they are still very small relative to the immense conventional, non-renewable programmes involving the use of fossil fuels. Using a novel methodology for bio-energy assessment which is both intensive and extensive, C. Seshadri puts forward a strong case for an even larger renewable energy programme in India. He supports his analysis by providing new evidence of the dominance of biomass in the country's energy picture. Sri Lanka seems unique in creating an institutional infrastructure specifically tailored for a national integrated rural energy programme. B. P. Sepalage gives details of this infrastructure, how it came to be put in place and what is expected of it in the future.

In Part V, the papers from Mexico and Jamaica present contrasting pictures of renewable energy situations in the Latin American and Caribbean regions. Manuel Martinez assesses the rural energy sector in Mexico and shows that in spite of the country's massive petroleum resources and the heavy subsidies that fossil fuels enjoy, the rural sector still depends heavily on traditional and renewable energy resources such as biomass and solar energy. After presenting the main renewable energy initiatives in rural Mexico, Martinez argues for a larger programme and outlines an action plan.

Dennis Minott argues that, with the exception of Trinidad and Tobago which is an oil-producing country, the renewable energy option is the most logical choice for most countries in the Caribbean. It is his contention that conventional energy systems which depend on imported fossil fuels are both vulnerable and expensive in comparison with the renewable energy which can be mobilized locally. And that the development of the region's abundant renewable energy resources is being hampered by conservative adherence to conventional energy systems. In Minott's view, renewables are, by their very nature, anti-monopolistic, more democratic and less amenable to centralized control, and thus eminently suitable for decentralized deployment in both the urban and rural areas of the Caribbean.

In Part VI, Eugenie Nadezhdin provides a long review of renewable energy activities in the Soviet Union and Eastern Europe. Given the acute energy shortages that have arisen in recent years in several areas of this vast region, Nadezhdine's paper is a timely contribution showing the potential renewables have for bridging energy gaps in today's world and in the future.

I KEY ISSUES

1 The Role of Renewable Energy Technologies in Rural Development

GUSTAVO BEST

Introduction

Although energy has always been a vital input in the process of economic development, its critical role in sustaining economic growth, particularly in developing countries, was not recognized until after the first oil price hike in the early 1970s. Since then, many developing countries have utilized a number of measures such as setting up institutional mechanisms, organizing programmes and evolving policies and plans for their energy sectors on the basis of assessment of their energy situations. This assessment has revealed the following significant common features:

- low per capita energy consumption, especially in rural areas;
- much higher elasticity of energy consumption with respect to gross domestic product than in industrialized countries, pointing to the fact that energy inputs are high in relation to overall economic growth;
- consumption of a major proportion of commercial energy in the urban, industrial and transport sectors, with the agricultural and the rural sectors getting only a small percentage of the total commercial energy;
- 'non-commercial' energy sources (fuelwood, cow dung, agricultural wastes) providing the largest proportion of the total energy, since these sources are typically outside the monetized economy and consumed mainly in the rural areas.

The above features bring out not only the sharp disparities between the energy situation in developing and industrialized countries, but also those between the rural and urban areas of developing countries.

The widespread shortage of energy in most developing countries, especially those that do not produce oil, has had most impact on rural areas. These areas have become trapped in subsistence-level economies characterized by inefficient use of 'non-commercial' energy, low agricultural productivity and poor standards of living. Sometimes, even fuel for cooking purposes is not readily available.

Many developing countries have, in the recent past, started programmes for the promotion of new and renewable sources of energy (NRSE)[1] to tackle

3

their rural energy problems. These programmes include biogas, improved cookstoves, social forestry schemes for fuelwood, low-grade solar thermal energy systems, wind energy, biomass and gasifiers. While these rural energy programmes are mostly at the demonstration stage, those for biogas, improved cookstoves and social forestry have made good progress in many countries. However, their overall impact in containing the rural energy crisis has been limited. One reason is that they are being treated as separate ad hoc activities, with little relation to one another, to rural development efforts, to the situation at the grassroots level, or to end-use requirements.

Another reason for the limited success of these programmes in promoting sustainable development in the rural areas is that they contribute mostly to meeting subsistence energy needs for cooking and heating (through biogas, improved cookstoves, afforestation). They rarely contribute directly to improving productivity or income in the rural sector, whether agricultural or non-agricultural.

Agriculture, for example, which contributes more than half the national income and provides employment for a large proportion of the workforce, gets only about one-tenth of the total commercial energy in most developing countries. Other non-agricultural income-generating activities (such as agro- and other rural industries) which provide employment for a growing labour force, thus helping to contain rural–urban migration, are often seriously constrained by scarcity of energy for rural development.

Energy policies and plans in most developing countries focus on the energy requirements of the agricultural and rural sectors only occasionally, and then on an aggregate, country-wide basis. This is due to the small impact these sectors have on the national energy balance because of their meagre energy consumption, and also to the inherent difficulty of data collection and management. The dispersed and, at times, non-monetized nature of energy consumption patterns in the rural areas also contributes to this neglect. Energy authorities rarely have institutional or operational mechanisms in the rural areas. On the other hand, most agriculture and rural development plans and programmes do not treat rural energy requirements explicitly, because of technical incapability and ignorance of options. Agricultural and rural development agencies are often incapable of negotiating with electricity utility companies and energy authorities regarding their energy requirements.

This situation has led to a vacuum of authority and lack of guidance for energy interventions in rural areas, resulting in the scarce allocation of energy resources and a low level of energy investment for rural development and agricultural activities vis-à-vis other sectors of the economy, such as the industry, transport and commercial sectors.

If overall energy development in rural areas is complex and linked to in-adequate policy and programming, the promotion of renewable sources of energy in this context is even more complex. The majority of NRSE technologies have a large utility potential in agricultural, fisheries and forestry activities, but this potential has not been realized. The reasons for this situation and possible solutions to it are the main themes of this study. In the first place, a series of technological issues need to be assessed regarding the level of development of NRSE applications; it is just as important, however, to review the overall development context within which these applications are imbedded.

A new approach to promoting energy for agriculture and rural development is thus required, which considers NRSE decentralized technologies and options in the same context and framework as commercial energy resources and conventional energy technologies. It is clear that only a mix of both conventional and renewable sources of energy can meet the basic needs of the rural people and improve production and income in the agricultural and non-agricultural economic sectors.

This new approach will integrate energy and economic development (including employment creation) with the environmental issues of the rural areas of the developing countries. This linkage of the environment with energy and employment through an integrated approach has become especially relevant in view of the present awareness of environmental issues. The rural energy crisis, rooted as it is in poverty, underdevelopment and resultant ecological destruction, cannot be wished away and must be tackled urgently through this multi-dimensional approach to ensure sustainable, ecologically sound development by providing planned inputs of all types of energy for the subsistence and production needs of the rural population. In this regard, NRSE's role becomes apparent.

The need for an integrated approach to agricultural and rural development has been discussed widely during the past few years. Increasingly, it is being accepted that only through a comprehensive integrated approach can rural energy problems be tackled effectively and the pace of agricultural and rural development accelerated. Many countries are adjusting their energy policies and development strategies to focus on the energy problems of the rural areas. Some countries have already integrated rural energy needs into overall energy and agricultural planning and development efforts, implementing policies which rely on local resources and institutional infrastructure and thus accelerating the entry of NRSE into rural areas.

Although there is consensus on the need for the integrated approach and the role of NRSE in this respect, many problems and constraints must be overcome to make the approach effective and operational. This chapter discusses the technological and non-technological issues which need to be considered. It also discusses the difficulties encountered in developing and implementing strategies to overcome these problems. It is hoped that the conclusions and recommendations presented will be useful in identifying actions to be taken by governments, donors and international cooperation agencies to promote the role of NRSE in rural development.

Rural Energy Requirements

Energy flow in the rural areas

Most household and economically productive activities in the rural areas are linked to an energy supply in one form or another. Cooking, heating, transport, planting and harvesting all require energy inputs; rarely are these characterized explicitly in either qualitative or quantitative terms. This 'implicit' integration does not mean that the full potential of energy in promoting rural development has not been realized. An assessment of the present energy flow and energy requirements in rural areas is needed in order to identify options and strategies to incorporate rural populations into overall national energy development.

The rural sector accounts for almost 40% of the total energy consumption of developing countries (excluding Asian centrally planned economies) according to FAO estimates. Energy-use patterns in this sector centre around the use of biofuels, mainly fuelwood. Conventionally reported energy balances, however, usually represent only monitored energy forms and hence greatly underestimate the actual energy consumption. This characteristic makes accurate assessment of the existing demand for rural energy very difficult (FAO, 1982). It must be noted that special attention has been paid to fuelwood utilization; methodological approaches are available to estimate the flow of this major energy source in rural areas.

Energy flow in the rural areas can be classified in various ways. One classification, proposed by El Mahgary and Biswas (1985), places rural energy in the nine categories illustrated in Figure 1.1. Energy can also be divided into commercial and non-commercial sources. Supply problems are related to lack of assessment of local resources, isolation of rural communities and resultant difficulties in distribution and supply of energy, wastage of available energy resources and lack of energy infrastructure. The main users of energy in the rural sector are households, small-scale industry, agriculture and fisheries, and commercial and other services. Fuelwood is the major source, representing more than 75% of rural energy consumed in developing countries (FAO/ SIDA, 1983).

The demand for energy in rural areas of developing countries could be much greater if accessible, inexpensive and sustainable resources were available. Energy planners often assess and develop resources on the basis of finite supply limits. These resources are not always fully exploited because of the various factors affecting demand. A more recent approach to energy planning is first to assess the energy end-use and then the resources that should be developed. In order to make these estimates, the mechanisms affecting present and future demand must be understood.

The energy consumed by rural populations varies from one region to another for geographical, agro-ecological and socio-economic reasons. Selected estimates of the energy budgets of different rural settlements are presented in Table 1.1. The types of energy utilized and the energy demand figures do

Figure 1.1 Rural Energy Supply and Demand

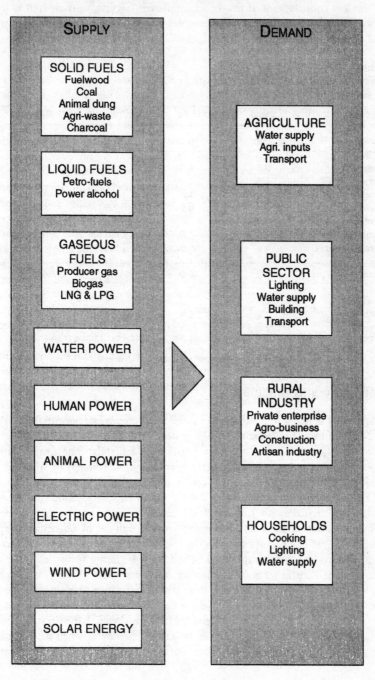

not necessarily reflect a country's commercial energy supply. This is illustrated by the low consumption of fossil fuel in oil-rich Nigeria, as compared to the other countries in Table 1.1. The complex factors influencing energy supply and demand are discussed in this chapter.

Table 1.1
Estimated rural energy flow for selected countries
(in GJ per person per year)

Countries	Thailand	India	China	Nigeria
Sources	8.2	10.7	11.5	19.4
Fuelwood	2.2	4.4	3.6	15.7
Crop residue	1.3	1.0	3.9	n.e.
Dung	n.e.	1.8	0.2	n.e.
Fossil fuels	2.1	0.9	2.5	<0.05
Electricity	0.2	<0.05	n.e.	
Human power	n.e.	1.0	n.e.	3.1
Animal power	n.e.	1.5	n.e.	n.e.
Uses	8.2	10.9	11.5	19.4
Household	3.9	7.0	7.9	15.7
Agriculture	1.8	2.4	2.5	2.9
Other	2.5	1.5	1.1	0.8

Note: n.e. = not estimated
SOURCES: FAO (1987); Revell, (1976); FAO/SIDA (1983); Makhijani & Poole (1975).

Demand considerations

The energy demand in rural areas of developing countries is primarily for the end-user to meet fundamental and basic needs. As mentioned before, there is a major difference between energy needs and demands. The former is an essential requirement, while the latter is an economic concept meaning what a person is willing and able to pay for (in monetary or non-monetary terms).

However, needs are relative to a given set of socio-economic conditions, which can change with time, and are usually much greater than market demand. Demand is therefore a much smaller sub-set of potential energy needs of rural communities in developing countries. Rural energy demand generally involves consumption of relatively few energy forms. Because of the poverty of rural areas in developing countries, most of the energy consumed is non-commercial, coming from the farmer's own production or from the countryside. Obviously, these energy sources are hardly ever present in accounts of national resources or energy balance sheets. Estimates or extrapolations are calculated sporadically by energy planners, when a particular proposal or project requires these statistics. At best, these are rough approximations, rarely integrated in the policies and plans at national level.

DEMAND-CREATING FACTORS

Several factors affect energy demand. One of the most important is the level of development of an area. Subsistence farmers usually do not use commercial energy. However, as living standards rise and agricultural productivity increases, the need for more energy becomes apparent. The use of fertilizers, pesticides and farm machinery leads, eventually, to agro-industrial activities. It can be said that the higher the level of development, the greater the demand for more and varied forms of energy, or vice versa. The appearance of a demand is a sign of development.

The price of energy and the financial policies regarding energy-producing equipment are key factors affecting demand. In general, rural populations are in an unfair situation as regards the price of energy. If autonomous power systems are required, rural people have to pay the entire cost themselves; connected to the electricity grid, they would pay only for the actual power used, the society as a whole meeting the cost of the infrastructure.

Climate is another factor affecting demand: space heating, for example, is sometimes required. The nature of rural activities also has an impact, with competition for resources from energy-intensive technologies. Technological innovation may also create a demand for energy forms hitherto unused. Such is the case when electricity is generated by local resources, or when solar, wind or biomass energy systems become available. Tradition may also affect demand. Taboos and fears associated with certain energy forms should not be underestimated in project planning or in assessing future demands. However, rural people are willing to accept new technologies when there are proven benefits. Increasing emphasis is being placed on people's participation in the planning and implementation process, without which effective and sustainable results are impossible.

Energy demand is also affected by demography. This refers not only to population growth or density but also to pressures resulting from migration out of rural areas, seasonal variations and resettlement programmes.

DEMAND STIMULATION – TURNING NEEDS INTO DEMANDS

Although rural energy demand and development are interrelated, there is some doubt as to which drives the other. The consumption of increasing amounts of commercial energy in the rural sector denotes positive changes in the level of development. However, should the consumption of energy be encouraged (or subsidized) as a means of promoting development? How can demand be made sustainable? Some of the ways in which energy demand can be stimulated are set out below.

Technological innovation, concerned with alternative forms of energy and new end-users, stresses research and development. Over the past 15 years, prototypes have been successfully adapted to local situations and, in some cases, have stimulated demand. The way in which these innovations are introduced and the soundness of their basic design are important with respect to their acceptance and sustainable impact. Technological improvements are adaptations of existing technologies making them more efficient or easier to use. Adaptations, since they do not involve changing an established enterprise drastically, may obtain local acceptance more easily than a new technology.

Extension, information dissemination and training help to sensitize rural populations to their energy resources; if adequate financial schemes are established at the same time, it may also be possible to introduce hitherto unknown sources of energy. The way in which the message is communicated is as important as the message itself. A rural development programme can be an effective vehicle for propagating energy training at various levels throughout a community.

Policies and legislation are often a government's tools to stimulate rural commercial energy demand. Governments can also encourage energy consumption through investment programmes, such as rural electrification schemes, which often operate at a financial loss until increasing demand can pay for the investment. Incomes are meagre in rural areas and consumption of electricity insignificant. Only when activities related to improving agricultural productivity appear, will demand be augmented.

Specific demand considerations for different sub-sectors in rural areas will be dealt with in a later section. One thing is certain, however: rural energy demand can only become greater and more diversified, and effective planning and management will be required.

Supply considerations

Traditionally energy planning and development have taken the supply-side approach, on the theory that if energy resources were available, demand would follow. This obviously does not work so easily in low-income rural areas. As a result, a demand end-use approach was adopted, as mentioned earlier. Supply considerations are nevertheless of fundamental importance in energy planning and resource development. A distinction must be made between the terms 'resource' and 'supply'. The former is defined as untapped and usable potential, while the latter implies that this resource has been made available to consumers. A raging waterfall is a resource of little use until it is harnessed through turbines to produce a supply of electricity.

Settlements develop where there are sufficient resources to sustain the basic human requirements. These resources include energy. As rural communities expand, energy supplies can become overstretched. Competition for fuel results in a flow of energy out of the rural areas, as urban centres (with more income) encourage marketing efforts. Rural people may be forced to switch to alternative fuels (of a less marketable variety), which also affects supply. Price, both local and neighbouring, has its impact on the amount of energy brought to the market. These market factors provide an entry point for non-monetary fuels to become commercialized.

As the demand grows, so does the search for alternative energy sources. Certain crops have been reclassified as energy crops: food crops such as sugar cane, cassava and maize are grown for conversion to ethanol. Technological change can have a positive effect on the supply of energy. This involves innovation and improvement in collection, production, distribution and utilization practices. Technology also has a role to play in enhancing supply through improved production and harvesting techniques. Many examples of increased energy supply can be traced back to technological advancements.

Land tenure and proprietorship laws can affect energy supply by promoting the production of energy crops over food crops, or vice versa. Legislation, as mentioned earlier, directly influences supply through the regulation of stocks, harvesting rights and the prices paid for the produce. Alternative land use may affect energy supply. Unexpected deliveries of fuelwood as a result of land clearing may cause a glut on the local market, whereas six months later, there may be a shortage caused by these same land-clearing activities.

Agricultural energy

In most developing countries, agriculture is a major economic sector, in terms of both employment and of gross domestic product. As rural populations advance through a process of development, technological improvements replace traditional agricultural methods. From an energy perspective, these changes bring about a need for more energy from both fossil and non-fossil sources. In many developing countries, however, the level of development has not yet reached the stage where any great utilization of agricultural machinery can be observed. For the majority of developing countries, agriculture represents only a minor part of the total national energy balance.

One of the activities with the greatest energy requirement is mechanized irrigation. A comparison of traditional and transitional practices for irrigated rice production in the Philippines showed a 37-fold increase in energy requirements when improved technological methods were practised. This involved the use of inorganic fertilizers, pesticides, farm machinery and a diesel pump for irrigation (FAO, 1977). Reported energy inputs were 6.39 GJ/ha compared with 0.17 GJ/ha for transitional/traditional practices. Rice yields were more than doubled with improved cultivation. Energy inputs for rice grown in the United States are about 64 GJ/ha, with yields twice as great as the transitional practices of the Philippines. The growing realization of environmental degradation due to energy-intensive agricultural practices is leading to a more rational approach to resource and productivity management. Although low-input farming is essential if sustainable agriculture is to be attained, clearly more energy inputs are still required in the farming systems of most developing countries.

The differences in agricultural practices with respect to energy flow and crop yield have been studied in the case of mixed farming in Senegal. Traditionally, one ox was used for cultivation of rice, peanuts and millet. Improved techniques introduced two oxen with a better-designed implement, agrochemicals and better horticultural practices. The human energy input was only slightly higher with improved technology. Total energy was raised by 0.11 GJ/ha, while production increased by 73% (CNEEMA, 1972)

Household energy

The household sector consumes the greatest amount of energy in rural areas, primarily in the form of fuelwood for cooking. Household energy consumption in developing countries is high compared to consumption in the rural sector as a whole. This is true despite the absence of space-heating requirements in tropical areas and the generally simple style of life. This relatively high consumption reflects the small amount of energy used for productive activities and is due in part to the inefficiency of end-use technologies. When analysing household energy-use patterns, the fuel type as well as the appliance used should be examined. In the majority of households, fuelwood is used on the open fire with a 'three-stones' arrangement.

Most authorities agree that as long as fuelwood remains available, it will continue to be used widely for cooking in rural areas of developing countries. Apart from the fact that fuelwood is the traditional source of energy in these areas, another reason for its popularity is that, while other fuels are unavailable or expensive, wood is generally a 'free' commodity in rural areas. An open fire provides the household with light and heat, and acts as a social focal point. Wood smoke both flavours and preserves food, and keeps insects from infesting the organic material of the house's walls and roof. Some societies have spiritual beliefs related to the household fire. Fuelwood is also easy to use and provides a wide range of cooking temperatures.

Some of the drawbacks are the daily drudgery and time wastage in collecting fuelwood, the seasonal difficulties in obtaining dry wood, the increasing scarcity of fuelwood, poor thermal performance and subsequent wastage of fuel, ailments related to smoke inhalation and eye irritations, usually afflicting women. Other problems, especially in arid zones, are the environmental degradation resulting from cutting trees for fuelwood, which can lead to deforestation, soil erosion, desertification and climatic changes.

Most rural populations have no choice but to use fuelwood for cooking. If this traditional fuel is unavailable, other less-valued sources are generally employed. If more efficient, clean, inexpensive and easy-to-use fuels were available, it is likely they would replace the problematic fuelwood. The role of other renewable sources has to be enhanced in this respect. In regions where space heating is required and where there is unrestricted fuelwood collection, consumption estimates are between 2.6 and 2.9 tonnes of fuelwood per person per year. In areas where space heating is not a necessity, the annual per capita consumption generally drops to between 1.2 and 1.5 tonnes. (Leach & Gowan, 1987) The percentage of biofuels in the rural household energy budget tends to be independent of income level, the factor which governs the pattern of energy consumption in urban areas.

Fuelwood is being substituted for cooking purposes by LPG, kerosene or coal in many countries which have established price policies to this end. Critical wood supplies or socio-economic development strategies have motivated these policies, which will have a strong effect in the medium term.

Energy for small rural industry

Small-scale industries in developing countries consume, on average, less than 10% of the total rural energy budget. The rural industry is characterized by its small size and decentralized nature, which complicates energy distribution from a centralized production facility. For this reason, the autonomous, small-scale energy generation of NRSE technologies can be a suitable solution for rural industry.

The main energy forms used by rural industries are process heat and mechanical power, supplied manually in most rural applications in the poorer areas. However, small motors using diesel or torque electricity are becoming more common. This is especially true of high-speed operations. Diesel is preferred for applications requiring power of 3 KW or above. Low-speed, high-torque requirements are often supplied by draught animals or water power. In many countries, small hydro-power and wood-fired energy plants are operating in selected sites. Large numbers of solar and wind systems are being demonstrated and windmill rehabilitation programmes are under way.

Process heat is supplied through the combustion of wood, coal, oil or bio-mass residues. Low-grade heat from solar energy for crop and fish drying is a widespread application. Consumption rates vary considerably from one process to another, with a vast range of power requirements. Drying processes need low installed capacities, while brick and cement making, forging and baking require much higher temperatures over shorter periods. There is a wide variation in thermal efficiency within any one process due to the techniques, equipment and energy forms used. Energy can be conserved by improved stove design, insulation, continuous as opposed to batch processing, recycling exhausted heat, and using downdraft convention flow.   Several NRSE technologies lend themselves to small-scale rural industry. The most obvious is biomass combustion in the form of gasification, biogas or direct combustion. Waste organic material can be used to process heat and electricity. Wind and solar energy may also have a role to play in specific locations.

Energy in fisheries

The energy requirements of fishing communities are of particular relevance in many developing countries. Renewable energy resources are well suited to the special energy requirements of the fisheries sector. Indeed, many NRSE technologies have been used for centuries in the fishing industry. Wind energy is perhaps the most obvious example. Recent activities concentrate on the introduction of sails for fishermen's boats. Sails have been redesigned, both in form and material, to make them more energy-efficient. Design improvements are also being introduced to hulls and fishing nets to reduce drag and conserve energy.

Fish curing and preservation, traditionally by smoke, salt, or sun drying, can be enhanced through improved techniques. Solar dryers can accelerate the drying time, protect the fish from flies, other contamination and inclement weather, and reduce the labour input in the drying process. Better designs for fish-smoking kilns use less fuelwood and improve the working environment in the smoking chamber. Recent improvements suggested for some FAO fishery projects include the establishment of fuelwood plantations adjacent to the smoking kilns.

In remote, medium-scale fisheries operations, photovoltaics or solar refrigeration can preserve fish destined for urban markets inland. Hybrid systems can also provided a form of production security for isolated fishing communities. There is a need, however, for large-scale, cost-effective absorption refrigeration systems than can be fuelled by renewable energy. Another area that could receive more attention is conservation and more efficient use of fisheries by-products and renderings, possibly as recycled energy. Other maritime produce could also be valorized. Seaweed could be solar dried and used as an energy source.

Technological Energy Options for Rural Development

Efficient use of energy

Having given an overview of the factors affecting supply and demand, and analysed some of the end-uses of energy in the rural environment, we can now assess the energy options available for rural development.

RATIONAL ENERGY UTILIZATION

In industrialized countries, large national energy conservation programmes have had significant success in instilling energy consciousness into end-users. The result is a lowering of the rate of overall energy consumption in most developed countries since the first oil shock of 1973 (Bach *et al.*, 1980). Such reductions were necessary because of excessive wastage of energy in all sectors of the economy.

There is, however, a belief in a many developing countries that the rate of change of national energy consumption and economic growth curves must be kept parallel and as close as possible if development is to progress at an adequate rate. A more recent approach is to qualify the type of energy being consumed and disengage these two curves while maintaining positive rates of development. This is obviously only possible after a certain level of development has been reached. As energy is often an imported commodity creating a heavy burden on the balance of payments, the amount of non-endogenous energy consumed should be used as efficiently as possible. Rational energy use is a necessary part of any national energy programme. While the rational use of the small amounts of energy presently available is not the answer to the energy needs of rural populations, any saving in energy will undoubtedly benefit rural inhabitants.

Various measures are required in advancing towards the efficient use of rural energy. The conventional approach includes a phase of sensitization using local extension networks, energy need surveys, project planning, pilot scheme implementation, evaluation and eventual expansion of the scheme.

Rural development programmes are especially suitable for local energy awareness and conservation activities, as a variety of sectors of the community are implicated. Energy efficiency can be taken as a general development theme for the entire community. At the operational level, development programmes can help in coordinating and implementing the multi-disciplinary activities through community participation in all phases.

Three stages can be identified in activities aimed at improving energy efficiency. These stages can be referred to as 'pre-use', 'use' and 'post-use'. The 'pre-use' stage includes production, harvesting, transportation, commercialization, collection and storage of energy resources. As the name suggests, the 'use' stage simply refers to the time when the energy source is utilized. The 'post-use' stage involves the use of by-products that can be recycled as energy. This stage also includes the secondary use of energy that has already served elsewhere. It is important to note that the disaggregation of energy-use activities results in a better understanding of how energy conservation can take place.

Improvements in efficiency in the 'pre-use' stage involve agricultural and reforestation techniques and transformation processes, optimizing the use of simple machinery for harvesting and transport, and some simple techniques for fuel commercialization and storage. Energy efficiency during the 'use' stage is a technological issue dealing with the 'hardware' installed and possible techniques for operating it. Better timing of activities may also be included. Energy resource mixes may be pertinent in this phase. Hybrid systems using different fuel types can alleviate supply problems by providing more versatility and choice for the end-user. The 'post-use' stage is the management of residues and by-products for re-use in the energy cycle or for other purposes. This could also include transformation of a by-product into a usable energy form such as ethanol or biogas.

SMALL-SCALE ENERGY SYSTEMS

The concept of integrated rural energy systems has been proposed as a way of developing autonomous production of rural energy throughout the year under varying conditions of supply and demand. The application of this concept results in indigenously produced, self-contained village energy coming from a variety of sources (usually renewable), and operated with the aim of sustainability (INRESA, 1985).

Much of the work in implementing this concept was undertaken by the United Nations University (UNU). Integration takes place at three levels. First, there is integration of several energy sources into a single energy system. Second, there is integration of traditional, improved and new technologies. Third, there is integration of the energy system itself into the social foundations of the local community. The aims of these systems are to decrease local unemployment, stimulate small-scale industry, increase agricultural production and benefit all members of the society, especially rural women. The systems encourage village participation in the decision-making process and stimulate development through increased use of locally produced energy (Shearer, 1989). In essence, these are more or less closed ecological systems. They require community spirit, commitment and collaboration. The mix of human and natural energy resources is a critical factor; in many cases, getting it wrong may limit successful implementation. The concept of an integrated rural system based on biogas and solar technologies has been well received in China.

Fuelwood

REFORESTATION

The basic energy problem of the rural poor is the fuelwood problem. About 80% of the wood harvested in developing countries is used for cooking, heating or small-scale industry in the rural sector. This represented 1,408 million cubic metres of wood in 1985. About 11.3 million hectares of trees are cleared each year from tropical forests (FAO, 1987a). FAO estimates that 50 million hectares of forest must be established by the year 2000 in order to sustain fuelwood requirements. At present reforestation programmes in developing countries plant less than one million hectares of trees annually (Kristofersen & Bokalders, 1986).

It is predicted that, within the next ten years, almost three billion people will be affected by fuelwood shortages in developing countries. They will either have reduced supplies or will lack fuelwood altogether. Already vast amounts of human energy and time are spent each day, usually by women, in the search for fuelwood to meet household requirements. Leach & Gowan (1987) compare 14 fuelwood surveys and report that weekly household collection time ranges from 8 minutes in Indonesia to 38 hours in Nepal. Considering that peasants must often work long hours to scratch out a subsistence living, this time factor is a significant burden.

Fuelwood scarcity is a crisis that cannot be neglected. While the technological know-how exists to meet this difficulty, the major challenge is to find long-lasting solutions, taking into consideration the complex social structure of rural communities. National efforts at reforestation for the purpose of meeting energy requirements have not had much success. One of the most serious constraints in organizing energy plantations is the nature of the fuelwood collection itself. It is estimated that less than 5% of the fuelwood

consumed comes from plantations (Anderson, 1986). State-run forestry programmes are generally understaffed and underbudgeted, further complicating
reforestation efforts.

A holistic view of rural development issues can show ways in which to
solve these problems. Different strategies using the holistic approach have
been adopted in an effort to increase the fuelwood supply. Agroforestry, for
example, attempts to integrate tree-growing with improved agricultural
practices to meet the requirements of food, forage, shelter and fuel. Trees
may be planted on land that normally does not support food crops. When
agroforestry is taken as a means of supplementing the farm with fuelwood,
there need be no loss of crop production. If 2% to 5% of arable land is
planted with trees, crop yields can be maintained and even increased through
improved agricultural practices (FAO, 1985a). Traditional agroforestry has
been practised for many centuries in various parts of the world.

The advantages of agroforestry when nitrogen-fixing trees are used are
soil improvement, wind protection for plants and buildings, 'live fencing' for
livestock, increased fodder production and closer fuelwood supplies (French,
1985). Trees can also be considered as a form of savings for the poor, providing
them with regular income from periodical harvests and long-term security in
cases of extraordinary cash requirements (such as marriages or deaths).
Obviously the question of land tenure and reform, as well as ownership rights
and government policy vis-à-vis tree planting and the usually landless rural
poor, have to be dealt with prior to large-scale acceptance of this concept
(Chambers & Leach, 1989). Also, different legislation with respect to agricultural and forestry lands can be a problem.

Social forestry is another concept that has been used to promote broad-
based integrated reforestation. In addition to forming the administrative and
extension capabilities to sustain such an activity, social forestry programmes
encourage community participation in reforestation, using communal nurseries
and plantations, improved cookstove technology and the development and
commercialization of wood products to meet local market requirements (FAO,
1986).

COOKSTOVES

As fuelwood is the major source of energy in rural areas of many developing
countries, special efforts have to be made to improve one of its most inefficient
end-uses, namely, cooking. One of the ways to do this is by replacing the
traditional 'three-stones' technique for cooking by improved cookstoves. These
cookstoves have been said to reverse the flow of deforestation by saving up
to 50% of the fuelwood consumed by traditional cooking. Nevertheless, the
success of cookstove programmes has been very modest. The whole question
of efficiency has led to much confusion in the dissemination of cookstoves.
A distinction must be made between efficiency obtained under research
conditions and efficiency as actually measured in rural communities by end-
users. Leach & Gowan (1987) proposed average efficiency values for different

cookstoves, which have been accepted by the World Bank. These range from 15% efficiency for the 'three stones' to 25% for the improved portable metal stoves.

As a result of the apparent failure of cookstoves programmes and in the light of cumulative experience, some recommendations can be made for future programmes. These have been selected with a view to their use in overall rural development programmes.

Cookstoves should be promoted at the grassroots level. There must be an ongoing dialogue between technologists and end-users in order to make the necessary design modifications according to local specifications. Any changes in the tested design should not decrease the overall efficiency of the cookstove. The active participation of women, artisans and local extension workers is essential. Training should be targeted at different socio-economic groups with follow-up evaluations to verify the impact of the programme. Ongoing field research should be undertaken to monitor cookstove developments. Some form of credit or incentives should be available to encourage the purchase and use of improved cookstoves (Manibog, 1984; Smith, 1989; Agarwal, 1983).

Cookstove programmes could also promote the non-monetary benefits of improved technology to encourage diffusion. The cost of cookstoves varies according to design and construction materials used, and even a small monetary outlay may be prohibitive for rural populations. For this reason, the cookstove should, where possible, be made of locally available materials.

While cookstoves may not have the secondary benefits of the open fire, which provides smoke for insect control and preservation of food, the direct benefits undoubtedly justify a change to the improved technology (Smith, 1989).

CONVERSION AND SUBSTITUTION

Fuelwood deficits can be met by reforestation and conservation efforts, or, as discussed earlier, by conversion or substitution of fuelwood.

The conversion technologies most widely used are charcoal production and, to a lesser extent, briquetting. Conversion can also take the form of gasification of wood for use in transport, process heat and mechanical power. However, this technology is not fully developed or commercialized, and is not generally accessible to the rural poor. Wood gasification has a proven potential in the context of rural development programmes in a forestry community. An example is the FAO project in Honduras, where gasification of forest wastes from a saw mill produces electricity for the entire community (Trosero, 1989). Other small-scale rural industries use agricultural wastes together with gasifiers to run their equipment. Examples of these installations are found in Asia, where rice and copra wastes are used to produce electricity for threshers, grinders and mills.

Charcoal production is of primary importance in urban areas where transportation of fuelwood is a major constraint. Although considered a wasteful conversion process, carbonization is of considerable economic importance to rural development. Strategies to conserve charcoal include the introduction of improved charcoal stoves and more efficient production techniques.

Traditional carbonization methods are not very energy-efficient and can be improved through better kiln design. Earthen kilns are the norm in rural areas and their efficiency can be improved by lining, chimneys and process techniques.

Although more expensive, brick and metal kilns can increase carbonization efficiency by as much as 30% while producing a better grade of charcoal. Naturally, the choice of technology depends on the capital and resources, both human and material, available locally (Kristofersen & Bokalders, 1987).

Charcoal manufacture is very decentralized; as a result, there is tremendous wastage of energy and capital because of duplication of human and material resources. If charcoal making were set in the context of overall rural development efforts, certain problems inherent in this technology could be alleviated. The first advantage is the opportunity of disseminating information on improved manufacturing and marketing techniques. Secondly, there are shared production inputs, better distribution and credit facilities and more organized marketing of the end product. Thirdly, this grouping of producers can have a positive impact on technology transfer.

Conventional forms of energy

According to the World Bank, the 25 wealthiest countries (about 16% of the world's population) consume roughly two-thirds of the globe's commercial energy. A survey of developing countries found that commercial energy represented roughly one-quarter of total rural energy demand (FAO, 1982). These figures differ from country to country, of course. In China, for example, conventional energy represents 20% of the energy used for production, and 11% of the energy in the residential sector (FAO, 1985b). These figures should be reviewed in the light of recent policies on the promotion of coal for cooking in China.

Conventional fuels have increasing importance in rural areas of developing countries, as rates of development increase. Liquid fossil fuels will continue to represent the largest proportion of commercial sources in agriculture, transport and small-scale industry. Inorganic fertilizers will be the most important commercial energy used in agriculture in developing countries by the year 2000, occupying nearly 60% of total energy consumed in this sector (FAO, 1981).

While rural electrification is a major direct energy initiative in most developing countries, a serious problem is the high cost of installing capacity vis-à-vis the small number of rural consumers. Many developing countries produce rural electrification at a financial loss. These investments are absorbed, albeit with difficulty, into their development effort. Some measures to recuperate the costs can be taken, such as load sharing, discontinuous operation, power reduction and single-phase lines (Menanteau, 1988). One issue related to the development of public utilities is the difference between what could be called 'national' and the 'personal' budgets. As mentioned earlier, those wishing to develop energy capacity at their own expense are disadvantaged compared to those connected to electricity grids, who pay only for the actual power used and not for the overall infrastructure. This inequity can only thwart the efforts of those wishing to promote autonomous development in the rural areas.

There is growing awareness of the need to promote links between rural electrification and rural development programmes in order to exploit fully the benefits of this investment and enhance agricultural productivity and the living standards of the rural inhabitants.

Renewable energy resources

It is widely accepted that technologies based on the use of renewable energy resources have a high potential in rural development. The selection of a NRSE technology is a site-specific exercise, but there is sufficient experience to be able to identify proven and mature technologies and, avoiding the problems that have plagued NRSE projects in the past, move towards their widespread utilization.

Hydrocarbons are playing an increasing role in many countries, especially oil-producing ones, with LPG, kerosene and, in some cases, natural gas being widely used in rural areas. Usually these fuels are promoted through subsidized pricing and efficient distribution schemes. Several non-oil producing countries are assessing the economic, social and environmental benefits at national level of substituting these fuels for fuelwood in both urban and rural areas. The high cost of reforestation, coupled with the socio-economic expectations of the rural people, are factors influencing institutional policies. Inter-country cooperation is important, as can be seen in Central America, North Africa and the Sahelian region.

Mineral coal has been promoted in some countries as a substitute for fuelwood and other biomass. As mentioned earlier, China's household energy balance is being changed dramatically through these policies.

Diesel provides mechanical and electrical power in many rural areas. The scarceness of fuel and absence of technical back-up for repairs and maintenance are considered to be the main problems of this energy option, but there seems to be a large potential for further expansion. Fuel conversion of diesel engines to operate with biogas, producer gas or biomass liquid fuels is receiving much attention and developments in this line are expected shortly.

An overview of the principle NRSE technologies is given below. Each energy source is subdivided into its various end-uses. From this list, a pre-selection process should indicate those applications best adapted to rural energy development.

Table 1.2
Evaluation of the potential of solar energy applications for rural sub-sectors

	Agriculture	Household	Rural industry	Commercial & services	Total rating
Cooking		1		2	3
Water heating		2	2	1	5
Space heating		2		1	3
Drying	2	1	2		5
Refrigeration			2	1	3
Distillation		1	1	1	3
Sterilization		1	1	2	4
Electricity					
photovoltaics	1	1	2	1	5
solar ponds	1		1	2	4

1 = limited potential   2 = strong potential

SOLAR ENERGY

Perhaps one of the biggest disappointments for NRSE researchers has been the limited success of an energy source so abundant in developing countries (more than 6000 MJ of solar radiation per square metre per year in many countries). The two main solar applications are process heat and electricity. The former is adapted for cooking, water and space heating, drying, sterilization, distillation and refrigeration. The latter is mainly used with photovoltaics to provide energy for pumping, lighting and refrigeration devices. Table 1.2 evaluates the different solar applications and the sub-sectors most likely to use them.

This simple analysis shows the technologies most likely to have an impact on rural development. Photovoltaics, solar water heating and solar drying appear to hold the greatest potential. The selection of a suitable technology depends on the site-specific, socio-cultural and economic environment and the amount of energy resources available. The sub-sectors where solar energy applications have the greatest impact are the rural industry and the commercial and services sub-sectors, followed by the household and agriculture sub-sectors. It should be noted that post-harvest agricultural technology has been included in rural industry.

WIND ENERGY

The two main applications for wind energy are mechanical power and generation of electricity. The latter is a relatively complicated technology requiring strong, steady wind, sophisticated equipment (often imported) and storage and transmission facilities. The participation of the public electricity utility or other technical back-up is needed in order to maintain these sophisticated systems.

Mechanical wind-powered systems are a simpler technology, can be manufactured and maintained locally, and require less technical expertise. Wind energy is used primarily for pumping water for rural use or irrigation purposes and, to a lesser extent in developing countries, for grinding grain. The sub-sectors mainly involved are the agriculture and commercial and services sub-sectors. Although wind pumps are simpler machines than wind-powered generators, they are still fairly complicated, requiring regular maintenance and replacement of worn-out parts. There are many locally manufactured designs, especially in Asia. Wind-pumping technology, however, has not been diffused widely, due perhaps to the absence of suitable locations or the high capital costs, prohibitive for small rural communities. Wind pumps by the thousands were displaced by the introduction of electricity, but there is growing interest in rehabilitation programmes in various countries.

BIOMASS TECHNOLOGIES

These technologies use organic materials as fuel, either directly, or through some transformation process. The organic material comes from a natural energy source, such as energy crops, fuelwood, peat or from waste products (agricultural, animal or human). Peat is site-specific, non-renewable and not widespread, and will not be dealt with here. Fuelwood has already been discussed.

The principal biomass technologies, either in bulk or by consolidation (briquetting), are direct combustion, biomass fermentation or gasification and alcohol production. These technologies have been analysed in the same way as solar energy, resulting in Table 1.3 which attempts to identify which processes are adapted to which sub-sectors in the context of rural development programmes.

This analysis indicates that direct combustion and biogas hold the most potential, followed by gasification and alcohol production. Again, rural industry appears to be able to make the most of these NRSE technologies, followed by the household, agriculture and commercial and services sub-sectors.

MIICRO HYDRO-POWER

Hydro-power, while site-specific, represents in many countries a major untapped potential for supplying electricity to isolated communities. Certain political issues related to autonomous power production will be dealt with elsewhere in this chapter. Micro-hydro (under 100 KW) and pico-hydro (under 10 KW) are technologies that correspond to the electricity needs of small villages. There are turbine designs and configurations corresponding to varying hydraulic heads and flow rates, many produced in developing countries. The cost of these small-scale power generation schemes must be kept to a minimum in order to achieve financially viable projects. Three factors contribute significantly to cutting the cost: locally available site-

Table 1.3
Evaluation of the potential of biomass energy for rural sub-sectors

	Agriculture	Household	Rural industry	Commercial & services	Total rating
Direct burning	1	2	2		5
Fermentation		2	2	1	5
Gasification	2		2		4
Alcohol	1		2		3

1 = limited potential   2 = strong potential

evaluation, engineering and management capabilities; locally provided construction; and, wherever possible, materials and diversified end-utilization by the greatest number of consumers (Kristofersen & Bokalders, 1987).

Other hydro-powered technologies that could meet the needs of rural development include hydraulic rams and vertical- or horizontal-axis stream-flow water wheels. These are used to lift water but the latter can also provide mechanical power or pico generation of electricity. Hydro-power schemes can have a positive effect on rural development because of their impact on all sectors of the economy and their multiple end-uses. Various developing countries have ambitious programmes in this field and ample technical experience is available. Further expansion of untapped resources can be predicted.

DRAUGHT ANIMAL POWER

Draught animals have been used for centuries in some countries, while in others their potential has not been exploited. Local breeding programmes and extension infrastructure for animal maintenance can enhance utilization of this energy source. Areas where improvements in age-old technology could have impact on rural development are in the local manufacture of agricultural implements and vehicles, in the use of draught animals for activities such as grinding and pumping, and in the better use of animal by-products for conversion to energy. The use of these animals can significantly reduce human energy requirements in agricultural production and raise productivity in areas such as swamps, where it is impossible to use machinery because of the soil conditions. China and India have the greatest numbers of draught animals, 50 and 80 million respectively.

Draught animal power is well adapted to many rural development schemes because of relatively low capital requirements, simple technology and complementary production of bio-energy, food, fertilizer and hides.

OTHER TECHNOLOGIES

There are a number of NRSE technologies that have not been discussed as they are not considered to be directly applicable to rural and agricultural areas. Among these are vegetable oil fuels, solar power plants, advanced solar thermal heating systems, technologies based on geothermal energy and ocean power (tidal wave, ocean thermal energy conversion) and sophisticated end-use equipment for external or internal combustion engines.

Nevertheless, small-scale vegetable oil fuel plants and low-grade geothermally heated greenhouses can be of interest in selected sites where resources and energy demand coincide.

Selecting viable technologies

Having gained an overview of NRSE and the rural sub-sectors where these technologies could be applied, we can now select energy end-uses with the most potential for implementation. Within each general application there are specific technologies that should be identified and evaluated according to their suitability for rural development programmes. Although an in-depth analysis is necessary for each project and each set of local conditions and constraints, certain general preferences can be expressed for technologies capable of responding to the most common energy needs of rural areas. The following technologies, selected in this way, have not been listed in order of priority:

- photovoltaics
- solar drying
- solar water heating
- wind pumping
- micro hydro-power
- draught animal power
- improved cookstoves
- biomass fermentation
- improved direct combustion of biofuels.

The applicability of these technologies to rural development activities is given in Table 1.4. The processes have been presented separately, though they could have been combined with other NRSE technologies or with conventional energy sources. Hybrid systems ensure back-up energy in case of supply difficulties and can promote more rapid development, with greater exposure to various technologies.

It is of paramount importance that the technology selected should be a viable option for the community. Therefore, factors such as the following should be assessed:

- acceptability of the technology
- financial resources
- economic/social benefits and feasibility
- environmental sustainability
- training and skill levels
- planning and management capabilities.

Table 1.4
NRSE technology in rural development programmes

	Agriculture	Household	Rural industry	Commercial & services
Photovoltaics	Pumping, lighting, cooling, grinding	Community battery re-charging for house-hold use	Lighting, cooling, electricity	Pre-electrification telecommunications
Solar drying	Crop preservation	Food preservation	Tobacco, timber, coffee, tea	
Solar water heating	Dairy, poultry	Bathing, cooking	Textile, process heat	Clinics, schools
Wind pumping	Irrigation, grinding, mech. power	Household water	Process water, mech. power	Rural water supply, clinics
Animal power	Ploughing, pumping, shaft power, transport	Transport	Transport, mech. power, pumping	Transport, pumping
Cookstoves		Cooking		Clinics, schools
Biomass fermentation	Fertilizer, electricity	Cooking, lighting	Electricity, heating	Cooking, electricity
Biofuel combustion	Electricity, crop drying	Cooking, heating	Electricity	Electricity, steam, process heat

The Roles of NRSE in Rural Development

The development role

Even if oil prices were to stay at their current low level, the dependence on commercial energy sources (often imported) is a continuing drain on the rural economy of many developing countries. This could slow down the adoption of new technologies and maintain agricultural output at the subsistence level. The concept of a balanced mix of energy resources, both renewable and conventional, is probably the best approach to stimulating rural development.

The socio-economic development needs of the rural areas of developing countries are so great that they require commensurate efforts to reduce the cost of energy and increase the dependability of supply. This would undoubtedly have a positive effect on the local level of development.

Rural development programmes can be effective only if they have sustainable and economical energy sources to power the infrastructural and technological improvements. While these programmes give impetus to new rural production and industry, NRSE can ensure that these developments will continue to expand. To this newly productive independence is added a certain amount of energy autonomy, which has a multiplier effect on the rural environment and other sectors of the economy. Locally produced renewable energy forms can encourage the diversification of energy uses, stimulating the consumption of other goods and services and resulting in economic growth.

The commercialization of locally produced energy resources within the rural sector or other sectors (e.g., urban or intra-regional) could have a beneficial impact on the rural economy. The synergetic effect of NRSE diffusion would encourage a new infrastructure to maintain, repair and expand these technologies.

The economic role

Many applications of NRSE technology, such as wood-energy systems, provision of electricity to national grids by sugar mills, or the industrial use of charcoal, are having a positive effect on the national economy. Other applications have strong potential.

In any assessment of the economic impact of NRSE on rural development, consideration must be given to the financial as well as the economic aspects. The economic role covers a gamut of variables for different perspectives. Macro-economic differences exist between countries and agro-ecological regions that may affect acceptance or rejection of a particular NRSE technology. As well as the varying perspectives of national government planners and local authorities, there are also micro-economic differences within countries and even within communities which influence the way in which a development initiative is implemented.

A financial evaluation of the energy alternatives, through an analysis of costs and benefits, must include estimates of local discount rates, risk assessment and credit availability. In this regard, some characteristics in developing countries are the high rates of return (often above 30%) expected by farmers; risk aversion and subsequent underestimation of the lifespan of capital equipment; the positive effects on internal rates of return of financial leverage when subsidized credit schemes are in place.

Accurate economic appraisal of these factors is difficult as it involves a valuation of the non-pecuniary development benefits and costs. The social costs of development projects may reflect the additional government services needed to prepare, implement , monitor and carry out a particular development activity. A more quantitative estimate is required of the social benefits of NRSE projects. These may range from improved health to benefits to the environment. Further work is required to standardize the way in which social costs and benefits are assessed (Hutzhusen & Macgregor, 1987).

NRSE have a critical role to play in improving the economic conditions of the rural sector in developing countries. On a national level, the promotion of agricultural production through locally generated energy and efficient use of fossil fuels should have a positive effect on the balance of payments and debt-servicing problems. The rural sector has been badly hit by falling agricultural commodity prices, rising energy import costs (including fertilizer) and poor agricultural output. By promoting the more rational use of indigenous energy through a holistic approach to rural development, an increasing number of farmers can move from subsistence cultivation to surplus agricultural production. Peripheral activities requiring energy, created through rural development, should also benefit from the reduced operational costs of NRSE. As the initial investment costs of many NRSE technologies are still too high for rural communities, financial mechanisms and credit schemes should be established to assist the rural people.

At the local level, simple NRSE technologies such as improved cookstoves can have an immediate positive economic impact by reducing various household costs. There are other possible economic benefits, such as improved family health, greater agricultural productivity and exposure to more advanced technology. It is clear that the economic role of NRSE has still to be fully exploited.

The political role

The political role of NRSE is two-fold: international and national. The international role is to increase agricultural exports. The use of cost-effective renewable energy forms has obvious implications for rural development, and direct consequences in the form of greater agricultural production, food and energy self-sufficiency. The relationships between the balance of payments, debt-servicing, and improved rural development have been discussed previously.

The national role centres on the political environment within the country. The role of greatest relevance to rural development is the inward-looking political orientation of NRSE. In many developing countries, while agriculture may be the main activity, the rural sector is not the top priority in terms of government spending. This is often due to capital-intensive primary and secondary industry, geared towards export earnings. Provided with abundant and cost-effective locally produced energy, the rural sector could contribute to the overall national development, a role which it still has to realize. Investment in rural development is necessary, both in terms of capital equipment and services.

The success of rural energy programmes depends on the government's policies and commitment to rural development policy. Nation-wide programmes that promote energy conservation and autonomous production can also benefit from such political support. Government commitment must be supplemented by legislation that encourages rural people to be more conscious of their energy resources and their environment. Here, too, the NRSE approach has a role to play in providing solutions within the context of rural development by reducing the migration of rural populations from the land and into already overpopulated cities. NRSE technologies also offer local and central governments the possibility of making political decisions that could reverse the trend of global deforestation and desertification, and promote socio-economic growth in rural areas through enhanced productivity in agriculture, fisheries and forestry.

The following are some critical questions that must be asked:

• Are governments prepared to allow local rural communities to have liberal access to energy sources? Are governments willing to address the problems of land reform and ownership, in order to alleviate rural energy problems?

• Are governments willing to invest in NRSE technology, training and transfer programmes, when there are institutional insufficiencies?

• Are governments prepared to take decisions on NRSE and rural development today, in order to avoid the more serious rural energy problems of tomorrow?

• What are the tasks and responsibilities at the different levels of government vis-à-vis implementing energy activities within an overall rural development strategy?

Different types of development will have varying approaches to incorporating energy policies and options into the rural sector. An institutional framework has to be established carefully, with clear-cut roles for all participants, if the concerted and multi-disciplinary action required is to be effective. FAO's integrated approach to energy assessment and planning for rural and agricultural development stresses the need for such concerted institutional action.

The environmental role

Although the strongest impact on the rural environment is caused by poverty, it is, nevertheless, necessary to assess the main environmental issues related to energy production and utilization in rural areas.

Wasteful agricultural practices and poor forestry management are degrading the environment (both locally and globally). Although fuelwood collection plays a small role in this respect, it must be thoroughly assessed in critical sites. The practices responsible for the passage from forest to desert, with all the disastrous environmental consequences, have been well documented. Traditional cooking practices continue to threaten rural women with polluting emissions which contribute to respiratory disease and cancer. Obviously, reducing this environmental menace will have a positive effect on rural development. The environmentally degrading side of other NRSE technologies must also be recognized so that preventive actions can be taken. Hydro-power, while having a positive impact on rural development, has had an irreversible negative impact on the environment: flooding of arable and forest land; disruption and resettlement of tens of thousands of people; and changes in the micro-climate. Micro-hydro does not cause all these repercussions, but the risks should be assessed carefully. The stillage effluent of ethanol and methanol production can pollute the water severely if not properly treated. The stillage produced by Brazil's alcohol programme represents a pollution risk equivalent to the daily sanitary waste of 44 million people (Trindade, 1980). Obviously it is not enough to invest in alcohol-producing equipment alone. Waste management and treatment capabilities are equally important.

Biogas plant effluents are also a potential environmental risk. Untreated waste materials can contain pathogens and parasites that plague rural populations in most developing countries. Processed and handled through appropriately designed biodigesters, however, the effluent contains fewer pathogens than fresh manure.

NRSE technologies should not create new sources of environmental degradation. Environmental impact assessment studies can minimize the risks of direct or indirect hazards.

The socio-cultural role

Perhaps the most difficult task in promoting rural development is to transfer a technical message accurately and fully to people from different socio-cultural backgrounds, and to ensure that the results benefit the target group. The whole socio-cultural question involves differences in tradition, social and economic levels, values, religion, beliefs, education, motivation, language and culture. Some of the differences relate to tribe, caste, religion, race, age group, political affiliation and gender.

Rural inequity and poverty have their roots in the conditions of landless, subsistence agriculture and age-old class structures (Lipton, 1977; Harris, 1977). Rural and urban classes compete directly for scarce energy resources. Usually, the more powerful party wins and rural development becomes stunted. This is particularly true of energy development; the industrial, commercial and transport sectors are usually well trained, organized and capable of evaluating and negotiating their energy needs with energy supply agencies and planners. This is not the case in the rural sector.

Criticism of the lack of NRSE penetration on socio-cultural grounds relates to the unwillingness of government bodies to respond to local energy problems or support village-level NRSE initiatives. Also mentioned is the inability of these same bodies to transfer simple technological solutions (Clay, 1974). Other researchers disapprove of the technology itself, claiming it to be ill-conceived or inappropriate in that it assists the rural rich, who in turn keep the poor in their misery. The marginality of the poor is perhaps the most fundamental and urgent problem in rural development. Rural women are a sub-set of this group, who are often discriminated against and are a critical target group for improved and effective development policy measures. A key issue in this respect is the integration of the energy requirements of rural populations into overall rural development on the one hand, and into national energy plans and strategies, on the other.

Conclusions and Recommendations

Conclusions

A great deal of effort is still needed to bridge the gap between the diffusion of NRSE and energy requirements in the context of rural development goals. Formal links should be established to tie energy options systematically to rural development programmes.

NRSE technologies have come a long way since the 'back-yard' prototypes diffused two decades ago. Today, proven technologies exist which can be promoted in rural development programmes. There is obviously still a need for technological research in order to take other technologies to a point where they can have an impact on rural development.

In the context of rural development programme implementation, all possible and viable NRSE options as well as conventional energy forms should be considered. In order to apply the technologies in the villages where they are desperately needed, technicians, energy planners and extension officers are required. Energy needs have to be assessed and suitable technologies identified by planners, implementers and the villagers themselves in order to find the best technological mix to meet local aspirations and constraints. Rural development is a slow process, but reliable and sustainable energy sources should hasten the pace to long-term improvements for rural people of the developing world.

The following recommendations for action give high priority to two specific fields of rural development: energy assessment and planning; and technological development and research.

Energy assessment and planning

The complexity of rural energy problems, and the number of possible solutions, point to the need for a coordinated decision-making system. In many countries, however, the rural sector has been left to fend for itself and the results have been scarcity of energy and stagnation of development. Many researchers and government authorities recognize the urgent need to set up a rural energy planning strategy. FAO, ESCAP, UNDP and various governments have been active in the development of ways to implement rural energy assessment and

Figure 1.2 Framework for RD & rural energy planning

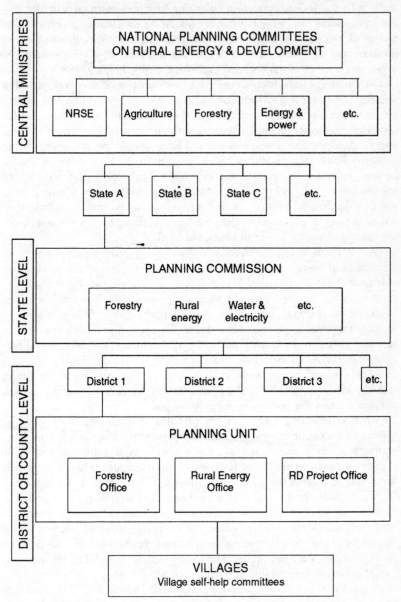

planning programmes. The experiences of Brazil, China, Colombia, Guatemala, India and Indonesia in energy planning have been instructive in identifying and tackling the particular constraints facing developing countries. The methodologies that have been developed must now be diffused, adapted and implemented on a wide basis in developing countries. FAO, accordingly, is organizing a series of national level activities (FAO, 1988b & 1989).

Certain stages have been identified in setting up a rural energy planning strategy. The first is political recognition of the need for action and greater public awareness, and the identification of a government body responsible for the plan's implementation. In keeping with an integrated approach to rural energy development, this top-level taskforce should be the coordinating authority linking the various ministries present in the rural sector; it should be complemented by regional and eventually local representatives working for the same goals. A typical framework for a rural energy planning unit, showing the linkages between sectoral authorities and government administrative structures, is presented in Figure 1.2 (p. 31). Basic energy planning units are suggested at the district or municipal level.

One of the first tasks undertaken by an energy planning unit will be an assessment of energy supply and demand and an analysis of the social infrastructure of the community. Macro-economic data are usually available for rural areas and can be combined with energy surveys in order to obtain the aggregate rural energy balance for the different regions. This will serve to identify the areas requiring urgent action. The use of micro-computers can facilitate this data processing phase. Several computer modelling packages have been conceived especially to assist planners from developing countries to assess current energy flows and predict what they will be in the future (LEAP, MEDEE, APENPLAN, ENERPLAN). Models specializing in rural situations are in the process of being developed.

When establishing a rural energy planning unit, consideration must be given to the existing institutional and organizational framework for rural and agricultural development, and its structure made as accessible as possible to energy planners at the various levels of participation. This is especially important as regards the 'basic unit of focus' (village, district, municipality). This top-down approach should be followed by bottom-up participation in determining local needs and aspirations. Efforts should be made to sensitize local populations about energy issues and the participation of villagers should be sought in the planning process to determine the local energy and development priorities. Care should be taken to consider the views of all the members of the society before establishing an action plan. Proposed solutions at this stage need not involve significant capital outlay, but should lead eventually to more substantial energy-related projects.

Pilot projects could be designed, planned and implemented jointly with regional and local participation. Project monitoring and evaluation are of key importance in order to learn from the project experience and rectify problems.

Replication of projects in other locations necessitates a careful appraisal of local conditions prior to the implementation. The success of pilot schemes and their expansion will accentuate the need for more dialogue between energy planners and decision-makers in rural development. Collaboration between these two groups is dependent on adequate access to information. The creation of rural development databases is an important step in this process.

Finally, while central governments have a critical role to play in coordinating these various activities, decentralized energy planning should also be encouraged. National energy planning budgets are often too small to deal with local issues. The motivation for implementing energy-efficient and capital-effective projects often lies at the local level. It is becoming increasingly necessary to give local groups the tools with which they can design and implement their own rural energy and development plans. FAO has launched activities in the field of energy assessment and planning for rural development in the Asia and Latin America regions which incorporate many of the issues raised in this section (FAO, 1990).

Technological development and research

Despite the many technological innovations that have taken place to date, NRSE have yet to be utilized widely in programmes promoting rural development. Certain technologies have to overcome economic limitations to be cost-effective. Other restrictions relate to the way in which a technology is diffused, ignoring local socio-cultural criteria. Still other problems relate to the technical deficiencies that prevent some technologies from having a sustainable impact. Research and development is needed in these three areas. There is a need to refine the process of economic and financial appraisal of NRSE systems. In many cases, these analyses have not been done, partly due to the absence of consensus with regard to project benefits. Innovation in the financing of projects should have a positive effect on technological diffusion. This effort should also address the question of the commercialization and marketing of NRSE technologies and other energy sources by both the private and public sectors. Mass production has the effect of lowering prices and promoting widespread NRSE use. This cannot happen, however, until economically feasible solutions are found. Innovations are also required in the financing of credit schemes tailored to different regional, ethnic and agricultural backgrounds.

Integrative, adaptive and participative are words that have been used to describe research into and promotion of technologies among different socio-cultural groups. These techniques need to be further developed and applied if NRSE are to have a long-lasting impact in rural areas. The mechanisms behind farmer motivation and the passage out of a subsistence life style need to be better understood.

The NRSE technologies chosen for rural development programmes must be mature, proven technologies. This, of course, does not mean that they cannot be redesigned and improved through more research. There is need to optimize existing designs in order to make them more affordable and efficient. Many NRSE technologies require more investigation before they can be considered as viable options by rural development planners.

From a purely technical perspective, research priorities have been expressed by different authorities. Table 1.5 lists one such case. The importance of these research topics varies from one country or region to another. In order to address these research priorities, an army of technicians will be necessary, working in both the industrialized and the developing countries. For this purpose, emphasis should be placed on the training of new energy researchers, technicians and planners. Expertise in this field will have to be mobilized to assist in the educational process. In-country seminars, training, research and exchange programmes will also have to be initiated in collaboration with existing institutions.

Table 1.5
NRSE research and development priorities

Priority ranking	Subjects
1	Solar photovoltaic technology
2	NRSE planning and management
3	Rural energy planning and management
4	Forestry for fuel
5	Solar thermal energy for heating
6	Small hydro-power
7	Wind water pumping systems
8	Solar crop drying and heating
9	Biogas plants for smallholder
10	Agricultural residues utilization
11	Solar refrigeration
12	Efficient cookstoves

SOURCE: ESCAP (1986).

Technological programmes rather than projects should be the aim. Energy programme objectives will have to be established for both the short and the long term. It is clear that in the short term activities will have to be centralized, operating through national programmes in which research, industrial, financial and commercial institutions participate in a concerted manner. There is an enormous task, in terms of local data collection for research purposes, that can be undertaken using existing manpower and limited extra capital inputs. In the longer term, as the programmes become established, the system can become more decentralized. Local solutions will replace imported technologies. Industry will face a major challenge in the commercialization of energy resources, as the focus shifts from household to small industrial applications. In the long term, if this programme approach is followed, the technologies themselves will be better suited to the needs, conditions and constraints of rural development.

Institutional issues

It is obvious that any attempt to set up a framework for the 'energy in rural development' issue will involve a great many institutions. The recommendations made here should be considered in the context of those made regarding energy assessment and planning.

In most developing countries, there are governmental institutions to coordinate development efforts in the rural sector. As has been stressed, a vacuum of authority exists in relation to the decision-making process for energy in rural areas; the energy ministries in most developing countries give low priority to rural energy due to its small impact on the national energy balance, while the agricultural and rural development ministries rarely deal explicitly with the energy requirements of their programmes and have no technical capability.

The perspectives of these different parties should be considered in the light of the integrated approach suggested. Distinct responsibilities should be assigned to all who are involved in implementation efforts. The local private sector should be involved so as to encourage the manufacture, marketing and distribution of NRSE technology. Grassroots organizations should be involved in the various stages of the programmes. These groups are often respected by rural people, who may look upon government officials with suspicion.

International cooperation should be further promoted for financing and implementing integrated rural energy projects. Rural energy assessment, planning and project design should be included in the explicit objectives of rural development programmes. International support should also come in the form of assistance to research organizations which address the issues of NRSE options for rural development. It is recommended that an international network be established to pool the experience of different researchers and field workers. This type of networking is essential to sensitize government authorities to the problems facing the rural poor, as well as to the possible solutions using local resources. The creation of an international network of research institutions dealing with different energy resources and/or end-uses has been suggested and should now be put in place.

Local credit at preferential rates should be available for energy technologies for the rural poor. This credit could be administered through cooperatives or government-sponsored programmes. Governments could contribute to stimulating energy efficiency and promotion of NRSE technologies through tax facilities, subsidies, land reform or other legislation. These measures will be necessary if any headway is to be made in increasing the energy inputs for rural development, and should be based on policy decisions emanating from the suggested integrated energy assessment and planning framework.

NOTE

1. Defined by United Nations General Assembly Resolution 33/148 as comprising 14 sources: hydro, solar, geothermal, wind, tidal and wave energy, thermal gradient of the ocean, biomass, fuelwood, charcoal, peat, energy from draught animals, oil shale and tar sands.

REFERENCES

Agarwal, B. (1983). 'Diffusion of rural innovations: some analytical issues and the case of wood-burning stoves'. *World Development*, Vol. 11, No. 4, pp 359–76.

Anderson, D. (1986). 'Declining tree stocks in African countries'. *World Development*, Vol. 14, No. 7, pp. 853–63.

Bach, W., Manshard, W., Matthews, W. H. & Brown, H. (1980). *Renewable Energy Prospects*. UNU, Pergamon Press, Oxford, pp. 771–1022.

Chambers, R. & Leach, M. (1989). 'Trees as savings and security for the rural poor'. *World Development*, Vol 17., No. 3, pp. 329–42.

Clay, E. (1974). *Planners' Preferences in Local Innovation in Tubewell Irrigation Technology in North-east India*. IDS Discussion Paper No. 40, University of Sussex.

CNEEMA (Centre d'etudes et d'experimentation du machinisme agricole tropical) (1972). *Machinisme agricole tropical*, No. 38, pp. 329–42.

de Lucia, R. (1983). 'Energy use in agriculture and industry', in:FAO/SIDA (1983), pp. 180–9.

El Mahgary, Y. & Biswas, A.K. (1985). *Integrated Rural Energy Planning*. Butterworths, London.

ESCAP (1986). *Report on the Consultative Meeting on the New and Renewable Resources Programme: Future Directives*. Bangkok.

FAO (1977). *The State of Food and Agriculture, 1976*. Rome.

—— (1981). *Agriculture: Toward 2000*. Economic and Social Development Series, No. 23, Rome.

—— (1982). 'New and Renewable Sources of Energy for Agriculture and Rural Development'. Paper presented to Thirteenth FAO Regional Conference for Europe, Sofia, Bulgaria, 4–8 October 1982, ERC/82/4, pp. 3–7.

—— (1985a). *Wood for Energy*. Forestry Topics Report No. 1, FAO Forestry Department, Rome.

—— (1985b). *Rural Energy Planning in China and Other Developing Countries of Asia*. FAO Environment and Energy Paper, No. 5.

—— (1986). *Developing Social Forestry in Peru*. FAO Forestry Department, Rome, p. 4.

—— (1987a). *The Tropical Forestry Action Plan*. Published in collaboration with WRI, the World Bank and UNDP, Rome.

—— (1987b). 'Rural energy in Thailand: demand supply and policy directions', in *Rural Energy in the Asia-Pacific Region*, RAPA Bulletin 1987/1. FAO Regional Office for Asia and the Pacific, Bangkok, pp. 1–9.

—— (1988a). 'How to make the most of draught animals and the use of draught animals in rural industry', in *Rural Energy in the Asia-Pacific Region*, RAPA Bulletin 1988/2. FAO Regional Office for Asia and the Pacific, Bangkok, pp. 31–4.

—— (1988b). *UNDP/ESCAP/FAO Expert Consultation on Energy Assessment and Planning for Rural and Agricultural Development: Final Report*, Rome.

—— (1989). *Energy Planning for Agricultural and Rural Development* (originally a paper presented by Chopra, S. K., at FAO/ESCAP/UNDP Regional Training Workshop on a Comprehensive Approach to Rural Energy Assessment and Planning, Beijing, China, 1989). Rome.

—— (1990). *Report of Expert Consultation on Rural Energy Planning in Latin America* (Buenos Aires, October 1989). FAO/Government of Argentina (in preparation).

FAO/SIDA (1983). *Wood Fuel Surveys*. Forestry for Local Community Development Programme GCP/INT/365/SWE, Rome.

French, D. (1985). *Agro-Forestry, a New Fashion or Old Tradition?* IFAD, Rome.

Harris, B. (1977). 'Rural electrification and the diffusion of electric water-lifting technology in

North Arcot District, India', in Farmer, B. H., *Green Revolution*. Macmillan, London, pp 102–203.

Harrison, B. (1980). 'Appropriate technology: how can it reach the village?' *New Scientist*, 20 November 1980, pp. 521-3.

Hutzhusen, F. J. & Macgregor, R. D. (1987). *A Multidisciplinary Approach to Renewable Energy in Developing Countries*. Horizons Publishing Company, Columbus, Ohio.

INRESA (1985). *INRESA Newsletter*, No 10.

Kristofersen, L. & Bokalders, V.(1986). *Renewable Energy Technologies: Their Applications in Developing Countries*. Pergamon Press, Oxford.

Leach G. & Gowan, M. (1987). *Household Energy Handbook*. World Bank Technical Paper, No. 67, Washington.

Lipton, M. (1977). *Why Poor People Stay Poor: a Study of Urban Bias in World Development*. Temple Smith, London.

Makhijani, A. & Polle, A. (1975). *Energy and Agriculture in the Third World*. Ford Foundation/ Ballinger Publications, Cambridge.

Manibog, F. (1984). 'Improved cooking stoves in developing countries: problems and opportunities'. *Energy*, No. 9, pp. 197–227.

Menanteau, P. (1988). 'Electrification rural dans les PED'. *Need*, No. 8, pp. 2–6.

Revelle, R. (1976). 'Energy use in rural India'. *Science*, Vol. 192, pp. 969–75.

Shearer, W. (1989). 'Integrated rural energy systems'. *Work in Progress*, Vol. 11, No. 1, UNU, Tokyo, p 2.

Smith, K. R.(1989). 'Dialectics of improved stoves'. *Economic and Political Weekly*, 11 March 1989, pp. 517–22.

Trindade, S. C.(1980). 'Energy crops: the case of Brazil'. Paper presented at International Conference 'Energy from Biomass', Brighton, 4–7 November. 1980, p. 17.

Trossero, M. A. (1989). FAO mission report (unpublished). FAO Forestry Department, Rome.

Wionczeck, M., Foley, G. & van Buren, A. (1989). *Energy in the Transition from Rural Subsistence*. Westview Publishing Company, Boulder, Colorado.

The Political Context of Rural Energy Programmes 2

IRENE TINKER

The political context of energy planning is often avoided in discussions about energy requirements and supply for rural development; yet the development policy choices of international donor agencies and national governments set the parameters within which energy planning and local implementation take place and so condition the success or failure of virtually all projects. In the past, many of these policies were premised on the assumption that the primary culprit in the growing environmental degradation of rural areas is the rural populace. This tendency has been intensified by the global environmental movement.[1]

In the search for new responses to rural energy demand, it is essential to avoid heaping all the blame for deteriorating conditions in rural areas on the backs of the rural inhabitants. While not excusing the rural populace entirely, this chapter identifies the major sources of land degradation as external to the rural poor and argues that to focus solely on their energy needs, without attention to basic developmental policy choices, is simply to blame the victim.

Further, project designs that have begun by identifying the wrong problem are unlikely to work, and may indeed exacerbate the life conditions of the rural poor. Such mistaken problem identification has been a constant issue ever since rural energy programmes were launched over a decade ago. Assuming that rural poor farmers and nomadic herders were destroying forest and savannah cover in their search for fuelwood for cooking, the development community designed two distinct programmes to alleviate the energy shortage: tree planting and improved cookstoves. These solutions utilized contemporary technology but overlooked local needs, particularly those of women.

This chapter will review the evolution of rural energy programmes using case studies to illustrate the current state of the art and raising issues relating to actual development programming which influence rural energy demand and supply – among these, local participation, particularly by women, in the planning and implementation of energy programmes.

The chapter will then address the political context of rural energy planning, identifying governmental development and pricing policies, rapid urbanization and population growth as critical issues driving rural energy requirements and supply. The conclusion is that increased understanding of the local social, economic, and cultural dimensions of rural energy requirements can lead to improved programmes that will assist rural women and men to survive in the short run. To achieve sustainable development in the long run, however, will require a paradigm shift in the approach to global economic development.

Rural Energy Programming

Improving the cookstove

Designing an improved cookstove for rural farmers was the response of the appropriate technology (AT) movement which was gaining adherents in the early 1970s as the development community turned its attention to the basic needs of the poor in developing countries (Manibog, 1984). Early enthusiasm was generated by the Lorena model[2] which incorporated energy efficiencies in optimal laboratory conditions, and was offered to the women on the assumption that saving fuel was a high priority for them. However, women resisted adoption because for the efficient running of the stove they had to cut wood, use high-quality fuel, and keep the fire lit continuously. Other complaints about this model include the size and hence immobility of this large mud structure, lack of lighting, lack of smoke to kill insects and cure foods, insufficient flexibility in use, and difficulty of repair. Nor did women necessarily value fuel-saving over time: faster cooking was often more important to the burdened subsistence household manager (Tinker, 1987b). Onyebuchi (1989) has documented this preference for convenience in a recent field study in Nigeria.[3]

AT organizations rapidly began to move away from the Lorena model and experiment with improving the efficiency of traditional models, consulting frequently with women users of both traditional and experimental stoves. Various models were carefully tested in the laboratory and the results widely disseminated (de Lepeleire *et al.*, 1981). In Africa the three-stone fireplace became a tripod metal frame with wind control on two sides. In India the traditional pottery stove was given additional cooking spaces and vented to provide the 'smokeless *chula*' and reduce indoor air pollution,[4] but adoption has been constrained by the slower cooking of the more efficient stove, which requires adaptation in cooking styles (Bajracharya, 1984; Joshee, 1986).

Portable charcoal stoves made from old kerosene cans, primarily for urban use, have been improved with ceramic sleeves. The all-ceramic Thai pot is also being diffused widely. Reflecting the escalating cost of fuel in cities and their ability to burn low-quality fuel as well as charcoal, these stoves have been adopted more widely than rural models (Ulluwishewa, 1989).

Many AT groups have experimented with solar heaters. Generally, reflected heat is a practical means of warming or even pumping water, but no good for cooking. In contrast, the solar oven/box cooker is enjoying a modest success for the slow cooking of cereals. Biogas digesters have not been adopted widely by individual farmer families in the absence of subsidies, owing to the high installation costs; another problem is the need for technological training to make repairs (Devkota, 1986). As the energy crisis escalates, however, community biogas digesters may provide a viable alternative for rural and urban energy needs.

In the short run, modern fuel substitutes for fuelwood may make sense. Subsidizing kerosene burners has been tried by NGOs in Java. In central Nepal, where low-cost electricity has been made available to local villagers near the Anda Khola dam, a locally made double pot with an electric coil inside has been marketed which is four times as efficient as heating a regular pot on an open coil.

The importance of understanding who benefits from government-sponsored cookstove programmes is illustrated by a project initiated in 1985 in Saliyan, a bazaar in the mountains of western Nepal, and reported by Randall Bluffstone, a Peace Corps volunteer (1987). The project was designed to increase the use of prefabricated smokeless *chulas* and its objectives were both to reduce fuel consumption in an environmentally stressed area and to provide a new source of income for potters after the market was saturated with water jugs. Residents of this district centre buy firewood from rural women who walk two to four hours each way to earn Rs 10–15, a daily wage about 25% below the average male rate. With energy efficiencies of 30%, the saving on the purchase of fuel per week was equivalent to the daily wage of a male labourer. The stoves had some success in the bazaar because this cash saving was significant and because they were sold at a 50% subsidized price. Also, the thin pottery walls were sturdy enough for the urban rice and lentil diet. In contrast, the time saved in fuel collection in the rural areas was an insufficient incentive for cash outlay even at the subsidized price. Further, the traditional corn hash eaten by subsistence farmers requires vigorous stirring likely to crack the clay pot. The project met its objectives: income to potters from selling *chulas* was three to four times greater than selling water jugs, which had reduced the skilled potter income to that of an unskilled worker; and many bazaar families were saving fuel and cash by using the smokeless *chulas*. On the other hand, like many development programmes, this one did not benefit the poorest families.

Increasing attention is given to the diffusion of innovation (Agarwal, 1983). Designers of cookstoves debate how to create an effective demand for new technology in response to national priorities (Joseph & Hassrick, 1984). Even where stoves are given away, as in parts of rural Nepal, one study found only 18% in use (Joshee, 1986). While some suggest that low acceptance is due to inadequate adaptation or sloppy installation (Wood, 1987), others believe that even a good design needs a network of suppliers and trained repairers.[5]

Inventing social forestry

Forestry departments developed a sub-specialty of social or community forestry to address the issue of tree planting for personal use. Because foresters are trained to plant fast-growing straight trees for commercial purposes and to police existing forests, this new focus was alien to them. Many of the early difficulties with social forestry programmes were due to misapplication of established forestry techniques to a very different situation. Monoculture of exotic species may provide locally needed timber and poles, but it overlooks the multiple purposes of indigenous bush and forests for food, fibre, fodder, fencing, medicines and fuelwood. Because timber is commercially traded, it tends to be under the control of men, while the household uses of forest products for subsistence and health are usually women's concerns.

Early social forestry programmes ignored women's expertise in the many-sided utilization of indigenous species and planted commercial varieties instead (Hoskins, 1983). A recent World Bank document on women and forestry notes that only one of the 22 Bank-aided social forestry projects and only four of 33 agricultural projects with a forestry component appraised between 1984 and 1987 mentioned women as potential beneficiaries.

Tree-planting schemes raise issues of use and ownership of the trees and their products. In many areas tree ownership was traditionally independent of land ownership; trees could be controlled by an individual on common land. In Burkina Faso men replant wild baobab trees and utilize its leaves in sauces for the family gruel made from millet or sorghum. But since the tree is owned by the man, if leaves are sold in the market the proceeds belong to him (Williams, 1984, 1985). As the commercial value of fuelwood increased, common land was often converted to social forestry projects. On paper such conversion may look like more intensive use of common land for common purpose. In fact it often meant that the use by women of tree and bush products on common land was abolished; scrubby, useful trees were replaced by commercial exotics with commercial value as firewood. Men sell this wood for private gain while their wives must roam further away to find fuelwood to cook their food (Fortmann & Rocheleau 1985).

Tree planting in refugee settlements in eastern Sudan was confined to individual family compounds at least partly because of confusion over land and tree rights. Even though the trees were distributed free by the development agency and planted within compounds, the survival rate of the trees reflected the economic level of the family. Poor recipients lacked the time to fetch sufficient water for the trees; rich settlers usually purchased water from local entrepreneurs who used wheeled carts or donkeys to transport the water. Besides water, tree seedlings need to be protected from chickens or goats within the compound; in this arid region, the poles and brush to construct fencing must be purchased. Despite the subsidies meant to equalize the access of all the refugee families to the trees, 'the project runs the danger of unintentionally increasing the gap between the rich and poor' (de Treville, 1985:11).

The importance of trees for fodder increases with pressure for 'zero-grazing' or stall feeding of animals. Unlike fuels for cooking which can be stored during the dry season to avoid collecting during the monsoon, fodder must be provided daily. In Nepal, where cattle are essential to hill agriculture because they process biomass into fertilizer which both binds and fertilizes the soil, 35% of the animal feed comes from trees. In the hills there is one large animal per person per family of five or six, a farming system that requires 1.3 hectares of forest land for each hectare of agricultural land (Applegate & Gilmore, 1987).

The stress of fodder and fuel collection in the fragile hills of Nepal has led to a concerted effort by the development community to address the issue. In 1987, there were 68 different agencies in this small country undertaking some sort of forestry programme (Carter, 1987) of which 35 included some sort of community forestry component.[6] The community forestry approach was begun by forester, Tej Mahat, in 1970.

The government of Nepal has passed legislation allowing transfer of national forest land to local village units (*panchayats*) under two distinct programmes. Forest lands under stress are to be enclosed and allowed to rejuvenate naturally: Panchayat Protected Forests. Degraded grazing land is to be fenced and reforested as Panchayat Plantations.[7] Village-level forest committees are to be set up to expedite this transfer, but from the first there was debate over the composition of the committees: should they consist of locally elected village officers, or of users? And if these are to be user committees, should not women be included? Early attempts to set up user committees with women on them were not successful because the women, and the poorer men as well, were dominated by the local elites (King *et al.*, 1988). But in this traditionally patriarchal society, even the attempt is significant, and efforts continue to include the women and men users on the committees.

The actual functioning of this programme frequently adds to the burdens of local women since the fencing of forest areas they use for fuel and fodder requires them to make longer trips, or to purchase these products if they can afford it, or to use agricultural refuse and dung, a practice which depletes the soil. Benefits from the sale of timber are most likely to accrue to the local power elite who head forestry committees. Not surprisingly, fencing does not always keep out the village women. Thus many programmes are experimenting with incentives to encourage cooperation with the government forestry programme. Perhaps the most successful innovation is to plant fast-growing fodder grass between trees in plantations and let the women harvest that instead of trees.

Household issues

Central to changing habits of procuring or using fuelwood are intra-household power relationships. For example, who makes household decisions about expenditure on items such as cookstoves? Given the usual sexual division of labour, with women responsible for both collecting firewood and cooking, men may have little interest in investing in new cookstoves unless status pressure is brought to bear. This approach may explain why so many unused cookstoves are found in rural areas: women are not consulted but men are forced to acquire unadapted stoves. In some African cities, however, men apparently have taken over the provisioning of firewood and are willing to buy improved *jikos* to reduce weekly expenditure (Tinker, 1987b).

Household decision-making also influences the use of renewable fertilizers based on nitrogen-fixing plants or algae rather than chemical fertilizers – so reducing both the energy costs of fertilizer production and the rate of land degradation. Another energy saving is a return to the use of rice husks or bagasse instead of fossil fuels for food processing.

Overlooked in most discussion of household energy use is the fact that many households are also production units for textiles, crafts or processed foods (Tinker, 1987a). Various studies show that the greatest demand for traditional fuels is often in the smallest industries; further, these enterprises are most likely to be run by women (de Treville, 1987). Because poor women are most likely to be at risk if the cost of traditional fuels increases, particular attention needs to be given to ways of subsidizing the adoption of alternative energy sources.

Experience gained in the 15 years of programming for rural energy requirements has clearly illustrated (1) the importance of adapting programmes to local social, economic and cultural factors; and (2) the importance of participation by the affected people in the solutions. Participation itself may be a burden, however, particularly for rural women whose days are already filled with survival tasks (Cecelski, 1985; Tinker, 1987b). Critical are the benefits which accrue from participation.

Political Context of the Rural Energy Crisis

Efforts by the development community to address the growing energy crisis have focused on social forestry and improved cookstoves. While these programmes are certainly important to many local residents, they are in no way sufficient. One discouraging assessment of the crisis in Malawi estimates that, for that country to meet its current demand for fuelwood, every family would have to plant 1000 trees, a most unlikely event as long as there are 'free' trees available in the indigenous forests (French, 1984). This raises the crucial question of pricing. It is well known that governmental pricing policies are often designed to encourage exports to support development or to reduce food costs for urban areas. These policies tend to keep rural areas poor, and so discourage investment in fuel-saving technologies.

Continuing to treat trees as a free good affects real costs of highway construction. The Swiss Aid Agency in Nepal has tried to encourage the use of cold bitumen surfaces on all new roads because current practices of using asphalt require the cutting of trees along the new highways, resulting in severe erosion throughout the hills. Even if contractors replaced the trees they cut, the cost of asphalt would exceed bitumen – and of course new trees do not have the value of mature growth. The extension of highways, especially over the fragile soils typical in Africa and Nepal, are major causes of deforestation but are seldom targeted for intervention by government policy.

By the year 2000, it is estimated that more than 3 billion people – half of the world's population – will live in urban areas. The spiralling demand of urban residents for fuelwood is too often overlooked. The women in Nepal who carry huge loads of firewood are most likely earning a livelihood by selling their loads to urban customers. In much of Africa it is the men who have taken over selling firewood. Programmes aimed at rural users are irrelevant to this type of forest exploitation.

Population growth is a major factor in putting stress on natural resources. Efforts to increase food production to feed this mass of people have led to many of the contemporary agricultural practices that have set up the cycle of destruction. The problem is to design sustainable development in the face of this population growth. The realization of the delicate balance of the global environment is leading to greater questioning of the dominant development paradigm. Vandana Shiva builds on a growing opposition to the values which support contemporary economic growth and encourage rape of the earth. She sees a parallel between the violence of 'the scientific and economic paradigms' created by the western patriarchy and the growth of violence against women. In her book, Shiva identifies the opposition to this western ideology of profit maximization as 'both ecological and feminist' (1989: xviii).

Government pricing policies, transportation programmes, rapid urbanization and burgeoning populations all put pressure on natural resources used by the rural poor. Most development programmes focus only on the victims of these policies rather than on the basic development paradigm and its underlying values. While energy-focused programmes are important in the short run to reduce energy consumption in rural areas, more attention at this level should be given to urban demand. Urban forestry and gardening should be encouraged, along with incentives to change cooking and other fuel consumption patterns. Exploitation of natural resources through corruption should also be identified and punished. But, for the long run, the search continues for a more sustainable development paradigm.

NOTES

1. See, for example, Sandra Postel, 'Halting land degradation', in Lester R. Brown *et al., State of the World, 1989* (W. W. Norton and Co., Washington D.C., 1989), p. 22, where she writes that 'the people themselves are not only degradation's victims but its unwitting agents. The four principal causes of land degradation – over-grazing on rangelands, over-cultivation of croplands, waterlogging and salinization, and deforestation – all stem from excessive human pressures or poor management of land.'
2. This mud and sand range was developed in Guatemala; pot holes are sized to actual utensils, cut firewood is enclosed in a firebox, and heat passes from one pot hole to another and past a receptacle for heating water before being exhausted through a chimney.
3. Efficiency is not a high priority in developed countries, either. A study conducted in the state of Michigan found that energy use could be reduced by 25% over a 20-year period through the purchase of more energy-efficient household appliances. Here convenience may simply be using a familiar appliance or in not having to shop for a new one, or not having to invest in an expensive item even though energy costs over time are higher.
4. Smoke inhalation is an enormous health problem in India. Kirk Smith (1984) reports that one day's cooking in the rainy season in a typical Gujerati rural hut results in inhaling particulates equivalent to 20 packs of cigarettes!
5. Development Alternatives in New Delhi is setting up a franchising system for innovations in building materials for rural use. Its founder, Asoke Khosla, argues that distribution is a key to the diffusion of technology.
6. The 68 projects may be conveniently divided into eight categories. Those with participatory activities include: major afforestation projects (6); watershed projects (15) and NGOs (14). Commercial timber programmes (11), policy research (9), field research (8), local consulting groups (3), and training programmes (2) complete the list.
7. See the special issue of *Banko Janakari, PS. A Journal of Forestry Information for Nepal* (devoted to community forestry management), Vol. 1, No. 4, 1987.

REFERENCES

Agarwal, Bina (1983). 'Diffusion of rural innovations: some analytical issues and the case of wood-burning stoves', *World Development*, Vol. 11, No. 4, pp. 359–76.

Applegate, G. B., & Gilmore, D. A. (1987). *Operational Experiences in Forest Management Development in the Hills of Nepal.* ICMOD Occasional Paper No. 6.

Bajracharya, Deepak. (1984). 'Organizing for energy need assessment and innovation: action research in Nepal', in Islam, M. N., Morse, R. & Soesatro, M. H., *Rural Energy to Meet Development Needs: Asian Village Approaches.* Westview Publishing Company, Boulder, Colorado.

Carter, Jane. (1987). *Organization Concerned with Forestry in Nepal.* Forestry Research and Information Centre Occasional Paper 2/87.

Cecelski, Elizabeth. (1985). *Rural Energy Crisis, Women's Work and Family Welfare: Perspectives and Approaches to Action.* ILO, Geneva.

Cecelski, Elizabeth, Dunkerley, Joy & Ramsy, William. (1979). *Household Energy and the Poor in the Third World.* Resources for the Future, Washington, DC.

de Lepeleire, K., Prasad, Krishna, Verhaart, P. & Visser, P. (1981). *A Woodstove Compendium.* The Netherlands: University of Technology, Eindhoven.

de Treville, Diana. (1985). *Refugee Reforestation Project Eastern Sudan.* USDA Forestry Support Program, Washington, DC.

—— (1987). *Fuelwood-Based Small-Scale Enterprise Assessment: An Analysis of Renewable Energy Users and the Informal Sector.* Equity Policy Center, Chevy Chase, Maryland.

Devkota, Govinda Prasad. (1986). *A Viable Alternative Energy for Rural Nepalese Villages: A Case Study of Gobar Gas.* Forestry Research Paper Series, No. 2, Winrock for HMG, Khatmandu.

Fortmann, Louise & Rocheleau, Diane. (1985). 'Women and agroforestry: four myths and three case studies'. *Agroforestry Systems*, No. 2, pp. 253–72.

French, David. (1984). *African Farmers' Behaviour in Tree Planting: Sociological and Economic Variables in Reforestation*. USDA Agriculture and Rural Development Department, Washington, DC.

Hoskins, Marilyn. (1983). *Rural Women, Forest Outputs, and Forestry Projects*. FAO, Rome.

Joseph, Stephen & Hassrick, Philip. (1984). *Burning Issues: Implementing Pilot Stove Programmes – A Guide for Eastern Africa*. Intermediate Technology Publications for UNICEF, London.

Joshee, Bharat Raj. (1986) *Improved Stoves in Minimization of Fuelwood Consumption in Nepal*. Forestry Research Paper Series No. 2, Winrock for HMG, Khatmandu.

King, G. C., Hobley, Mary & Gilmour, D. A. (1988). *Management of Forests for Local Use in the Hills of Nepal*. Nepal/Australia Forest Project, Khatmandu.

La Rovere, Emilio Lebre. (1986). *Food and Energy in Rio de Janeiro: Provisioning the Poor*. United University Food/Energy Nexus.

Leitmann, Josef. (1989). *Women and Forestry: Operation Issues*. World Bank WID Working Paper, Washington, DC.

Manibog, Fernando R. (1984). 'Improved cooking stoves in developing countries: problems and opportunities'. *Annual Review of Energy*, No. 9, pp. 199–227.

Mayer, Judith. Series of letters written on South East Asia as a Forest and Society Fellow of the Institute of Current World Affairs, 4 West Wheelock St., Hanover, NH 03755 USA.

Onyebuchi, E. I. (1989). 'Alternative energy strategies for the developing world's domestic use: a case study of Nigerian households' fuel use patterns and preferences'. *Energy Journal*, Vol. 10, No. 3, pp. 121–38.

Repetto, Robert, Magrath, William, Wells, Michael, Beer, Christine and Rossini, Fabrizio. (1989). *Wasting Assets: Natural Resources in the National Income Accounts*. World Resources Institute, Washington, DC.

Shiva, Vandana. (1989). *Staying Alive: Women, Ecology and Development*. Zed Books, London.

Smith, Kirk. (1984). *Biomass Fuel Consumption and Health*. WHO, Geneva.

Tinker, Irene. (1987a). 'Street foods: testing assumptions about informal sector activity by women and men'. *Current Sociology*, Vol. 35, No. 3 (monograph: entire issue).

—— (1987b). 'The real rural energy crisis: women's time'. *Energy Journal*, No. 3, pp. 125–46.

Tyler, Stephen R. (1990). 'Urban household energy use in Thailand'. PhD dissertation draft. University of California/Berkeley.

Ulluwishewa, Rohana. (1989). 'A case study of energy use for domestic cooking by urban dwellers in Colombo City'. *Energy*, Vol. 14, No. 6, pp. 341–3.

Williams, Paula J. Series of letters written on Sub-Saharan Africa as a Forest and Society Fellow of the Institute of Current World Affairs, 4 West Wheelock St., Hanover, NH 03755, USA. (1984). No. 12, 'Traditional agroforestry'. (1985). No. 17, 'Women's participation in forestry activities in Burkina Faso'. (1989). No. 32, 'Despite many voices, African women unite'.

Wood, Timothy S. (1987). *Assessment of Cookstove Programmes in Nepal*. VITA, Arlington, Virginia.

3 Energy Technology Options for Rural and Agricultural Development: The Major Issues

STEPHEN KAREKEZI

Over the past two decades, numerous technical options for the generation and distribution of energy for agriculture and rural development have been developed and field tested in a large number of developing countries. Available options include:

- Diesel-powered machinery for mechanized agriculture, transport, agro-processing and the generation of electricity;
- Fuelwood-fired cookstoves, kilns and baking ovens;
- Micro-hydro plants for electricity generation and shaft-power;
- Biogas units for cooking and lighting;
- Wind-powered equipment for water pumping and electricity generation;
- Direct solar energy devices for water heating and crop drying;
- Photovoltaic equipment for lighting, refrigeration and communication;
- Grid electricity for lighting and for providing power to rural agro-processing and manufacturing units.

Numerous energy activities utilizing one or a combination of the above options were initiated in developing countries over the last 15 years. These initiatives were in part a response to world-wide concern over the emerging energy crisis after the oil shock of the early 1970s. The rationale for these initiatives was based on a belief that the wide-scale application of appropriate energy technologies would have a significant ameliorative impact on the energy problems faced by a large majority of the rural inhabitants of the Third World.

While the experience to date has significantly increased the existing stock of knowledge on possible technical options for the rural energy sector, the results of many of the above initiatives have often been below expectations. The primary reason for the disappointing results was the unexpected complexity of developing, selecting and implementing appropriate technical options that adequately address the rural energy question. Key issues that contributed to increasing the complexity include:

1 Urban bias vis-à-vis rural development in general and rural energy issues in particular;
2 Access to information on the rural energy sector and energy technology options;

3 Specialized sub-sectoral approach to energy for agriculture and rural development;
4 Integrated rural development;
5 Endemic poverty of rural areas;
6 Needs and effective demand;
7 Equity issues;
8 User needs and participation.

Urban bias vis-à-vis rural development

The rapid urbanization of developing countries is one of the most significant demographic changes that is taking place in the South. In the case of Asia and Latin America, urbanization is a long-established trend. In Africa, the continent that historically has been the least urbanized, the urban population is expected to double in the next 12 to 15 years (World Bank, 1989). A recent report on African energy policy (Soussan, 1989) states:

> Urban growth rates of up to 10% per year are the norm in Africa and what were rural societies are becoming increasingly urban focused. . . . The corollary of this conclusion is that urban energy demand is of increasing importance, and for some countries may become the dominant energy policy issue in the near future.

This demographic shift is strengthening the historical bias on developing urban areas and has continued to push rural energy issues to the background. From this perspective, mobilizing support for developing and implementing technology options for rural areas has been and will continue to be an uphill task.

Access to information on the rural energy sector and energy technology options

The scarcity and difficulty of obtaining information on the rural energy sector is arguably the single most important constraint in the selection and diffusion of appropriate technology options. Past attempts to collect rural energy data have often been static in nature and content (Barnett et al., 1982). Results provided snapshot pictures of the energy situation and were unable to capture the dynamic and fluid nature of rural energy. Most of these attempts were heavily dependent on formal questionnaires that were often based on questionable assumptions and rationales. To compound the problem, the questionnaires were in most cases administered either by external experts with limited local knowledge or by local personnel with limited training in the collection of survey data.

Partly as a result of this information shortfall, inadequate access to relevant data on energy technologies continues to be one of the key constraints that face decisions makers at both policy and field levels (Board on Science and Technology for International Development, 1984). The information required may vary from an in-depth review of national energy resources to design drawings and specifications of a particular energy technology device. Unavailability of sufficient information has led to increased reliance on external technical assistance which could, in the long term, stifle local development and initiative.

Specialized sub-sectoral approach to energy

Past attempts at addressing the rural energy question tended to focus on specific technologies for generating energy, whether it be a micro-hydro plant or a biogas plant (Bhatia, 1987). Insufficient attention has been paid to other equally vital components of the rural energy system such as:

- The national or district (as the case may be) energy balance;
- The transportation and distribution of energy;
- The manufacture and maintenance of equipment and spare parts;
- Training of users, maintenance personnel and manufacturers;
- Involvement of entrepreneurs in the manufacturing process, and in the marketing and servicing of associated equipment.

As a result, current understanding of how stand-alone energy technologies perform is not matched by an adequate appreciation of the systems environment that is necessary for the successful introduction of rural energy technologies.

Integrated rural development

In the 1950s and 1960s, rural and agricultural development were approached from a perspective that was focused on a single technology: intensive use of fertilizer, for example, or increased use of mechanization. This approach was, in many cases, energy-intensive and required the outlay of costly and high-tech equipment and expertise. A typical example is provided by the numerous large-scale power and irrigation schemes that were initiated in many developing countries.

Within a high-tech environment, the selection and provision of requisite energy services is relatively straightforward. In most cases, there exist adequate and well-tested conventional energy technologies and resources that are available and well understood. The major constraint is usually availability of sufficient financial resources to underwrite the normally large investment that conventional energy technologies entail.

In recent years, a consensus has developed that sees rural development as a multi-faceted issue requiring a diverse range of interventions. The increased reliance on integrated rural development projects is, in part, a strategy to respond to the diversity of the rural and agricultural development sector.

The development ethos that stressed diversity and multiplicity in approaches and objectives has led to the investigation of a wider range of energy sources, technologies, and production and marketing systems. Thus, in addition to conventional energy sources, there is now increased emphasis on conservation options and renewable energy sources such as biomass, solar power, wind and biogas.

Integrated rural development appears to be more amenable to decentralized energy technology options, while the energy needs of high-tech, single-technology rural development initiatives such as power or irrigation schemes are met by centralized energy technology options. The table below, adapted from a recent United Nations report (Hurst, 1986) illustrates this dichotomy.

Table 3.1
Nature of energy technology

	Decentralised technology option	Centralised technology option
End-uses		
Mechanical power electricity generation	Windmills, small hydro-turbines	Power stations/ supplying grid electricity
Heat	Solar heaters, wood heaters	Natural gas distribution
Transportation	Animals	Fuel alcohol, refineries
Investments	Small investments by individuals or groups	Large investment by utilities over long time periods
Technical complexity	Simple manufacturing and metal working	Often complex with 'turn-key' installations
Foreign exchange requirements	Generally low	Often high

Endemic poverty of rural areas

The poverty that is prevalent in most rural areas of the developing world was found to be a major constraint on the successful introduction of energy technologies. In this respect, rural energy was not the only sector to face this problem. Virtually all development efforts in rural areas find that the very limited purchasing power of most rural inhabitants is in certain cases the single most important constraint.

Whether it is a solar photovoltaic lighting unit or a small diesel generator, the rural poor are often unable to raise the required investment finance. An aid agency or the government may provide the initial investment cost but finance for operation and maintenance may still present an insurmountable barrier.

Needs and effective demand

The problem of poverty has another important dimension: the difference between need and effective demand. For example, the rural households in developing countries that need electricity far exceed those who can afford to pay for it – the effective demand. Thus, conventional marketing surveys which focus on the effective demand are of limited use. Too often the underlying need, or what is often referred to as suppressed demand, is ignored.

To address the issue of needs, attempts were made to initiate energy interventions that address basic needs of the rural populace. A typical example is shown below (adapted from a matrix developed by Ashworth *et al.*, 1980):

Table 3.2
Basic needs for energy

Type of activity	Identified need	Available energy technology
Food preparation	Cooking Drying Processing	Wood stoves Solar dryers Diesel-powered equipment
Health maintenance	Provision of potable water Refrigeration	Wind pumps
Agricultural & village industrial production	Irrigation	Micro-hydro

Numerous technology matrices have been developed. These are rarely comprehensive, containing one or more gaps in most cases. For example, the matrix above does not include transport, communication and lighting – which are all basic human needs. While most energy technology matrices have limitations, they provide a conceptual framework for analysis and for planning policy and field-level initiatives.

Equity issues

The need to address basic needs is closely intertwined with the question of enhancing equity in the rural areas. It appears that the introduction of rural energy technologies is not in itself sufficient to address the question of equity.

In certain cases, rural energy technologies can widen income gaps rather than narrow them.

For example, the biogas programme in India is said to have made it more difficult for the rural poor to have access to cattle dung for use as fuel and fertilizer because of the competing demands of the rural middle class, who now use cattle dung as biogas feedstock (Prasad *et al.*,1974; Moulik *et al.*, 1975; and Barnett *et al.*, 1978).

Equity is not only an issue at the field implementation level of rural energy technology. It is of increasing concern at the level of research and development. Hoffman (in Barnett *et al.*, 1982) explains:

> a massive inequality is being built up in the international distribution of capabilities relevant for the exploitation of alternative energy technologies. The pattern of R&D expenditures indicates that substantial research and development capabilities are being accumulated in a handful of industrialised economies, and that their scale far outweighs those being accumulated in the whole of the Third World. . . . In short, this scenario will need little development or elaboration before it looks remarkably similar to the present costly state of affairs with respect to conventional energy technology. . . .

User needs and participation

Addressing the needs of the users and ensuring their participation is increasingly perceived to be of critical importance in the development and wide-scale dissemination of rural energy technologies. A recent study on the development and dissemination of improved cookstoves in Sudan (Gamser, 1988a) is more emphatic on this issue and states:

> Bringing artisans, housewives, and retailers into the technology development process in its stoves programme was, in itself, an institutional innovation for the ERC (Energy Research Council of Sudan). It represented a departure from previous, more insular laboratory-based ventures. This institutional innovation to facilitate a more user-interactive technology development programme was a critical factor in the success of the overall stoves project.

The study goes on to stress that rural energy technologies are no different from more conventional technologies. In both cases, user needs are paramount and user participation is an essential component of technology development.

User needs and participation are no longer in the category of development buzzwords but are prerequisites for the successful implementation of rural energy technologies. This is true of virtually all rural energy technologies, a selection of which are discussed in greater depth in the next section.

Efficient Energy Use

Energy conservation has several intrinsic advantages. First, energy conservation does not entail the high investment and costly financial outlay of exploration and energy production. Energy conservation involves increased efficient use of the existing energy resources. Secondly, a good deal of energy conservation is generally not an equipment-based or machine-intensive technology.

On the other hand, energy conservation is in many ways an information-intensive and management-intensive technology. It requires an in-depth understanding of current energy use patterns in order to identify the most cost-effective and promising conservation opportunities and the management and organizational skills for exploiting these. There the problem lies. Energy use patterns in the rural areas are poorly understood. A global review of energy research issues (International Development Research Centre & United Nations University, 1986) explains:

> Energy statistics in most developing countries are sparse and poorly organized, and permit only aggregated and imprecise analysis . . . efforts should also be made to improve the data base for estimating more detailed and reliable relationships.

Energy for rural and agricultural development is often dominated by biomass-based fuels whose supply, distribution and marketing are very poorly understood. The problem is compounded by the low energy consumption levels of rural areas in general. A recent United Nations report (Centre for Small Energy Resources, 1988) states:

> The low level of energy use [in rural communities] is both a cause and an effect of poverty in rural Africa and improving the efficiency with which this energy is delivered will simply serve to entrench poverty. Energy consumption therefore has to increase if poverty is to be alleviated.

Energy conservation has great potential in energy-intensive sectors such as industry or in developed economies. This in part explains the relative success of energy conservation in the industrialized nations of the developed world (Lovins, 1989). Despite the above problems there are still some unexploited opportunities for energy conservation in rural development. These include:

- Transport;
- Mechanized agriculture;
- Agroprocessing industry;
- Biomass resources utilization (discussed below).

Transport is an important input to rural development. It brings in essential agricultural inputs such as fertilizer, improved seeds, packaging materials and the all-important consumer goods for the rural populace. Transport is also required to deliver agricultural surplus to local and external markets. An energy-intensive activity, it also offers opportunities for fuel saving.

Transport in rural areas is often carried out by means of motorized vehicles that use either petrol or diesel. Technology options for energy conservation include energy audits to optimize transportation routes and enhanced logistics and improved maintenance to reduce fuel consumption of vehicles. These options can be implemented easily by entities that own large fleets.

In the margin, handwritten: *Topofcropping?*

In the case of smaller vehicles such as pick-ups and vans, the standardization of models and the establishment of improved service centres in the rural areas might be the best strategies for energy conservation. On a larger scale, switching the mode of transport – for example, from road to rail transport – can result in substantial energy savings.

Similarly, mechanized agriculture offers opportunities for energy conservation. Improved tractor maintenance can generate substantial energy savings. Likewise, energy savings can be realized by optimizing irrigation systems: drip irrigations can dramatically reduce the energy needs for water lifting and transportation.

Agroprocessing industries based in rural areas offer excellent opportunities for energy savings through audits and greater use of insulation for those industries that require process heat.

At the household level, too, there are opportunities for conservation. But since the most important fuel in the rural areas of developing countries is fuelwood, possible conservation interventions will be discussed in the next section.

Fuelwood

An estimated two billion people, many of whom reside in rural areas, depend on fuelwood to meet their cooking and space heating needs (FAO, 1985). Other rural uses of fuelwood include charcoal production, post-harvest crop processing (e.g. tea drying and curing of tobacco) and brick manufacture.

Fuelwood technologies that have been developed to date can be subdivided into three categories, namely production and supply, conversion and end use. Research and development work in the above categories has concentrated more on enhancing the efficiency of the above three processes than on the development of further innovations.

In the case of fuelwood production and supply, attention has been aimed at the development and promotion of fast-growing species (National Academy of Sciences, 1983); interplanting fuelwood with food and cash crops (agroforestry); and development and wide-scale dissemination of multi-purpose species for fuelwood, fruits, fencing, shade and the extraction of pharmaceutical and industrial raw materials (El Mahgary, 1985).

While substantial progress has been registered in identifying fast-growing and multi-purpose tree species, tree planting for fuelwood production is still faced by many constraints. These include the poor returns of plantations or plots of fuel trees, unfavourable land ownership patterns that discourage tree planting or any other land improvement measures (O'Keefe *et al.*, 1988), lack of sufficient supplies of water (a critical factor in the case of newly planted trees) and inadequate access to technical assistance and support.

Of equal importance has been the work done on improving the efficiency of fuelwood conversion (Yamba, 1986). Particular attention has been paid to the production of charcoal, often cited as one of the main causes of deforestation. There are now a multitude of designs of energy-efficient charcoal kilns for use in both small-scale and industrial-scale charcoal production units (Foley, 1988). In the case of small-scale charcoal production, the introduction of improved techniques and equipment has been severely hampered by the informal and, in some cases, illegal nature of charcoal production.

In addition, significant efforts have been expended in developing more efficient briquetting techniques and processes. In particular, substantial investment has been made in developing appropriate binders for briquettes and small-scale equipment suitable for rural areas. The main constraints on briquetting include the high cost associated with collection of the raw material and with purchasing, operating and maintaining briquetting machines.

At the end-use level, extensive laboratory-based and field-based work aimed at designing improved cookstoves that use a wide range of fuels including wood, charcoal and a variety of biomass residues (rice husks, maize stalks, etc.) has been undertaken (Prasad, 1985). The continued use of wood as a 'free good' is a major constraint on the wide-scale adoption of improved cookstoves in the rural areas of the developing world (Krugmann, 1987). A large number of rural households traditionally buy neither stoves nor fuel (Karekezi, 1988). Wide-scale dissemination is also limited by the prohibitive costs associated with establishing sustainable dissemination networks for rural stoves (Caceres *et al.*, 1989).

Conventional Sources:
Constraints and Limitations in the Rural Context

Conventional energy sources for rural development include grid electricity, coal and petroleum products such as diesel and kerosene. Conventional, well-established energy technologies usually have access to trained manpower for installation, operation and maintenance of associated equipment.

Electricity provided via an interconnected grid or a stand-alone diesel generator continues to be one of the most sought-after amenities in the rural areas of developing countries. The demand for electricity is often higher than the existing installed capacity by several orders of magnitude.

The main constraint appears to be the availability of adequate financial resources to finance the usually high investment cost of rural electrification. A recent global review of rural electrification (Foley, 1989) showed that the technical options for rural electrification are well known and generally available.

Innovation in rural electrification is required at the financial and institutional level. The aforementioned review found that the establishment of institutions with specific responsibility for rural electrification is a vital step in bringing electricity to the rural poor.

Diesel-powered equipment for agriculture, post-harvest processing and transportation has been and increasingly will be a vital component of rural development. As with electrical equipment, diesel-powered technology has a long and established track record. The technical options are therefore well understood and available – but at a price. Due to the rapidly dwindling convertible currency reserves of most developing countries, the availability of adequate supplies of fuel and spare parts for diesel-powered equipment is far from satisfactory in many rural areas.

One advantage shared by electrical and diesel-powered rural technologies is standardization. Due to their long-established market presence, electrical and diesel equipment have a reliable spare parts procurement and maintenance system in most developing countries. This is usually backed up by formal mid-level and high-level technical training for operators, technicians and engineers in the relevant disciplines.

Both these conventional technologies are heavily dependent on external inputs either in the form of fuel (petroleum) or machinery and/or spare parts. As a result, conventional energy technologies require adequate access to imports. With most of the developing countries facing chronic shortages of convertible currency, the security of conventional energy options for rural areas cannot always be assured.

New and Renewable Energy Technologies

New and renewable energy technologies (NRETs) have, in the eyes of many, failed to fulfil their promise. In the early 1970s, NRETs were a panacea for the developing world's deteriorating energy situation. They were perceived as a low-cost and appropriate alternative to conventional energy technologies and, most important of all, as suitable for use by the rural and urban poor of the Third World (World Bank, 1980).

Over the last 15 years, significant financial resources have been invested in NRET projects. Today, NRETs continue to face daunting hurdles. A large number of NRETs are beyond the financial reach of their principal target groups, the rural and urban poor sector. Some others that are low-cost (e.g., solar water heaters) continue to face enormous problems in mobilizing support at the policy level and in engineering large-scale dissemination at the end-user level (Karekezi, 1988).

In the early 1980s, a number of NRETs have, despite the aforementioned obstacles, demonstrated an unexpected level of success in addressing energy problems faced by agriculture and development initiatives in the rural areas. In particular, the following technologies have done well:

- Small hydro plants for shaft power and electricity generation;
- Wind pumps for water lifting;
- Biogas plants for cooking and lighting;
- Photovoltaic units for lighting and refrigeration.

This chapter will confine itself to brief discussion and comment on the above NRETs and attempt to identify a number of key issues that are of relevance to the potential of NRETs in rural and agricultural development. A comprehensive review of NRETs can be obtained from a 1988 Beijer Institute global report, *Renewable Energy Technologies – Their Application in Developing Countries* (Kristofersen and Bokalders, 1986).

Small hydro

Small hydro has a long and established track record of success as an energy technology for rural areas. The best-known examples are the small hydro programmes in China and Nepal. It is estimated that there are over 90,000 small hydro plants in China while Nepal has at least four manufacturers of small hydro plants with the largest making over 50 units per year (Hurst, 1986). In both countries, but in particular in Nepal, the small hydro programme was built on existing traditional water management know-how and expertise. In the case of Nepal, the government allowed any individual or institution to generate, distribute and sell power of less than 100 KW (Hislop, 1987). This measure is credited with a large part of the success of the Nepal small hydro programme. A recent study carried out in Ethiopia (Mariam *et al.*, 1987) showed that small hydro was competitive with electricity supplied from the grid or a diesel generator.

While small hydro offers significant opportunities for the generation of both shaft power and electricity in rural areas, it has several inherent technical limitations. Topography is an important criterion (Inversin, 1986). Suitable small hydro sites can be far from demand centres, in which case the cost of transmission can be prohibitive.

In addition, highly skilled civil engineering skills are required to keep the cost of civil works within affordable limits while ensuring a satisfactory level of plant safety and durability. The mechanical components of small hydro plants usually require access to well-equipped mechanical workshops, a rarity in many rural areas of developing countries.

Windpumps

Windpumps have registered notable successes, particularly in Kenya and Argentina. In Kenya, the manufacture of windpumps is now an established industry. By 1982, an estimated 37 windpumps were in operation (van Lierop *et al.*, 1982), while in Argentina an estimated 2000 wind machines are produced every year. The Argentine wind technology industry is estimated to account for a fifth of world production (Hurst, 1986). In both Kenya and Argentina, wind-powered technologies have increased the productivity of rural agriculture and, in addition, contributed to industrial development by giving rise to a new manufacturing industry.

Wind-powered technologies require favourable wind conditions and access to well-equipped engineering workshops. A certain minimum density of units is required if maintenance and service is to be provided on a cost-effective basis.

Biogas

Biogas technologies for rural areas are perhaps the best-known NRETs. Extensive use of biogas has been undertaken in the rural areas of India and China. In both countries, the government role was important. Biogas technologies developed in China and India are now being replicated in many other developing countries.

Perhaps the most important merit of biogas is its ability to use biomass to generate a fuel for energy while maintaining the potential to use the residual sludge as a fertilizer. Biogas technologies are not as low-cost as it was initially thought, however. Depending on the design, investment required for a biogas plant can be prohibitive. So can the cost of collecting biomass necessary to run the plant.

Photovoltaics

Photovoltaic technologies have experienced one of the most exciting developments in the last ten years. The cost of photovoltaic cells has dropped dramatically. It is estimated that in 1978 the cost of a photovoltaic cell was US$ 25 per peak watt. In 1988, the cost in the USA (for large orders and excluding the additional cost of delivery and taxes) is estimated to have dropped to US$ 4–5 per peak watt (Derrick *et al.*, 1989).

The dramatic drop in cost of photovoltaics is bringing a much larger market within the reach of photovoltaic equipment – in particular, photovoltaics for lighting and refrigeration. Photovoltaics are now increasingly the energy technologies of choice for rural clinics, hospitals and schools in developing countries. The current market for photovoltaics is expected to increase dramatically if systems cost can be brought down to US$ 5 per peak watt.

Proposed Actions for the Future

Of the eight issues raised earlier in this paper, four appear to be of special relevance to the question of energy technology options for rural and agricultural development. On the basis of the discussion of these issues, a number of actions can be recommended in response to the problems posed by the selection of appropriate energy technologies for rural and agricultural development.

Access to information on the rural energy sector and energy technology options
The flow of information on energy technologies for agricultural and rural development between developed and developing nations and among Third World countries can be enhanced through the establishment of and/or continued support for international and local information networks. Examples of existing networks include the AFREPREN/SAREC network on African Energy Policy Research, the UNDP/World Bank/Netherlands Government global Windpump Evaluation Programme, the FWD improved cookstove network and the UNDP/World Bank Gasifier Monitoring Programme.

Specialized sub-sectoral approach to energy for agriculture and rural development
Broaden the base of knowledge from which decisions on energy technology
options are taken. A specialized sub-sectoral approach to energy technology
can result in sub-optimal decisions and initiatives. Energy planning can provide
a broader understanding of available energy options across different sub-
sectors and thus assist in eschewing the problems associated with a narrow
focus on a specific sub-sector. This can be realized through increased support
for energy planning initiatives such as the two (francophone and anglophone)
annual ENDA energy planning courses.

Equity issues
Assist the development of South-based energy institutions to strengthen local
know-how in the selection and adoption of energy technologies. This may
include increasing the support for specialized energy agencies in developing
countries and providing in-country and external training in relevant subject
areas.

User needs and participation
Ensure that ongoing and planned energy initiatives for agricultural and rural
development pay greater attention to the needs of users and increase the level
of user participation in the process of identifying and selecting energy
technologies. This can be achieved through the strengthening of existing
extension networks or via greater recourse to decentralized market mechanisms.

REFERENCES

Ashworth, J. H. & Neuendorffer, J. W. (1980). *Matching Renewable Energy Systems to Village-
Level Energy Needs* (SERI/TR-744-514). Solar Energy Research Institute, Colorado.
Barnett, A., Pyle, L. & Subramanian, S.K. (1978). *Biogas Technology in the Third World: A
Multidisciplinary Review.* IDRC Report No. 103e, International Development Research Centre,
Ottawa.
Barnett, A., Bell, M. & Hoffman, K. (1982). *Rural Energy and the Third World – A Review of
Social Science Research and Technology Policy Problems.* Pergamon Press, Oxford.
Bhattia, R. (1987). *Economic Evaluation and Diffusion of Renewable Energy Technologies – Case
Studies from India* (MR 162e). International Development Research Centre, Ottawa.
Board on Science and Technology for International Development, Office of International Affairs,
National Research Council (1984). *Diffusion of Biomass Energy Technologies in Developing
Countries.* National Academy Press, Washington, second edition.
Caceres, R. *et al.* (1989). *Stoves for People – Proceedings of the Second International Workshop on
Stoves Dissemination.* IT Publications, CEMAT & FWD, London.
Centre for Small Energy Resources (1988). Final Report of the Experts' Group Meeting on
Energy for Rural Areas of Africa Held in Rome 15–17 March 1988. Centre for Small Energy
Resources (UNITAR/UNDP), Rome.
Derrick, A., Francis, C. & Bokalders, V. (1989). *Solar Photovoltaic Products – A Guide for
Development Workers.* Intermediate Technology Publications, London.
El Mahgary, Y. (1985). *Role of UNEP in Renewable Energy Development in Africa. Renewable
Energy Development in Africa.* Vol. 1 – Proceedings of the African Energy Programme Conference,
25–29 March 1985, Mauritius. Commonwealth Science Council, London.
Foley, G. (1988). Discussion Paper on Demand Management. Proceedings of the ESMAP Eastern
and Southern Africa Household Energy Planning Seminar, Harare, Zimbabwe, 1–5 February
1988 (Activity Completion Report No. 085/88). Joint UNDP/World Bank Energy Sector

Management Assistance Program, Washington, pp. 72-3.
———— (1989). *Electricity for Rural People*. Panos, London.
Food and Agriculture Organization of the United Nations (FAO) (1985). *Wood for Energy*. Forestry Topics Report No. 1 (I/Q4960/E/3.85/2/2000).
Gamser, M. S. (1988). *Power from the People – Innovation, User Participation and Forest Energy Development*. Intermediate Technology Publications, London.
———— (1988). 'Innovation, technical assistance and development: the importance of technology users'. *World Development* (Great Britain), Vol 16, No. 6, pp. 711–21
Hislop, D. (1987). *The Micro-Hydro Programme in Nepal – A Case Study*. Paper produced for the IIED Conference on Sustainable Development. Intermediate Technology Development Group and Biomass Energy Services and Technology, London.
Hurst, C. (1986) *Transfer, Adaptation and Diffusion of Mature Renewable Energy Technologies in Developing Countries* – Report for the Meeting for the Intergovernmental Group of Experts on the Transfer, Application and Development of Technology in the Energy Sector, Paying Particular Attention to New and Renewable Sources of Energy (TD/B/C.6/AC.10/ 2/Supp.1). United Nations Conference on Trade and Development, Geneva.
International Development Research Centre & the United Nations University (1986). *Energy Research – Directions and Issues for Developing Countries*: A Report of the Energy Research Group (IDRC-250e). International Development Research Centre, Ottawa.
Inversin, A. R. (1986). *Micro-Hydropower Sourcebook – A Practical Guide to Design and Implementation in Developing Countries*. NRECA International Foundation, Washington.
Karekezi, S. (1988). *Review of Mature Renewable Energy Technologies (RETs) in Sub-Saharan Africa*. An AFREPREN Research Report. NIR/SAREC/IDRC, Gaborone.
Kristoferson, L. and Bokalder, V. (1986). 'Renewable energy technologies: their application in developing countries'. Pergamon Press Ltd., Oxford, England.
Krugmann, H. (1987). *Review of Issues and Research Relating to Improved Cookstoves* (IDRC – MR 152e). International Development Research Centre, Ottawa.
Lovins, A. B. (1989). *End-Use/Least-Cost Investment Strategies. Energy for Tomorrow*. Compilation of Papers for the 14th Congress of the World Energy Conference, Montreal, Section 2.3.1.
Mariam, H. G. & Tebicke, H. (1987). *Small Hydro and/or Grid Extension for Rural Electrification – Alternatives and Complimentaries*. An AFREPREN Research Report. NIR/SAREC/IDRC, Gaborone.
Moulik, T. K. & Srivastava, U. K. (1975). *Biogas Plants at the Village Level: Problems and Prospects in Gujarat*. Centre for Management in Agriculture, Ahmedabad, monograph. Indian Institute of Management, No. 50.
National Academy of Sciences.(1983). *Firewood Crops – Shrub and Tree Species for Energy Production*, Vol. 2. National Academy of Sciences, Washington.
O'Keefe, P. & Munslow, B. (1988). *Resolving the Irresolvable – The Fuelwood Problem in Eastern and Southern Africa*. Proceedings of the ESMAP Eastern and Southern Africa Household Energy Planning Seminar, Harare, Zimbabwe, 1–5 February 1988 (Activity Completion Report No. 085/88). Joint UNDP/World Bank Energy Sector Management Assistance Program, Washington.
Prasad, K. K. (1985). *Stove Design for Improved Dissemination. Woodstove Dissemination*. Proceedings of the Conference Held at Wolfheze, the Netherlands. Intermediate Technology Publications, London.
Prasad, C. R., Prasad, K. K. & Reddy, A. K. N. (1974). 'Biogas plants: prospects, problems and tasks'. *Economic and Political Weekly* (Bombay), Vol. 9, Nos 32-34, pp. 1347–64.
Soussan, J. (1989). *Formulating African Energy Policy – A Discussion Document*. ETC, Leusden.
van Lierop, W. E. & van Veldhuizen, L. R. (1982). *Wind Energy Development in Kenya*.
World Bank (1980). *Energy for Developing Countries*. World Bank, Washington.
———— (1989). *Sub-Saharan Africa – From Crisis to Sustainable Growth*. World Bank, Washington.
Yamba, Y. D. (1986). *Determination of Techno-Economic Viability, Reliability and Durability of A Charcoal Retort Prototype. Renewable Energy Development in Africa*. Vol.2, Proceedings of the African Energy Programme Conference, 25–29 March 1985, Mauritius. Commonwealth Science Council, London.

4 Making Renewable Energy Programmes More Relevant

ERNESTO N. TERRADO

My main purpose in this chapter is to provide some observations, hopefully useful, on the situation and prospects of renewable energy sources (or non-conventional energy, as it is called in the Philippines) as an option for the Philippines and other developing countries. These observations arise from my own experiences as one of the originators of the Philippines' non-conventional energy programme in 1976, and later as an energy planner at a unit of the World Bank. In keeping with the terminology adopted by the UN, I shall henceforth use the phrase 'new and renewable sources of energy' (NRSE) to describe direct solar, wind and biomass energy sources.[1]

It may be recalled that the oil shock in the early 1970s led to the first serious efforts by countries and international agencies to identify and develop non-oil fuel alternatives. NRSE were among a number of alternatives which were widely considered promising and deserving of more intensive development efforts. When the Ministry of Energy was created in the Philippines in 1976, the country's energy consumption was about 96% oil, with hydro supplying the rest. Nuclear, coal and geothermal resources seemed to be the main alternatives; it was thought that NRSE were an energy option which should be developed for local applications. A Non-conventional Resources Division (NCRD) was created within the Ministry. Shortly thereafter, a national non-conventional energy development programme was formally launched, with initial funding of 10 million pesos for research, development and demonstration projects.

As well as contributing towards overall efforts to find non-oil alternatives, the Philippines programme on NRSE had other justifications. The country is situated in the tropics and has immense solar and biomass energy resources. It has 7,100 islands, implying a highly decentralized energy demand structure and high delivery costs for conventional fuels in many areas. The problem was to identify NRSE application particularly suitable for the country. It may be appreciated that at that time there was still little experience world-wide in this field. NCRD's research, development and demonstration programme was therefore initially a learning curve where all technologies and approaches thought promising were tried and tested. In the first five years of the programme, projects were financed to investigate the technical and cost characteristics of, *inter alia*, solar water heating, biomass gasification, dendrothermal power systems, windpumps, photovoltaics, alcohol for motor fuel and the use of geothermal heat for drying agricultural products. Some of these efforts generated useful results. Many did not, for reasons I will dwell on later. Today, the Philippines non-conventional energy resources development programme is still ongoing, albeit reduced in size and with a different emphasis. On the positive side, it is more focused, having benefited from lessons learned in early trials. In general, however, it can be said that NRSE activities in the Philippines in the 1980s became more subdued and received less local and international financial support than at the beginning. This development is not unique to the Philippines programme and, with few exceptions, mirrors the international scene.

NRSE Activities by the World Bank

In a similar vein, the evolution within the World Bank of activities related to NRSE reflects changes in global perception of the realistic role of NRSE. To help the developing countries adjust to higher energy prices, the Bank in the mid-1970s not only expanded its lending but diversified it to include areas that traditionally it had not financed. In the area of renewable energy, the Bank supported the world's largest alcohol from biomass production programme with a loan of US$250 million to Brazil in 1981.[2] The Bank also stepped-up its lending for fuelwood projects in response to the growing realization that deforestation in many parts of the world, especially Africa, poses a severe threat to a principal source of energy for about half of the world's population.

As for other renewables, the Bank provided financing for a number of small hydro projects, including financing for private sector manufacturing of hydro equipment by the Bank's affiliate, the IFC.[3]

However, Bank lending for other biomass technologies and for solar and wind energy has taken the form mainly of the financing of pilot and demonstration projects. Two factors account for this. First, for intended 'commercial' applications, the technologies in question often were not mature enough to meet Bank project lending criteria for performance track record and for economic and financial viability.

Second, the institutional and policy framework for the evaluation and commercialization of NRSE has been weak in many countries. Indeed, the greater need in many cases clearly has been for intensive pre-investment work rather than for investment financing. This type of work – studies dealing with the technical, financial and economic viabilities of selected NRSE technologies – was conducted in the Bank by the New and Renewable Energy Sources Unit of the Energy Department. The Unit was created in the late 1970s with what was essentially a monitoring and advisory function.

Since then, although as a matter of policy the Bank continues to support efforts to develop economic applications of NRSE, its overall involvement in renewable energy, except in the case of fuelwood, has tapered off. Again, this turn of events is not unique to the World Bank and closely mirrors those which occurred in other international financing agencies.

The Problems

Many factors contributed to the pronounced downward shift in international attitudes to the role of NRSE in the mid-1980s. In my opinion, the two most important ones are the drop in oil prices which started in 1982/83 and has just begun to stabilize, and the 'overselling' of NRSE application in the mid-1970s.

During the period 1972–83, international oil prices increased fivefold, then dropped steeply so that by 1987 they were again roughly at the same level, in real terms, as in 1972. The softening of oil prices had two major effects on renewables. Firstly, it made uneconomic various NRSE options that compete directly in the modern sector as relatively large-scale petroleum substitutes.

These include, among others, fuel alcohol projects, dendrothermal power plants, wind farms for electricity generation and industrial-scale solar water heating systems.[4] The Bank's first loan to the Brazilian alcohol programme, for example, was made when the oil price was over US$30 a barrel. The second loan was made in 1983 when the oil price was about $29 a barrel and projected in the appraisal report to rise to $38 by 1995. At the present international oil price of about $16–18 a barrel, the Brazilian fuel alcohol programme could be justified only marginally, at best. The Brazilian government, indeed, has suspended further expansion in fuel alcohol distilling capacity. Secondly, the softening of oil prices gave rise to a new *perception* that oil was again cheap and plentiful and that there was no need to examine other less familiar fuel options. This was regrettable because many important NRSE applications which are small-scale and with low fuel-cost components (such as photovoltaic applications) remain viable alternatives in many situations even at low oil prices.

Renewables were 'oversold' in the late 1970s and early 1980s not only by aggressive equipment suppliers, but also by well-meaning NRSE promoters world-wide who raised the expectations of the general public to unrealistic levels. A particular type of overselling occurred in many developing countries whereby technologies which were not commercially ready, by reason of economic or technical difficulties, were prematurely deployed in large national programmes and propped up with subsidies. The Philippines dendrothermal power programme is a case in point. The idea of generating large-scale power by using wood grown in dedicated, short-rotation tree plantations was sensible: wood combustion technology was well-established. Using managed plantations would enhance rather than deplete forest resources. The system would utilize an indigenous, renewable resource and, being labour-intensive, could generate significant employment opportunities in rural areas. On the other hand, it was recognized that many questions needed to be answered: since biomass yield is a critical factor in the economics of the project, would use of marginal lands produce enough biomass to make the system viable? If good land is used, what would be the opportunity cost? Would the oil-substitution objective be offset by transport fuel requirements for wood hauling? A period of field research was clearly indicated. For this purpose, NCRD financed a 500 KW pilot dendrothermal plant in Mindoro islands in 1978.

Before this pilot plant was even built, the national Electrification Administration launched its Dendrothermal Power Development Programme in 1979 with the ambitious goal of constructing 200 MW of capacity by the early 1990s, requiring over 70,000 hectares of tree farms at 63 sites.[5] The change of government in 1985 and consequently the loss of the programme's managers was a major cause of the abandonment of this programme. However, technical and organizational problems which could have been addressed in a properly paced research programme were also responsible for the failure. As noted in a recent Bank appraisal report,[6] the tree planting programme had

> poor results due to inadequate site selection and preparation, lack of fertilizer and generally careless farming. The wood processing equipment was poorly operated and maintained so that the quality of timber chips was uneven. In turn, the boilers were unable to burn the chips properly and achieve the rated output of steam. The Rural Electrification Cooperatives who were supposed to manage each plant were not provided adequate technical support in planning, designing and implementing generation plants of this type.

Of the 17 projects initially planned, only six were completed but are presumably not in commercial operation. Apparently the National Power Corporation has now been given responsibility for the programme.

Similar cases involving various prematurely deployed technologies have been observed in the programmes of other developing countries. For example, in Thailand, the Thai Ministry of Interior, through its Department of Public Works (DPW), embarked on a programme to supplement rural electrification with biomass gasifiers in 1980.[7]

The objective was to install 4000 power gasifier units by 1991. Over 140 15 KW charcoal gasifiers were deployed at a cost of about US$1 million. Today, none of these installations are working in any practical fashion, if at all. The difficulties encountered included technical problems with the gasifier design, economic non-competitiveness with alternatives and a host of social acceptance and institutional issues.[8]

The unfortunate result of such experiences world-wide was the generation of a backlash against NRSE in various quarters, including national planning agencies and international donors, which – coupled with the softening of oil prices – severely dampened world-wide interest in NRSE in the mid-1980s. The more cautious stance towards NRSE adopted by many was justifiable. In my view, however, the overall backlash was excessive and served to reduce support even for those NRSE applications which succeeded.

Future Prospects

On the positive side, the lessons learned in the last decade and a half have made most NRSE programmes, including the Philippines', more selective and more realistic in their goals. Gains were made in terms of training and institution building. There are now more people in both public and private sectors with NRSE expertise. National energy planning in general has been enriched by the availability of such expertise. Globally, many NRSE technologies *did* mature and are being commercialized in many countries. In Brazil, heat gasifiers are widely used in the industrial sector on a commercial basis. In India, the use of bagasse in sugar mills to generate surplus electricity for export to the grid (a biomass energy project) is seriously being planned for the State of Maharashtra as part of a Bank project for the industrial sector. Photovoltaics has emerged, not only as a power source for telecommunications projects, but as a cost-competitive power source for lighting, small-scale irrigation, water supply and refrigerators for medical supplies in remote areas in many countries, both developed and developing. In the Philippines, NCRD's programme (assisted by GTZ) to promote photovoltaics for use in small islands seems to have been well received by the island communities. The programme is being run on a minimal subsidy, with local 'solar cooperatives' established and able to obtain loans from the Development Bank of the Philippines.

Photovoltaic applications may well become the most significant economic application of NRSE in the near to medium term. According to a recent industry report, private companies and government-owned entities around the world now plan to bring on line entirely new or expanded PV modules between now and 1995.[9] A major reason for this development is the rapid fall in PV prices from a high of US$30–70 per peak watt in the early 1970s[10] to only about $5–7 (retail) today. PV cost in large projects could drop to about $3.50 per peak watt and, if manufactured locally, could drop to $0.50 to $1 in direct manufacturing cost.[11] The drop in PV prices unquestionably generated wider demand. But it can also be said that wider demand created by careful identification of the right 'niches' for PV applications over the years probably contributed to the decreased prices.

Finally, the recent upsurge of concern over environmental degradation at the global level – acid raid, global warming, destruction of the ozone layer – has resulted in more questions being asked about the environmental costs of conventional power generation systems.

Energy production is responsible for a large proportion of these adverse environmental impacts. Consequently, efforts are now under way in various lending agencies to develop acceptable ways to calculate and factor in such costs in the economics of energy projects. Although some NRSE applications also have negative environmental impacts, they are, in general, a much cleaner energy source. Along with projects which promote energy efficiency, it is highly likely that in the 1990s considerably more resources will be made available internationally to support efforts to make promising NRSE applications economically competitive with more familiar but less environmentally benign alternatives.

Conclusions : Making NRSE Programmes More Relevant

The main conclusion to be drawn is that despite the mixed experience in the last decade and the decline in oil prices, NRSE continue to have an important role to play in the energy sector of developing countries and should not be left out of national energy planning. Although many oil-substitution applications may have become marginally economic at present oil prices, it must be recognized that NRSE applications cover a potentially wide range of objectives, many of them related not just to energy production but to the delivery of a service, which in turn enhance the quality of life or provide new economic opportunities. It is not pertinent to say, as NRSE critics often have, that in the national context renewables can hope to account for some very insignificant fraction of electricity generation or oil consumption. Clearly, a kilowatt of PV power which enables the refrigeration of vaccine in a remote village is not 'equivalent' to a kilowatt of power delivered by the grid in the city.

The key to accelerating competitiveness and acceptance of NRSE is to do one's homework in identifying the appropriate 'niches' for applications. Since NRSE applications are highly site-specific, it means that there must always be careful resource assessment coupled with full knowledge of the end-use requirements of a particular area. It means being prepared to do good economic analysis and objectively compare alternative ways of achieving the same end. After the initial experiences described above, by and large there are less technology-driven NRSE projects to date. However, the quality and impartiality of comparative economic analysis can be improved in many projects.

To avoid overselling, NRSE programme managers must distinguish between R & D and commercialization activities, being patient not to push immature technologies into practical applications too quickly. Although the goal is to commercialize NRSE technologies in the immediate term, it is not unjustified in a developing country to expend some resources on R & D, especially 'adaptive' research. Commercialization initiatives must be based on achieving sustainability through market forces. This does not mean, however, that all forms of subsidies should be avoided since many NRSE applications, although mature, require a certain amount of support at the beginning. It does mean being careful that initial investment support does not become a permanent subsidy. As early as possible, the participation of the private sector must be encouraged.

NRSE programmes must always be formulated within the context of overall energy sector planning. One way to achieve this is to link up NRSE activities with broader, more urgent development issues such as rural energy planning or 'household energy'. The latter term, as currently used internationally, refers to issues related to overdependence in developing countries on traditional fuels, mainly wood; the grossly inefficient way in which such fuels are produced, distributed and used; the adverse impacts on the environment and on the well-being of households dependent on traditional fuel supplies; and the need to raise the very low levels of energy use in many developing countries and improve productivity. Considering that over half of the world's population still relies on wood as a principal fuel, these issues are indeed significant and urgent.[12] Fuelwood, of course, is a renewable energy (biomass) and NRSE programmes which do not address issues related to fuelwood use are, to say the least, incomplete.

Finally, NRSE programmes should look beyond the technologies and pay equal attention to social, institutional and financing issues, the resolution of which is often the prerequisite to commercialization. For example, even for commercially-ready NRSE technologies, the high initial cost of equipment and the dispersed nature of projects pose constraints to consumer acceptance and lender interest. It must be recognized that these constraints will remain in spite of advances in technology. Instead of regarding these as an insurmountable barrier, the attitude should be to develop innovative management and financing packages to handle small-scale, dispersed projects. Efforts should be made to eventually establish in the developing countries the institutional framework required to identify, appraise, finance, manage and operate small-scale decentralized NRSE projects.

NOTES

1. Other energy sources, such as geothermal, are included in the UN definition. In the Philippines, however, geothermal energy is considered a conventional energy source due to the large geothermal power generation capacity already established in the country.
2. A second Bank loan of US$300 was made to this programme in 1985.
3. Large hydro-electric projects comprise a major area of Bank lending in the energy sector. Although technically an NRSE, large hydro-power is a well-established technology and is treated in this paper as a conventional source.
4. This statement is made in a general sense. Since the economics of NRSE applications are extremely site-specific, some projects in this list may still be viable in their particular context.
5. Georgia Institute of Technology, *Dendro Thermal Power Generation Program Evaluation Study*, Volume 1 (1984), p. 9.
6. World Bank, *Philippines Rural Electrification Sector Study: an Integrated Program to Revitalize the Sector* (Report No. 8016-PH, November 1989).
7. Naksitte Coovattanachai, *Final Report on Assessment of the Performance of the Technical Problems of DPW's Gasification System* (Bangkok, January 1988).
8. The Bank's own monitoring of biomass power gasifiers conducted over several years in the Philippines and Brazil indicated many problems with this technology. Although technically developed (thousands of gasifier-powered vehicles were used in Europe and Asia during the Second World War; many gasifier installations have been demonstrated operationally in other countries), it is a complicated option compared to diesel. The monitoring results indicated few gasifiers were operated continuously. Many were in a research environment or highly subsidized operations.

9. *PV Insider Report* (December 1989).

10. National Academy of Sciences, *Energy for Rural Development* (Washington, DC, 1976), p.102.

11. Massachusetts Photovoltaics Center, *Photovoltaic Workshop for Latin America and the Caribbean* (Lowell, Massachusetts, July 1988).

12. Few countries today count non-commercial energy when reporting national energy balances. The Philippines lists non-conventional energy in its energy balance but, so far, includes only bagasse, coconut husks and other biomass used in agro-industries. In 1988, these biomass sources accounted for 15 % of total energy consumption. If fuelwood was included, the figure would probably be around 35–45%.

5 Assessment of Rural Energy Supply and Demand

DOMINIC J. MBEWE

In the last decade and a half there has been rising concern over rural energy needs in developing countries. Following the oil 'crisis' whose effects were global, another 'energy crisis' was identified that particularly affected developing countries (Eckholm, 1975). This crisis tended to be more pronounced in the rural areas and gave an impetus to efforts at understanding the rural energy problem.

Initially, the rural energy problem was described merely as a situation where biomass fuels were consumed at a rate faster than production (Barnett, 1983). Deforestation, which was thought to be due to woodfuel consumption and led to negative ramifications such as soil erosion, desertification, flooding and silting of rivers, dominated the rural energy debate.

Later, a clearer picture of the rural energy situation emerged. Although it is generally accepted that biomass fuel supplies (particularly fuelwood) are diminishing, deforestation is largely due to other factors such as forest clearing for agricultural expansion, overgrazing and commercial cutting of trees. In effect, the problem cannot be dealt with from the energy perspective alone. A multi-sectoral and indeed a multi-disciplinary approach to rural energy issues is needed.

With a better understanding of rural energy issues has come a better appreciation of the role of energy in rural development. Rural development is an important long-term objective of most developing country governments (Chambers, 1974) since the majority of their people reside in the rural areas, and yet, as R. Chambers (1983) rightly laments, 'the extremes of rural poverty in the Third World are an outrage.' Much still remains to be done to improve the lot of the rural population.

Energy greatly influences the quality of rural life (Morse, Soesastro & Schlegel, n.d.). Consequently, its contribution to the rural development process must be enhanced. Since energy may be an integrating dimension for rural development planning, an understanding of rural energy supplies and needs is of the utmost importance. To ensure the minimum conditions of well-being for rural communities, a significant amount of energy is required, coupled with changes in access to that energy.

From an energy resource point of view, new and renewable sources of

69

energy [1] appear well placed to make a significant contribution to rural development. Renewable energies are amenable to decentralized small-scale applications since they have, in general, a low spatial concentration. This aspect fits well with most rural situations where communities are often widely scattered, making a centralized supply of energy both difficult and uneconomic.

Significant progress has also been made in the development of renewable energy technologies. A number of these technologies are mature enough for application but the installations must be made under carefully selected conditions. Early efforts in promoting renewable energy technologies met with failure due to the preponderance of 'technology push' rather than 'demand pull' factors (Barnett, 1983). Suppliers sought to promote renewable energy technologies which they considered appropriate without prior appreciation of the real needs of the rural community. Experience has shown the importance of people's participation from the outset in any rural energy programme.

Rural energy systems are typically small-scale activities that are heavily dependent on local resources. An assessment of energy supply and consumption, together with the associated constraints on any rural community, is an important first step towards enhanced energy development.

This chapter aims to highlight some of the important principles that govern assessments of rural energy supply and demand. It is based on observations made from a number of rural energy research results. The focus of the discussion is on new and renewable sources of energy.

General Rural Energy Perspectives

Rural areas are highly heterogeneous. Rural people live and work in diverse and widely varying ecological and social settings. Within each community/ village there will often be divergent interests.

On rural energy issues the advantage of knowledge lies with the rural dweller (Morse, Soesastro & Schlegel, n.d.). Rural people, however, need information on technology, skills and other related inputs to facilitate local energy innovations.

Biomass is the principle indigenous energy source and its supply, use, familiarity and potential for increased productivity are enormous. Biomass is obtained as a non-monetized (freely collected), partly monetized or fully monetized commodity.

Rural Energy Supply

Conventional energy sources

Conventional fuels such as centrally supplied electricity, petroleum products or coal are not widely available in rural areas. Reasons for this include:
   • High cost of grid extension (for electricity) due to long distances and

the scattered demand for power;

- High transportation costs for other fuels and non-accessibility of these areas during certain periods of the year;
- High cost of equipment using conventional fuels and scarcity of maintenance and technical skills;
- Low rural incomes which limit the ability to turn energy needs into effective demand.

The scarcity of conventional sources of energy in rural areas contributes to the poor conditions of life and low agricultural productivity. Renewable sources of energy offer promise in contributing to rural development since they are often available in rural areas.

Renewable energy sources

Renewable energy resources are highly heterogeneous – they differ in their spatial concentration and in the degree to which they may be said to be natural (Energy and Development, 1985). Due to low spatial concentration, most renewables require dispersed extraction and their low density means that they conflict with other uses of land. The potential for renewables such as agricultural waste and energy crops is highly dependent on human activity. Agricultural wastes are a by-product of other economic activities, while energy crops depend on the potential of the soil which may have other uses assigned to it.

The potential for conflict over land use is a major factor. An integrated assessment of renewables must address the potential for land conflicts, not only among land-intensive renewables, but also with other resources and other uses of land. Since some renewables are also labour-intensive, conflict with regard to labour should also be addressed.

Biomass

Biomass is the dominant energy source for rural areas and will continue to be so for the foreseeable future. It is the most readily available and abundant local energy resource. Consequently, assessments of rural energy supply have often focused on estimating biomass availability.

Biomass has two outstanding features, namely, its dependence on land (soil) and its high labour intensity in extraction and conversion (Energy and Development). Biomass resources may be categorized as organic wastes, natural forests and energy crops. Organic wastes (animal and agricultural) are by-products of other activities and hence their dependence on land is less significant. Natural forests are the only truly natural biomass and suffer from various pressures that include demand for energy and other uses of wood and land. Energy crops (including planted forests) depend on land as a productive factor.

The determination of fuel availability from each of these categories differs. It is more difficult for natural forests and relatively easier for the other categories. Fuel availability largely depends on the patterns of land use of a particular society (Howes, 1984).

Energy crops, being neither natural nor a residue of productive functions but an autonomous productive activity that actively competes with others in the use of land, require a resolution of conflicts for land and, possibly, labour. Fuel availability from crop residues is relatively simple to assess since flows are a proportion of crop stocks (Howes, 1984). Care must be taken, however, to account fully for the seasonal nature of crop organic wastes. This means that measurements must be conducted on more than one occasion.

Solar energy, wind and hydro-power

Measurement of the availability or potential of solar, wind and hydro energy differs from that of biomass. Assessment involves installing equipment at specific sites to measure daily flows which are then aggregated to give the potential during a certain period of the year. It is important to ascertain the seasonal variations in the potential for these resources. There are few methodological problems since standard methods of measurement are available.

Most developing countries lie in the 'sunshine belt' of the world and hence solar energy is an abundantly available resource. Wind and hydro-power are more location-specific and the latter depends on topography and precipitation.

Rural Energy Demand Assessments

Desegregation

Because rural energy consumption is dominated by the domestic sector, most rural energy surveys have concerned themselves mainly with assessing the energy consumption of this sector (Howes, 1984). More specifically, the consumption of biomass (particularly fuelwood) by this sector has been the main preoccupation of most surveys.

Non-desegregated surveys do not reveal the influence of one sector on fuel availability to other sectors (resulting from competing uses). It is also impossible to determine the total energy consumption of that locality. Future determination of consumption levels cannot be assessed accurately (Howes, 1984). It is important to distinguish – at least – the domestic, agricultural, small-scale and commercial sectors.

Rural energy assessment must be desegregated at end-use level. The aim here is to identify the type and quantity of energy used for each given end-use. For instance, in the residential sector, various fuels such as kerosene, firewood, candles, etc. may be used for lighting. Identifying the various fuels used for an end-use is fairly straightforward; what is difficult is to determine the relative quantities of each fuel used for a given period of time. This is only possible where there is a high degree of user collaboration (Bialy, 1978) so that users monitor the consumption of different fuels over a period of time without, it may be hoped, influencing their normal pattern of consumption.

Energy consumption over time

Another important factor to consider in the assessment of rural energy is the variation of energy use and supply over time. This variation is either cyclic or non-repetitive. Cyclical variations may be those of a short duration (day to day), seasonal or annual (Howes, 1984). Many surveys conducted in rural energy have lacked a clear appreciation of variations in energy flows over time. Instead, a 'snapshot' rather than a moving picture is given, failing to capture seasonal and annual variations (Barnett, 1983).

The reasons for the variation of energy consumption over time are numerous. It could be due to the type of activity dominant in a given period, for example, or to change in the number of people eating at or away from home. Fuel availability is influenced by seasonal variations. During the rainy season accessibility or reliability of supply may be low, while during and after the harvest residues may be more abundant than at other times of the year.

Temperature variations also affect the amount of fuel consumed since space heating may be required during cold days. There may also be seasonal dietary changes and festivals that require more cooking may take place during certain times of the year. Home and small-scale industries may have seasonal variations due to labour changes in relation to agriculture. In the long term, there may be yearly variations arising from climatic changes. Time variations should not be taken lightly in energy assessments and any assumption that the period chosen to undertake an assessment is typical must be well grounded.

Residential energy consumption

In assessing household energy consumption, one does not only have to identify the quantities of energy from different sources which are allocated to specific end-uses, but to account for variations in household sizes and composition to reach standard consumption figures (Howes, 1984).

In determining family size and composition care must be taken to ensure that the respondents and the enquirer mean the same thing. For instance, in a village, a household member may mean an unmarried daughter who may not be actually living with the family at that time (Fleuret, 1978).

In order to make rural energy demand projections, other data on household characteristics such as income, occupation and education are required. The household characteristics must then be related to distinct energy consumption by amount, type and purpose in order to gain an understanding of the variations in consumption among the different household groups. The linking of household characteristics to energy consumption is useful in evaluating the likely consequences of an intervention, and also in future projection.

Agriculture

Improved agricultural production through the provision of adequate amounts of energy is a key objective of rural development. Determination of energy needs of local farming systems must be a priority in rural energy research so that the energy constraints on improved production can be removed. The method used to assess the energy requirements of a local agricultural system will depend on the local context but generally it involves tracing the energy flow in food production, processing and delivery (Stout, 1979).

A common feature of subsistence agriculture is the low intensity of energy utilization. The aim of an energy assessment should be to explore ways and means of increasing energy use in this sector.

Small-scale industries

Small-scale industries represent an important stage in rural development. Together with agriculture, they form the two critical sectors which require increased energy inputs to boost production and hence raise the economic welfare of rural people. In this regard, rural energy studies ought to explore ways of increasing productivity through adequate provision of energy to small-scale rural industries.

Energy consumption in this sector is relatively easier to assess than in the agricultural and domestic sectors due to the distinctive nature of individual production processes through which energy flows can be traced. Fuel for this sector is often purchased, which can generate an appreciable level of energy accounting. For this reason, the introduction of fuel conservation methods or other energy technologies is relatively easier.

There is a wide range of small-scale rural industries. These must be distinguished and the type of energy used in each type identified. It is not unusual for energy demand from rural industries to be in competition with household fuel needs. They both depend on local energy resources.

In most cases, the commercial sector in rural areas is rather insignificant and usually consists of small shops, village bars and restaurants. Kerosene for lighting and wood for cooking are the main energy sources. The consumption of energy is dependent on the demand for the goods and services rendered which, in turn, depends on the density of population and the economic level of the community.

It is important to understand the energy consumption of this sector and assess its overall influence on the existing local energy resources. In small-scale industries, fuels are often purchased, which increases the chances for successful energy interventions.

NOTE

1. This includes biomass, solar, hydro and windpower resources.

REFERENCES

Barnett, A. (1983). 'Rural energy needs and the assessment of technical solutions', in *Rural Energy and the Third World*. Pergamon Press, Oxford.

Bialy, J. (1978). *Firewood Use in a Sri Lankan Village*. University of Edinburgh School of Engineering Sciences, Occasional Papers on Appropriate Technology.

Chambers, R. (1974). *Managing Rural Development: Ideas and Experience from East Africa*. Scandinavian Institute of African Studies, Uppsala.

—— (1983). *Rural Development. Putting the Last First*. Longman Inc., New York.

Eckholm, E. (1975). *The Other Energy Crisis: Firewood*. World Watch Paper No. 1, World Watch Institute, Washington DC.

Energy and Development (1985). *What Challenges? What Methods?* Research programme and results by network of research centres on behalf of the Commission of European Communities.

Ernst, F. (1978). *Fuelwood Consumption among rural families in Upper Volta, West Africa*. Voluntary paper, Eighth World Forestry Congress, Jakarta, pp. 2–3.

Fleuret, P. & A. (1978). 'Fuelwood use in a peasant community. A Tanzanian case study' in *Journal of Developing Areas*, p. 317.

Howes, M. (1984). *Rural Energy Systems in the Third World: A Critical Review of Issues and Methods*. IDRC.

Morse, R., Soesastro, H. M.& Schlegel, C (n.d.). *Energy for Rural Development, Principles, Issues and Methods*. East West Centre.

Stout, B. A. (1979). *Energy and World Agriculture*. FAO.

Agricultural Residues as Energy Sources 6

J.G.M. MASSAQUOI

Integrated rural development programmes normally feature increases in agricultural production, encouragement of rural and small-scale industries, expansion of employment opportunities and satisfaction of basic needs. The success of any of the components of the programme is critically dependent upon ready availability of different types of energy. Furthermore, the quantitative and qualitative shifts in energy requirements resulting from increases in population and structural changes in the economy lead to intensive competition for all forms of energy supply. At present, the major part of this energy comes from woodfuel. However, in countries where the demand for energy has outstripped the wood supply, more people are turning to the use of agricultural residues as a substitute. Most developing countries have agriculture-based economies. In some countries, the contribution of agriculture to the economy exceeds 60% of the GDP. It is therefore expected that wastes (or by-products) associated with agricultural activities could represent a very significant product within the economy if properly utilized. Already several countries in Asia and Eastern Africa are using large quantities of these residues as fuels for various economic and domestic activities.

This chapter discusses the role played by agricultural residues in the rural energy scene. It gives an analysis of the energy consumption pattern in developing countries on the basis of both the type of fuel used and the activity for which it is used. It then goes on to highlight the potential and limitations, in technology terms and otherwise, of the role of agricultural residues as fuel in rural development.

Agricultural Residues

As a first step in examining the role of energy from agricultural residues, it is important to define the materials that constitute this class of fuel. The term agricultural residue as used in this chapter represents the full spectrum of organic materials produced as by-products in agricultural operations. These can be divided into two broad categories: crop residues and animal residues. The latter include cow dung and poultry and pig manure. Crop residues include (1) woody residues such as corn cobs, millet stalks, jute sticks, cotton stalks, etc.; (2) crop straws such as rice, wheat and barley straws; (3) green crop residues such as the tops of root crops (e.g., groundnut tops) and (4) crop processing residues such as rice husk, coffee husk, peanut shells, etc.

Whereas crop processing residues are normally generated off-farm, the other crop residues (straws, tops, etc.) are normally generated on-farm. This raises the problem of collection for use as energy source in non-farming activities. When the cost of the logistics of collection from the farm exceeds the economic value of the residue as a fuel it is normally abandoned on the field and therefore plays no role in rural energy supply.

Another factor which affects the use of any particular residue is the bulk density. Lower bulk density results in higher transportation cost, thus making logistics of collection and utilization very expensive. This, in effect, renders the residue inaccessible. The issue of accessibility of on-farm residues is complex and depends on several parameters including collection cost, opportunity cost of the residue and the distribution of farm-community distances. This issue has been dealt with by Massaquoi (1988a).

On the whole, large quantities of residues are produced in every developing country. The quantity and type produced depend on the agricultural practice of the country. The amount of residue produced is directly related to the total crop yield by a factor called residue index. The latter is the quantity of residue generated per unit weight of crop yield. Tables 6.1 and 6.2 give a list of residues associated with various crops and their respective residue indices. The list is by no means exhaustive. It only gives the ones common to several regions of the developing world.

Demand Pattern for Energy from Agricultural Residues

Agricultural residues, except when converted, usually exist in solid form. They are therefore suitable for use mainly as substitutes for food fuel. Furthermore, in the rural areas, they are used in only three sectors of the economy: industry, agriculture and the household. In any country, the extent to which each of these sectors consumes agricultural residues as fuel will depend on many factors, some of which are:

1　*The agriculture product mix*: some agricultural crops generate residues which have very low energy value in their fresh state. The country or region producing such crops may not resort to the use of residue as fuel. Furthermore there are some crops which require a lot of heat energy in their farming operation and this energy could be provided by crop residues. In such a case the demand for crop residues as fuel will be high. Crops whose processing also generates a lot of residues could use these to supply the energy requirement for processing. Thus the amount of residue used as fuel in the rural economies of any country depends on the nature of the major crops produced in the country.

2　*Agricultural practices*: in some countries, especially in the equatorial

Table 6.1
Some crops and their associated residues

Crop	On-farm	House	Factory (crop-processing)
Maize	Stems & leaves	Cobs	Parchment
Rice	Tough straw/ tender straw	Tender straw	Husk
Millet, sorghum	Stalk	Chaff	–
Wheat	Straw	Tender straw	Husk
Barley	Straw	–	Husk
Potatoes	Leaves & roots	Potato peel	Potato pee
Cassava	Leaves & stem	Cassava peel	–
Yams	Leaves & stem	Yam peel	Yam peel
Pulses	–	Stem	–
Groundnuts	Straw	Peanut shell	Peanut shell, oil, mill effluent
Coconuts	Leaves	Husk/shell	Husk/shell, oil, mill effluent
Palm kernel	Empty fruit bunches, leaves	–	Husk/shell, fibres fins/oil mill effluent
Cotton	Stem	–	Husk
Sugar cane	Cane tops & leaves	–	Bagasse
Coffee (dry process)	–	–	Husk
Coffee (wet process)	–	–	Cherries
Plantain, banana	Stem	Fruit stem	–
Jute	Stalks	–	–
Cocoa	Pods	–	–

Table 6.2
Value of residue indices for various crops

Residue	Primary crop	Residue index
Maize stover and leaves	Maize	1:0-2.5
Maize cob	Maize	0.2-0.5
Maize parchment	Maize	0.2
Rice straw	Rice	1.1-3.0
Rice husk	Rice	0.3
Millet stalk	Millet	2.9-3.7
Sorghum stalk	Sorghum	0.9-4.6
Wheat straw	Wheat	0.7–1.8
Barley straw	Barley	0.6-1.8
Cassava stem	Cassava	0.2
Coconut shell	Coconut	0.65
Coconut husk	Coconut	1.60
Coffee husk	Coffee	1.0
Cocoa pod husk	Cocoa	1.0
Bagasse	Sugar cane	0.1-0.3
Cotton stem	Cotton	3.5-4.0
Groundnut straw	Groundnut	23.0-2.9
Groundnut shell	Groundnut	1.0

SOURCE: Barnard and Kristoferson (1985); Openshaw (1986); World Bank (1985); Massaquoi (1985); Muller (1978).

forest regions of Africa and Asia, the bush fallow farming system is still practised. This involves clearing large areas of forest/woodlands for farming. Usually a substantial quantity of woodfuel is generated in the course of the operation and this supply of woodfuel discourages the use of residue. For instance, a study by Massaquoi (1985a) of a West African country showed that enough woodfuel was generated from the clearing of farm land to supply all the rural energy requirement for woodfuel.

3 *The scarcity of other traditional fuels*: since residues tend to compete directly with woodfuel as an energy source, their demand and extensive use will depend on the supply of the latter. Thus forested regions of the world are less likely to utilize residues in the energy supply.

4 *Energy demand pattern*: the nature of the economy, and in particular the economic contribution of the various sectors, determines the demand for various types of fuel. For instance, countries with a large industrial base usually have big industries whose demand is normally for conventional energy. This factor is especially important with reference to rural development programmes. When integrated rural development programmes are introduced, initially the increase in economic activity will lead to a rapid rise in the demand for energy for which residues may be substituted. As the programme becomes more and more successful, the rural economy may assume a structure wherein a greater contribution comes from small-scale industries whose demand for energy may be for electricity and other conventional energy sources. Similarly, the demand for energy for the household sector may change to fuel oil and electricity as the income of the population increases. Thus, after a rural development programme has succeeded for a while, there is a possibility that demand for residues may actually decline unless efforts are made to convert them to electricity or gas.

5 *Competing demands*: in most countries residues are used for purposes other than as fuel sources. For instance, rice husk may be used as animal food and rice straw could be used as fertilizer if left on the field. Some other residues are also useful as raw material for industries such as the paper industry. Under these circumstances the amount of residue used as fuel will be quite small.

The above factors are by no means the only determinants of the use of agricultural residues as fuel in rural areas. However, they could be used to explain some of the disparity in the level of use of residues as fuel in different regions. Other factors such as the cost of the end-use technologies, etc. are universal and independent of location.

Energy consumption pattern in developing countries

It is quite difficult to estimate the national energy consumption pattern in a developing country because some of the biggest sources of energy are non-commercial and hence do not enter into the trade and production records.

Therefore, data on the contribution of residues to the energy supply are usually quite old, and sometimes non-existent.

There are major differences in the level of the use of residue as fuel from region to region. Historically, the major users have been countries in Asia. In China, for instance, nearly 40% of the rural household energy consumption is from crop residues (FAO/RAPA, 1987a) and in Thailand 25% of the total rural energy requirement comes from residues such as bagasse and rice husks (FAO/RAPA, 1987b).

The contribution of residue to energy consumption in some African countries is also significant. One of the biggest users of residue is Ethiopia, where it supplies 15% of the total energy requirement. Table 6.3 shows the energy consumption pattern of three African countries from the different regions of the continent. Each of the countries have geographical areas facing the threat of deforestation and hence the inhabitants of these areas rely on residues for supply of fuel.

In Latin America, the contribution of residue is very small because of the availability of good forest cover which encourages the use of woodfuel in rural areas; another factor is the large industrial base in most of these countries.

Although it is quite difficult to determine the amount of agricultural residue used as energy in various sectors of the rural economy, it is at least possible to identify the activities of each sector of the economy for which they could be used as an energy source. In subsequent sections we shall discuss the types of residue used in various activities and the state in which the residue is used.

Table 6.3
Energy consumption by source for three African countries (%)

Source	Ethiopia	Swaziland	Ghana
Woodfuel	80.0	35.5	69.7
Petroleum	4.3	19.2	22.3
Hydro-electricity	0.5	6.7	3.38
Coal	–	13.8	–
Draught power	9.4	–	–
Residues	15.0	23.85	4.54
Others	–	0.84	–

Source: Massaquoi 1988b

Use of residue as fuel in rural industries

One of the useful consequences of any integrated rural development programme is a spurt in rural industrial activities. The scope for generating rural income from a variety of small- and medium-scale rural industries is quite significant. These range from agro-industries to manufacturing industries for soap, bricks, metal products and leather goods. All these require considerable inputs of energy. Usually most of the energy required is provided by woodfuel. And since it is quite easy to substitute certain types of agricultural residue for fuelwood, there is great potential for the use of residue in rural industries. Table 6.4 supplies a summary of the types of rural industries and the forms of energy they require. The table also shows those types of industry which could use residue directly as a substitute fuel. By far the biggest users of residues in the industrial sector are the agro-industries. These industries generate a lot of processing waste which they end up using as energy without incurring any additional cost. Examples of residues used in agro-industries are palm fruit fibres and husks, bagasse, and rice and coconut husks. These residues are usually used to generate process heat in boilers. In some cases the residue is used to generate electricity which is sold to the grid system. An example is Mauritius, where electricity is generated from bagasse. In Thailand, 5.5 million tons of bagasse is used in the sugar industry while 1.3 tons of husk is used in the rice mills. (FAO/RAPA 1987b)

As rural industrial development progresses, the type of energy in growing demand will be suitable for shaft power to run industries such as wood and metal works and grinding mills. In such a case the direct use of residue in industry will decline but indirect use, mainly in the form of electricity or gas, will increase.

Table 6.4
Industrial energy uses of agricultural residues

Activity	Types of energy	Suitability of agricultural residue	Examples of residues currently used
Heating, cooking	Process heat	Direct combustion of any solid residue	a Bagasse in sugar industry b Nut shells in oil processing industry.
Wood working	Shaft power	Not suitable except converted to electricity or gas	None
Metal working	Shaft power	Not suitable except converted to electricity or gas	None
Forging, smelting	Process heat	Not suitable	None
Brickmaking	Process heat	Direct combustion	Husks
Mineral processing, other manufacturing operations (e.g. soap making)	Process heat	Direct combustion	Cocoa pods
Agro-industry	Process heat	Direct combustion	Husks, shells, bagasse

Use of residue as fuel in agriculture

Table 6.5 shows the types of activity involved in agriculture and the nature of the energy required. From this table, it is observed that only two main activities in the agriculture sector can utilize residues directly without conversion to gas. These activities are drying/curing and rice parboiling. Both sets of activities require only process heat which is obtainable from the combustion of residues. Despite its suitability, residue is used very little in drying operations. This may be surprising considering that the residue is generated on the farm where the drying also takes place. Drying of most food crops, except where large quantities are involved, is carried out with solar energy in the traditional way (i.e., spreading in the sun). Residue is used in the drying of most non-food (or cash) crops, on the other hand. For instance, in Ivory Coast some of the 150,000 tonnes of coffee husk generated annually is used in drying the beans.

Table 6.5
Energy uses of residues in the agricultural sector

Activity	Types of energy	Suitability of residues of fuel for activity	Examples of residues currently used in the activity
Planting and cultivating	Shaft power	Not suitable except converted to gas	None
Pumping	Shaft power	Not suitable except converted to gas	None
Harvesting	Shaft power	Not suitable except converted to gas	None
Drying	Process heat	Direct combustion	Coffee husk for drying of coffee cherries
Parboiling	Process heat	Direct combustion	Rice husk
Milling	Shaft power	Not suitable except with gasifier	Gas from rice husks

In rice-growing countries in Asia and West Africa, some rice husk is used in parboiling. In general the quantity of residue used as fuel in agriculture (not including processing activities) is quite small, since agricultural activities tend to require shaft power which is provided by liquid or gaseous fuel.

Use of residues as fuel in the household sector

Rural energy demand is concentrated in the household sector and its supply comes mainly from non-commercial energy. However, significant structural changes should be expected to occur in future as a result of rural development policies.

Depending on the size of the industrial base, the consumption of energy in rural households can range from 50% to 80% of the total rural energy demand. In Thailand, for instance, 50% of the energy demand is consumed in the household sector, whereas in southern African countries this figure is usually about 80% (Massaquoi, 1988b).

Most of the energy demand in rural households is for cooking. Thus the residues used in the household sector are usually those which are dry in the fresh state. Hence, the most common types of residue used as fuel in rural households, apart from cow dung, are those connected with the cereal crop. Among the cereal crops, maize has residues with particularly good energy characteristics: a low ash content (1.6%) and a higher than average bulk density. In addition, maize cobs can be used in normal woodstoves and hence reduce the cost of inter-fuel transition (this is also true of sorghum stalks). Thus countries which grow large quantities of maize and sorghum are more likely to use residues as fuel in the household sector. This clearly underlines the earlier statement that the type of crop produced in a country is a very significant determinant of the extent to which residues will be used as fuel.

Table 6.6 gives the rural household energy use pattern for five countries in Asia and Africa. The African countries listed in the table are reportedly the biggest users of residue on the continent. In Asia, China uses very large quantities of sorghum stalks and maize cobs and stalks as fuel. By contrast residues are very little used in rural households in Thailand because the large quantities of rice husk and bagasse produced in the country are more suitable for use as fuel in the industrial and agricultural sectors than in the household sector.

Table 6.6
Household energy use pattern in selected countries

Fuel	Ethiopia	Ghana	Swaziland	Thailand	China
Traditional fuel	98.3%	93.4%	78.3%	92.0%	89.0%
a Woodfuel	(80.9)	(87.1)	(75%)	–	(40.0)
b Residues	(17.3)	(6.28%)	(3.3%)	–	(49.0)
Electricity	0.1%	1.68%	5.0%	3.0%	1.5%
Petroleum products	0.27%	4.93%	6.67%	5.0%	0.7%
Draught power	1.23%	–	–	–	–
Others	–	–	10.34%	–	8.8%
SOURCES:	Sheriff (1987)	Opong and Gomez (1987)	Richards (1987)	FAO/RAPA 1987b	FAO/RAPA 1987a

We can thus conclude that the role of residues in the rural household energy sector depends on the nature of the crops produced. In particular, crops which produce dry and monolithic (rather than pulverized) wastes encourage the use of residue because the cost of inter-fuel transition is limited.

Potential and Constraints

There is considerable scope for the use of residues in rural energy supply. In fact, in countries where surveys have been conducted it has been found that the supply of residue fuel is large enough to meet a substantial part of the energy requirements of the rural communities (Massaquoi 1985) – at little or no cost in the case of direct transition from fuelwood to residue. This advantage of forward and backward transition from wood to residue enhances the potential for its use as fuel, since consumers will not have to acquire any special end-use technology for the purpose.

The high potential of residues as fuel cannot be properly utilized, however, because of constraints on its development. These problems include: the cost of conversion and end-use technology, the non-availability of the technology, the lack of information on the resource base, and the social/cultural inhibitions of the population.

The range and choice of available technologies for a particular end-user or conversion process is very important to the viability of any operation. In the case of residues, all the hardware components of the technologies required are available. The problems are the availability of skills to operate and maintain the hardware and the cost of the technology. In the case of cost, we distinguish between the cost of end-use equipment and the cost of conversion systems. These two costs together, or independently, make it difficult to deliver the energy at affordable prices.

Thus the transition from conventional energy to agricultural residues becomes difficult. In some developing countries the lack of skills in the rural areas to operate gasifiers and other conversion and end-use technologies makes the switch to residues very difficult even when there is money to afford it. It is only when a community produces monolithic fuel where there is little transition cost or when conversion and end-use technologies are subsidized that the problem posed by the cost of technology becomes tractable.

In countries where there is an acute shortage of fuelwood, the transition to residues as a source of energy occurs without any promotional effort. However, for those with abundant forest cover there is usually no fuelwood deficit, and in such countries the problem is one of aborting an impending disaster rather than coping with a crisis. In such a situation the population is not likely to embrace the use of fuel of lower quality enthusiastically. As long as there is wood they will continue to use it until it starts to run out and its price shoots up. To promote the use of residues as fuel in such a situation would therefore require policy at a very high level. However, any policy on the use of agricultural residues as fuel will require reliable estimates of the supply potential and the characteristics of the available residues. For it is obviously useless and difficult to promote something about which very little is known. It is in recognition of this fact that several international and national organizations have carried out programmes to develop and standardize assessment methodologies and also to carry out projects leading to the evaluation of supply potential of residues.

Although the method of assessing the resource base of agricultural residues is fairly straightforward (Massaquoi, 1985a & 1985b), that of assessing supply potential is a little more complicated because of the problem of estimating the fraction accessible (Wereko-Brobby, 1986a and 1986b).

Concluding Remarks

The following general remarks briefly sum up the existing situation regarding the role of residues in rural development projects.

Details on the level of contribution of residues to energy supply are not readily available because of the non-commercial nature of this type of fuel. However, most rural communities in developing countries, especially in Asia and some parts of Africa, are known to be using large quantities of residue. Most crop processing wastes are used almost everywhere they are produced.

The disparity in the patterns and levels of utilization throughout the developing world is determined by several factors among which the extent of the scarcity of other traditional fuels and the type of residues generated locally are paramount.

The promotion of the use of agricultural residues as sources of energy in integrated rural development is constrained by the lack of data on the resource base and supply potential, and by the high cost of the transition to this fuel.

The potential of residues as sources of energy is considerable and most developing countries have good supplies of the material. The potential of this fuel resource has increased recently because of developments in conversion technology which facilitate the delivery of various types of conventional energy from residues.

REFERENCES

Barnard, G. & Kristoferson, L. (1985). *Agricultural Residues as Fuel in the Third World*. Earthscan, London.
FAO Regional Office for Asia and the Pacific (RAPA) (1987a) (1987b). 'Rural energy in China: demand, supply and development'. *RAPA Bulletin*, Nos 1 & 2, Bangkok, Thailand.
Massaquoi, J. G. M. (1985a). *Biomass Resources Assessment: A Survey of Sierra Leone's Energy Potential from Agricultural and Forestry Wastes*. Commonwealth Science Council, Technical Publications Series, No. 160, London.
———— (1985b). 'Assessment of Sierra Leone's energy potential from agricultural wastes' in *Renewable Energy Development in Africa*, Vol. 1. Commonwealth Science Council, London, pp. 141–52.

———— (1987). *Biomass Resources Assessment Phase II – Economic Value and Supply Potential of Rice Residues in Sierra Leone.* Commonwealth Science Council, Technical Publications Series, No. 220.

———— (1988a). 'Assessing the energy potential of agricultural residues'. *RERIC International Energy Journal,* Vol. 10, No. 2.

———— (1988b). 'Use of agricultural residues in small-scale energy supply in Africa'. Paper presented at Expert Group Meeting on Small scale Energy Sources in Rural Africa, Rome (available from UNITAR/UNDP Small Energy Resources Centre, Italy).

Muller, Z. O. (1978). *Recycling of Organic Wastes for Production Purposes.* UNDP/FAO Projects publication.

Openshaw, K. (1986). 'Concepts and methods for the compilation of statistics of biomass used as energy'. Working paper presented at ad-hoc expert group meeting, 29 September–3 October 1986. Available from UN Statistic Office, New York.

Opong & Gomez. (1987). 'Ghana energy policy issues'. Unpublished working paper presented at World Bank regional energy policy analysis seminar, 26 October–8 November, Nairobi, Kenya.

Richards. J. (1987). 'Energy situation in Swaziland'. Unpublished working paper presented at World Bank regional energy policy analysis seminar, 26 October–8 November, Nairobi, Kenya.

Sheriff, A. Y. (1987). 'Energy policy issues in Ethiopia'. Unpublished working paper presented at World Bank regional energy policy analysis seminar, 26 October–8 November, Nairobi, Kenya.

Wereko-Brobby, C. Y. (1986a). 'Common accounting procedures for biomass resources assessment in developing countries'. *Biomass,* 10, pp 265–390.

———— (1986b). *Proceedings of the Biomass Technical Working Group Meeting in Mauritius, 3–13 December 1986.* Commonwealth Science Council, London.

II SUB-SAHARAN AFRICA

7 Renewable Energy Research and Development in West and Central Africa

MICHAEL W. BASSEY

Commercial energy supply in the urban areas of countries in West and Central African countries is in the form of fuel oil and electricity generated largely from hydro-power. Most of the electrical energy is used in mining activities, industrial sectors, urban households, and private and government buildings.

Less than 10% of the electricity generated is used by the rural population. Considering that over 80% of the population reside in rural areas, where the bulk of national food output is produced, there is a gross disparity in the use of conventional energy between urban and rural areas.

There is a correlation between quality of life and energy consumption. Developing countries' use of fuel is about 5%–10% of that in industrialized countries. Developing countries, which account for about 50% of the world population, use only about 9% of the available commercial energy (UNIDO, 1979).

Developing countries' energy consumption growth is about 5%. The demand for commercial energy is increasing faster than the GNP in these countries. There is insufficient foreign exchange to import oil products needed to stimulate growth in the urban, industrial and transportation sectors. The countries of West and Central Africa are among the poorest in the world, most of them without conventional energy sources and nursing ailing economies. All in all, this is an alarming situation.

Energy Requirements

Energy demand in West and Central Africa is for activities in the household and for the public, transportation, industrial, agricultural, processing, mining and construction sectors. In rural areas, energy is needed for integrated rural development in agriculture, processing, small-scale industrial activities, transportation and social services. Some of the main activities in rural areas are outlined in Table 7.1.

Oil-importing developing countries are expected to consume about twice as much oil in 1990 as they did in 1980 (World Bank, 1980). There is a strong dependence on oil compared to other sources of fuel. Given the low production

Table 7.1
Some uses for energy in rural areas

Agriculture	Land preparation, planting, water pumping, harvesting, fertilizer production
Processing	Drying, dehulling, grinding, cooking, grating
Industry	Workshops for manufacture and repairs
Conservation	Drying, cooling
Transportation	Marketing, social and health services
Social Needs	Medical treatment, lighting, entertainment, education
Home	Lighting, cooking, ironing

of other fossil fuels, it is not possible for them to replace oil without fundamental changes in various areas.

The majority of countries in West and Central Africa are oil importers. Most of the countries also have actual or potential fuelwood problems, since the present annual consumption cannot be sustained without damage to the environment by the year 2000. Oil is used mainly for electricity generation and transportation in the urban, industrial, mining and large-scale processing sectors. Little of this energy is used by the rural population. It is estimated that non-commercial energy accounts for 80%–90% of the total energy use in these countries.

With the exception of Congo, Nigeria, Gabon and Zaire which are net oil exporters, nearly all of the countries in West and Central Africa import between 76% and 100% of their commercial energy in the form of oil.

Energy Supply

Commercial energy

Available energy supplies in these countries can be classed into three main categories:
- Commercial energy: oil, gas, coal, hydro-electric power;
- Traditional energy: fuelwood, charcoal, agro-waste, animal power;
- Renewable energy: solar, wind, ocean and wave power, small-scale hydro.

Very few countries in the region are net exporters of commercial energy. Statistics of proven and exploitable reserves of oil, coal and hydro indicate that, with substantial investment, several countries can reduce dependence on imported energy for commercial use.

Biomass energy

Traditional energy sources such as fuelwood, charcoal, agro-waste, animal waste and animal power are used by the majority of the populations for home and small-scale processing needs. For most countries, estimates of the availability of traditional energy sources are not widely available. Results are, however, available for some countries on the assessment of biomass resources (Wereko-Brobby, 1986; Viaud, 1984). The situation in Sierra Leone (Massaquoi, 1985) is representative of the resources available in the humid countries in the coastal region. In the Sahelian countries, there are fewer traditional energy sources due to the low rainfall and the resulting limited vegetation. Table 7.2 gives an indication of the various types of biomass that can be put into productive use for energy generation. This list is not exhaustive as the importance of any form of energy depends on the particular local conditions. For example, in the Sahelian countries, where people in the rural areas have cows which produce waste that dries quickly in the dry and hot environment, dung is used for cooking. In humid areas, where there is more vegetation, woodfuel is more abundantly available. Other crop residues and animal wastes are not used significantly.

Alcohol production for energy in the region is non-existent. The potential for this fuel is enormous, given the wide-scale production of carbohydrate-based crops such as cassava. For example, Nigeria produced 1,621,000 tonnes of cassava in 1978/79 (Bagpai *et al.*, 1986). This crop is grown in large quantities in other countries such as Zaire, Togo, Ivory Coast and Sierra Leone. The use of food crops for the production of alcohol implies competition between food and fuel but there exist policy instruments to stimulate large-scale production of crops for both food and alcohol production.

Table 7.2
Available biomass in West and Central Africa

Source	Description
Agriculture & Forestry	Fuel wood, charcoal, rice straw, rice husk, coffee husk, cocoa pods, bagasse, peanut shells, palm fruit fibres, palm kernel shells, cassava peels, sorghum and millet straw, maize cobs.
Animal waste	Cattle dung, pig manure, poultry waste
Animal	Traction power

Solar energy

Solar energy is abundant in the region. All of the countries have some sort of programme to monitor its availability. The intensity of solar energy depends on various factors such as latitude, atmospheric conditions and the time of year. In the Sahelian zone, solar radiation is available throughout the year, but in diminished quantities during the harmattan period due to dust storms. Countries in the coastal regions have significantly lower levels of solar radiation during the rainy season because of abundant cloud cover. The range of solar energy availability in the region is shown in Figure 7.1.

Solar radiation data for the region suggest that technologies such as flat plate collectors suitable for diffuse insolation can be used effectively. In locations which have significant cloud cover, technologies such as parabolic collectors are not effective during most of the year. Nevertheless, the abundance of solar radiation makes it practical to use simple thermal and photovoltaic devices in rural areas.

Wind energy

Wind energy is very site-specific. It is not attractive for the region as a whole because wind speeds in most locations are less than five metres per second. But in certain areas of the Sahel, and at higher elevations, continuous wind speeds make wind energy an attractive alternative to water pumping and electricity generation.

Information on the wind resource potential of various locations in the region is less available than in the case of solar energy. It is possible to map out the solar potential of a country on the basis of a relatively small number of strategically located measurement sites. This is not the case for wind energy which depends on altitude, surface contours, location, time of year, etc. Although several wind measuring stations exist in many countries, the collected data are often kept in archives for decades without any analysis being carried out to determine the potential of wind resources.

Energy Assessment

Experience with energy in West and Central Africa indicates that a missing link in most attempts to promote the use of non-conventional energy sources is adequate energy assessment studies. In the interest of sound planning, adequate knowledge of the energy requirements in all sectors of the economy, as well as knowledge of the energy options (supplies) that can fulfil the requirements, are prerequisites.

Current information suggests that none of the countries under discussion has comprehensive documentation on its energy situation. Some countries, however, have limited data on the use of energy in certain sectors of the

Figure 7.1
Daily total solar radiation available in some countries.

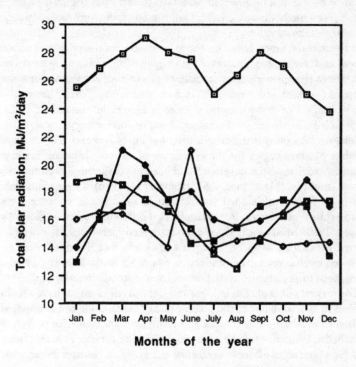

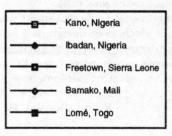

SOURCE: Bassey & Schmidt, 1987.

economy such as household, agriculture, services, industry and commerce (Davidson, 1985). The absence of adequate information on energy use is explained by the lack of qualified personnel to carry out the studies, inappropriate survey methodologies, lack of continuous follow-up for updating, and improper documentation.

In the past ten years, however, the identification of the types and quantities of new and renewable sources of energy has received greater attention. Publications that provide solar insolation information are available for several countries (Ezekwe and Ezeilo, 1981; Amouzou et al., 1987; Akinsete, 1986; Bassey, 1982). For many countries, there is enough information available on which to base decisions on the potential use of solar energy.

Reliable data on quantities and distribution of biomass are not as easily available. Methodologies for the estimation of various forms of waste, wood resources, etc. have been developed and used to obtain more preliminary data in some countries (Massaquoi, 1985; Bagpai et al., 1986). These methodologies need to be further developed and refined so as to obtain consistent results and to explain differences. For example, two different studies in Sierra Leone (Bassey, 1980; Massaquoi, 1985) gave estimated quantities for sawdust that differed by a factor of three. It is not known whether the differences can be attributed to changes in the production of timber in the country, or whether one or both of the studies rested on an inaccurate methodology.

The majority of countries in West and Central Africa either have a fuelwood problem or will have one at the present rate of exploitation of firewood. While the fuelwood situation in the hot and humid coastal countries is disturbing, the Sahelian countries face an even more alarming future. This reinforces the need for a concerted effort to determine the available biomass in each country on a more continuous basis.

Conventional needs assessment studies often use very structured methodologies which, even though they have their merits, miss certain important supplementary information. There is, therefore, a need to modify some of the existing survey methods to take into account the less quantitative aspects that are very germane to the information being sought. A possible methodology is the Rapid Rural Appraisal technique, which requires an inter-disciplinary approach (Khon Kaen University, 1987).

Technological, Social, Cultural and Environmental Issues

The end result expected from any technology using any energy source is satisfactory performance. With this as an ultimate goal, certain basic steps have been proposed which, if followed, will increase the possibility of achieving a positive impact.

The first and perhaps the most crucial is the assessment of the needs of the beneficiaries and possible technical solutions. It is here that issues related to social, cultural, environmental and technical concerns should initially be dealt with. This is an element that is consistently missing in the use of alternative energy sources for rural development. Technology development projects in the region have failed and continue to fail due to this lacuna (Bassey, 1987). Certain fundamental considerations which should be investigated are discussed below (Barnett, 1982).

CLEAR DEFINITION OF THE RURAL ENERGY PROBLEM
There is usually no need to defend the need for energy but it has to be articulated within the context of the rural system as a whole. For example, the lack of fuelwood could be a consequence of desertification. However, the problem may not be rectified by planting trees if there are underlying socio-cultural and political constraints related to land ownership and food production.

HOW USER NEEDS AFFECT CHOICE AND DIFFUSION OF TECHNOLOGIES
Rural dwellers have been known to reject technologically sound systems. Solar cookers and solar dryers are well-known cases in point. Certain cultural, social and economic aspects of the potential users must be understood for effective development and adoption of any technology. For example, women used to cooking in a kitchen in the evening cannot be expected to spend the afternoon outside in the sun, using a solar cooker. Nor can farmers used to burning firewood be expected readily to accept gathering cow-dung for use in what they may consider to be a smelly biogas digester. On the other hand, the pig farmer who is used to the smell and collection of the waste of his animals may more easily adapt to such a digester. The question of how the user will pay for a technology needs to be carefully considered as this is a prerequisite for a viable technology.

OPTIMUM LEVEL OF PARTICIPATION OF INTENDED BENEFICIARIES
The present trend in development projects is consciously to involve the potential users of a given technology in all aspects of its development. There is substantial interest in 'participatory action research' in which all activities are carried out with the active participation of the target beneficiaries. It is, however, important to optimize this level of collaboration in order to maximize efficiency. The rural population should be involved in the needs assessment study and they should be made to realize that the success of the investigation depends on them. As pointed out in a study to determine farmers' perceptions of their drying needs in Sierra Leone (Bassey, 1989a), even if the farmers' point of view is not justified, it is important for research and development workers to understand it. Such knowledge may be the key to the successful introduction of the technology. Relevant information can be collected quickly by allowing for active consultation between the developers of a technology and the potential users (Kpakote et al., 1988).

USE OF APPROPRIATE SURVEY TECHNIQUES

Methods used to collect information, on which to base decisions regarding the choice of energy options, are often inadequate. They often do not obtain information relevant to the problem. In view of the range of qualitative and quantitative information required on social, cultural, political, technological, marketing, historical and other aspects, conventional survey techniques that only use enumerators to record answers to questions are inappropriate. What is needed is a combination of the traditional survey techniques that collect quantitative and qualitative data, and other less rigid methodologies. A method which has been found to be intensive, iterative, cost-effective, expeditious and interactive is the Rapid Rural Appraisal (RRA) technique (Khon Kaen University, 1987). Essentially, it involves small inter-disciplinary teams that are interested in obtaining information from the rural population using semi-structured interviews which are frequently checked and refined. As a result, a lot is learned in a relatively short time about rural problems.

Considering the wide scope of energy assessment for rural development and the need to obtain and constantly update information, RRA is a useful tool for needs assessment studies on new and renewable sources of energy.

TYPE OF TECHNOLOGY TO BE DEVELOPED

Technological options should be determined during initial assessment studies. Technology selection will be guided by factors such as: the type of energy being proposed; the expertise of available manpower; technical skills in the immediate area where the technology will be used; available materials and tools; production facilities; level of sophistication desired; technical viability (repairs and maintenance); fuel supply; possible impact on people; cost of technology; familiarity with the new fuel; and the potential change in social activities as a result of the intervention.

EXISTING LOCAL ADMINISTRATIVE STRUCTURE

It is useful during the problem identification stage to determine the overall administrative structure that is already in place. Many countries have rural management systems which may not be considered 'progressive' in terms of Western standards of democracy and freedom of expression, but which work and fulfil the needs of the rural population. While improving them may be desirable and may improve the chances of making a technology viable, such changes are best carried out with the consensus of all concerned in order to minimize the chances of failure.

ROLE OF INTER-DISCIPLINARY TEAMS

The wide range of the subjects that need to be covered during the assessment study calls for inputs from various disciplines. In the past development of new and renewable sources of energy, technologists often worked in isolation, with little or no contact with the intended beneficiaries. The developed technology was then 'introduced' to users with little preparation or follow-up to determine crucial cultural, social and economic effects (Bassey, 1987). Evaluations of such projects by social scientists highlighted the lack of inter-disciplinary collaboration. This is largely due to academic training where disciplines are highly compartmentalized and which produce professionals (technologists as well as social scientists) who are unwilling to venture out of their realm of training and expertise. This situation is undesirable and should be rectified.

Some environmental issues

Environmental concerns are perhaps one of the most pressing issues in the use of alternate sources of energy. As already mentioned, most of the countries of West and Central Africa face or will soon face fuelwood problems. Fuelwood, the main source of energy in rural areas, is being depleted at an alarming rate. Charcoal production using traditional methods is about 25% efficient. Improved stoves which increase the utilization efficiency of wood or charcoal are expensive and unaffordable for the majority of the population who use traditional stoves with less than 10% efficiency. In addition, programmes for re-afforestation are either limited in scope or are not successful.

In the area of hydro-electricity production, special efforts have been made to reduce the damage to the ecology. In a fragile Sahelian environment, the diversion of even small streams can have a negative impact on human, animal and plant life. Sources of income such as fishing and hunting can be adversely affected.

Each source of energy has its environmental advantages and disadvantages. The development and use of any form of energy should be based on a compre-hensive analysis of its environmental impact.

Research and Development Activities

Research and development institutions

A significant amount of work on the research and development of new and renewable sources of energy has been carried out in countries of the region. Research institutions in some countries e.g. Senegal (Centre d'Études et de Recherches sur les Energies Renouvelables – CERER), Mali (Laboratoire sur l'Energie Solaire – LESO), Niger (Office de l'Energie Solaire – ONERSOL), Togo (Laboratoire Solaire – LESO), Ghana (Food Research Institute), Sierra Leone (University of Sierra Leone) and Nigeria (University of Nigeria, Nsukka) have accumulated years of experience in new and renewable energy sources. Several other institutions based in industrialized countries – such as Groupe de Recherches et d'Échanges Technologiques (GRET) and Groupe Energies Renouvelables (GRES) in France, VITA in the United States and Intermediate Technology Development Group (ITDG) in the UK – have also made useful contributions to the use of renewable energy in the region (UNESCO, 1982). Information on much of this work is not accessible, however, because of inadequate documentation and circulation.

Scope of activities

It is not possible in such a short paper to attempt an in-depth review of the work done in West and Central African countries. A sample of the types of research and development studies undertaken has been compiled by the Commonwealth Science Council (1986). An estimated quarter to one-third of the work carried out was on the use of solar driers in agriculture. Solar technologies such as cookers, water heaters, stills, ponds, refrigerators and sterilizers have also been investigated. In the area of biomass, the production of biogas from various animal and plant waste has been investigated in several countries, and so has charcoal production. Use of agricultural crop residues such as rice husk and sawdust has received less attention.

Crop drying

Drying of agricultural crops is the most widespread method of preserving foodstuffs. Bassey and Schmidt have compiled results of work done in several countries in Africa (Bassey & Schmidt, 1987). Due to the lack of electrical power farms, natural convective dryers of the direct, indirect and mixed mode types have been studied for the drying of a wide range of crops. The majority of these studies, however, have taken place at the laboratory level. A major constraint on the use of natural flow dryers is low airflow rates through the crops, resulting in low drying rates. Technical progress has been made in this area recently (Oosthuizen, 1988; Oosthuizen & Sheriff, 1988). Some of the reasons for the limited use of solar dryers include (Bassey, 1989b): poor problem identification; poor technical designs; high cost of the drying technology; low levels of production on farms; inadequate storage facilities; poor transportation facilities; underdeveloped distribution systems; non-existent government policies to improve product quality; lack of locally produced construction materials; inadequate technical expertise; absence of an inter-disciplinary approach; lack of electricity supply; and inadequate financial resources and planning. Efforts by the Commonwealth Science Council (CSC) and the International Development Research Centre (IDRC) have helped to promote dialogue between various African institutions on this subject. More recent input by IDRC has been aimed at developing better performance dryers and adopting a truly inter-disciplinary approach in the development and promotion of activities.

Solar water heaters

Solar water heaters have been developed in countries such as Niger, Senegal,

Nigeria (Chandra and Oguntuase, 1986) and Sierra Leone (Bassey and Brown, 1982). In Niger, for example, some designs have been manufactured for both private and public use. While it is one of the solar technologies that can gain rapid use in rural development, it still has not made an impact even in the urban sector, where a solar water heater can register significant savings in electricity heating bills. One of the reasons cited for lack of progress is the limited promotion of the technology due to a shortage of information on the economics of its long-term use. The author is unaware of systematic studies in countries of the region aimed at collecting performance data so as to determine the economic and technical viability of solar water heaters. These studies are needed in order to assess the effect on overall performance of factors such as the harmattan period, the rainy season and supplementary electric heating.

Solar stills

Solar stills are of interest to several researchers due to their potential use in the automotive, health and food sub-sectors. Designs have been developed and tested at the laboratory level in several countries but, due to high cost, no meaningful use has been made of this technology in the region.

Solar cookers

Cookers using solar energy (Chigbundu, 1986) have not made an impact in rural areas owing to their complexity and high cost; prevailing culinary practices also make them unacceptable. Efforts to develop steam cookers that can be used indoors, a characteristic that would increase the chances of adoption, have so far failed to overcome the low efficiency of such devices (Bassey, 1985). Further research and development work should concentrate on low-cost cookers with heat storage to suit traditional cooking practices.

Solar ponds

In view of the need to obtain continuous power for various activities, solar ponds are an attractive proposition in rural areas because they can store heat energy for long periods. Only one study on solar ponds has been undertaken in the region (Gnininvi & Amouzou-Abiba, 1985). This work, which is being carried out at the Université du Benin in Togo using a pond with an area of 200 square metres, has recorded working temperatures of about 80° Celsius throughout most of the year. It is presently being used as the source of heat in the development of a large-scale maize storage system.

Solar pumps

Solar pumps using flat plate collectors for heating a thermodynamic fluid that produces the pumping power have been tested in rural areas of the Sahel for many years. Many of them, however, have ceased to function due to technical as well as socio-economic factors. The availability of cheaper and more reliable solar cells offers a more attractive solar technology option for rural applications. The Centre d'Études et de Recherches sur les Energies Renouvelables (CERER) in Senegal is carrying out research on solar pumps (IDRC, 1986).

Solar refrigeration

Solar refrigeration research has not had any significant impact. Several imported refrigeration systems have been field tested in countries such as Senegal. The results of such tests are usually unavailable locally. Owing to lack of funds, work carried out at local institutions tends to be limited to the testing of components of the system (Arinze *et al.*, 1986; Toure & Niare, 1985).

Use of biomass

Both animal and vegetable waste have been used in the production of biogas using anaerobic digesters in several countries (e.g., Viaud & Preveral, 1986; Menanteau & Peultier, 1985). The activities have ranged from laboratory-scale testing to larger systems on farms using waste from cows, chickens, pigs and straw. Unfortunately, information on the testing of such biogas plants is not readily available, making it difficult to determine the merits and drawbacks of various systems used. The main problem with biogas plants is the collection of the waste and their operation. While the technology can be applied in some rural areas with little difficulty, long-term performance data are needed to undertake comprehensive technological and economic evaluation of biogas.

Efforts have been made in Ghana on the pyrolysis of biomass such as sawdust and wood shavings (Hagan, 1986). Useful gaseous and liquid fuels and charcoal were produced. Economic analysis of pyrolysis is, however, not available due to lack of maintenance of the plant. The use of this type of technology needs a substantial amount of raw material and good process control.

Charcoal production from wood is an active income-generating activity in all countries of the region. Generally wasteful traditional methods of processing are used even though improved technology is available; there is no known country in the region which uses improved techniques for large-scale charcoal production. It is possible to produce charcoal from waste such as rice husks, groundnut shells and sawdust, using controlled burning and then compacting the carbon product into briquettes. There has been no such development in the region, however. Burning of substances such as sawdust is also possible in a 'hole-through-packed-bed' type burner (Bassey, 1983b) and has been successfully used in the operation of dryers, water heaters, cookers and ovens (Bassey, 1983a). Results of these studies have still not been promoted in areas where they can make an impact.

Work done in Ghana (Ayegman & Oldham, 1986) showed the possibility of using the liquid that drains from cocoa beans to produce alcohol. Similar possibilities exist for other by-products of many agricultural residues but they have not been followed up.

One of the areas in which active research and development has been carried out, particularly in Sahelian countries, is improved wood/charcoal-burning stoves. Projects supported by many donors in Senegal, Mali and Burkina Faso, to name no more than a few countries, have shown the technical superiority of improved stoves over traditional ones. The sustained use of improved stoves has not been easy to achieve, however, due to various social and economic constraints.

Photovoltaics

In the area of photovoltaics (PV), research to study some basic scientific aspects of PV, or to develop fabrication processes for solar cells, has been undertaken in several universities. This has not, so far, led to the manufacture of solar cells for commercial use in any country. Photovoltaic cells have been used for electricity production at various sites to assess the technical and socio-economic viability of PV technology. One of these projects, which has been in operation since commissioning in 1982 in Senegal, uses a 5 KW solar panel and a 4 KW wind generator (United Nations Environment Programme, 1984). It has been performing satisfactorily while providing villagers with a basic electrical supply. Other PV installations are in place in several Sahelian countries.

Some constraints on research and development

Within the framework of attempting to solve some of the problems outlined above, certain basic conditions must be fulfilled before significant progress can be made at the research and development stage. Some of the constraints which have impeded progress in this area are: (1) poor problem definition; (2) lack of qualified manpower; (3) weak or non-supportive institutional infrastructure; (4) poor collaboration between different disciplines; (5) lack of funds; (6) lack of collaboration with the intended beneficiaries; (7) the absence of a systematic methodology in developing technologies; (8) academic isolation of research and development workers; (9) lack of peer review; (10) lack of proper documentation of results; (11) inadequate reference sources; and (12) poor economic conditions. This list of constraints is by no means complete but it gives a good indication of the range of problems to be tackled. It also indicates the need to look at the problem from a holistic perspective since many of the constraints are interrelated.

One of the main reasons for the slow progress of research and development in new and renewable energy in West and Central Africa has been the unsystematic and unscientific manner in which many problems were tackled in the 1970s (Bassey, 1987). Well-intentioned individuals, inadequately trained in energy systems and lacking knowledge of local conditions, introduced inappropriate technologies. Many of the early problems continue to prevail.

Many institutions do not provide the moral support needed by researchers and development workers. Bureaucracy often prevents funds being paid on time, causing work to be delayed and researchers to become disillusioned. Personal professional jealousy also frustrates the pace and quality of work.

Many institutions do not have the necessary material support for basic prototype construction such as lathes, welding equipment, a reliable electricity supply and expendable supplies. Library facilities are often outdated and basic reference sources non-existent. Transportation is usually unavailable, which prevents workers establishing, let alone maintaining, contact with rural target groups. This, in turn, leads to lack of participation by the intended users and the non-utilization of results.

A major bottleneck in research and development in the region is insufficient collaboration between various disciplines. Most of the activities in the development of new and renewable resources have been under the leadership of technologists/scientists. Concentrating on technologies and processes, they often neglect other critical aspects. For example, solar water heaters have not been used successfully on a wide scale because engineers or physicists have often developed the technology with little thought to who will use it, the acceptable cost of the system, the size of the storage tank that would suit the users' needs, and the installation problems. Work is often carried out without the input of other specialists such as economists or architects, who would have prompted the designer to take these aspects into consideration. On the other hand, even when the opportunity for collaboration exists, many experts, narrowly educated in a specific area, are unwilling or unable to interact with professionals from different disciplines. This is a serious problem in the region: until it is rectified, research and development will continue to produce too many inappropriate results.

Socio-Economic Climate for Intervention

In several instances, potentially useful developments have not been used on a widespread scale because of the unfavourable socio-economic and political climate existing in the region. Many countries do not have the mechanisms in place for effective energy planning in the area of new and renewable energy. Most of the planning is focused on conventional fuels such as oil. Even though energy planning units do exist in many countries, 'the decision-oriented state of energy planning' inhibits a long-term, phased transition to new and renewable energy forms (Foell, 1985).

Due to the lack of capital, useful results cannot be commercialized by interested entrepreneurs. Even when credit facilities are available, interest rates and conditions imposed by several governments for registering business are prohibitive.

The production of a given technology which uses renewable energy sources usually needs simple imported equipment or materials. Economic crises in many countries often make it impossible to buy simple materials such as galvanized iron sheets, plywood, transparent plastic or glass sheets in the local market. Prices are often unrealistically high, making the finished product uneconomic. Since these countries do not have steel and other building material industries, it seems likely that this problem will persist – and that the use of new and renewable technologies will continue to stagnate.

Recommended Strategy for Implementation

A proposed strategy for the use of new and renewable energy sources in integrated rural development is outlined below.

AN EFFICIENT ENERGY PLANNING AGENCY WITHIN EACH COUNTRY
Given the importance of planning in the use of energy, countries which do not have a government agency for energy planning should establish such a body as a first step. The agency should be staffed by adequately trained personnel with a good background in the relevant social science and technology disciplines. The unit should also be able to draw on a competent inter-disciplinary team of specialist advisers – from research and business institutions, for example – to help in the formulation of appropriate policies. Government decisions would thus be based on up-to-date and complete information on the various options available within the country.

ASSESSMENT OF AVAILABLE RESOURCES AT NATIONAL AND LOCAL LEVELS
Countries should carry out studies to document, as accurately as possible, the types, location and quantities of the various forms of new and renewable energy sources. This should first be done at the national level to enable broad policies to be formulated on the possible role of these various energy sources. Once this is done, detailed assessments will then have to be carried out at the specific locations where energy will be used. Information obtained from such studies needs to be updated on a regular basis.

ASSESSMENT OF ENERGY USE PATTERNS
Energy use patterns for all forms of energy should be determined at national level, in all sectors of the economy. Given the dynamic nature of the existing energy situation in various countries, such studies will need to be updated regularly with supplementary studies. More detailed assessment on energy use will need to be done in locations where specific sources will be used.

ENCOURAGEMENT OF APPLIED RESEARCH AND DEVELOPMENT

Research and development on the use of new and renewable sources of energy should be encouraged by governments and funding agencies through (1) the provision of grants to qualified researchers in various disciplines to carry out studies aimed at developing technologies that are economically and technologically viable for rural use; and, (2) the improvement of resources such as equipment, transportation, manpower and reference material within research institutions in order to enhance the quality of the results obtained and increase the chances of their adoption.

PROMOTION OF THE UTILIZATION OF RESULTS IN APPROPRIATE LOCATIONS

Government and funding agencies should choose, on the basis of studies of energy availability and use, specific locations for the integrated and effective use of various energy sources. Energy centres should be developed at these locations with the aim of carefully monitoring and documenting all the various technical, social, economic and cultural aspects over a substantial period, so as to determine their impact. It is imperative that these centres be under local management as this develops the experience needed for future activities.

DEVELOPMENT OF AN INDUSTRIAL BASE FOR THE PROVISION, ACQUISITION AND SUSTAINED USE OF VARIOUS TECHNOLOGIES

Governments should, through objective analysis of prevailing economic and social conditions, develop and implement policies that would encourage local entrepreneurship in the production, acquisition and use of technologies. Policies should be aimed at facilitating the setting-up of local manufacturing business through the reduction of bureaucracy and provision of loans; local processing, where possible, of raw materials needed for manufacture; and providing incentives through soft loans and/or reduced taxes for rural processing industries that use renewable energy sources.

COLLABORATION BETWEEN REGIONAL AND INTERNATIONAL INSTITUTIONS IN THE PROMOTION OF ENERGY USE

Organizations such as the Economic Community of West African States (ECOWAS), the Organization of African Unity (OAU), United Nations agencies and foreign aid agencies from developed countries should work more closely to integrate the support they provide in the development of new and renewable energy. They should encourage governments to document all past and current activities and results. This would serve as a basis for making decisions on future support, avoiding duplication of efforts. Regional and national centres such as the Centre Regional sur l'Energie Solaire (CRES) in Bamako, Mali, CERER in Dakar, Senegal, ONERSOL in Niamey, Niger, and several others should be evaluated and strengthened as appropriate. They could, in turn, be used as centres for training other research personnel as well as helping to solve the urgent energy problems facing the region.

Finally, local and international organizations should promote collaboration through the judicious development of links between developing and industrialized country personnel at all levels.

REFERENCES

Akinsete, V. A. (1986). 'Estimation of solar radiation for Nigeria and Cameroon', in *Renewable Energy Development in Africa*, Vol. 1. Commonwealth Science Council, London, pp. 119–27.

Amouzou, K., Gnininvi, M. & Kerim, B. (1987). 'Solar drying problems in Togo', in Bassey, M. W. & Schmidt, O. G., eds, *Solar Drying in Africa*. International Development Research Centre, Ottawa (IDRC-255e), pp. 252–71.

Arinze, E. A., Adelifa, S. S., Folayan, C.O., Bugaje, I. M. & Ajiboye, V. A. (1986). *Nigerian Journal of Solar Energy*, Vol. 5, pp. 42–60.

Ayegman, K. O. G. & Oldham, J. H. (1986). 'Utilization of cocoa by-products as an alternative source of energy'. *Biomass*, Vol. 10, No. 4, pp. 311–8.

Bagpai, S. C., Jasdanwala, R. T., Musa, M. & Sulaiman, A. T. (1986). 'Biomass resources in Nigeria and their energy potentials', in Wereko-Brobby, C. Y., ed., *Assessing Biomass Energy Resources in Developing Countries*. CSC Technical Publication Series, No. 188, Commonwealth Science Council, London.

Bassey, M. W. (1980). *Variables Affecting the Performance of Sawdust as a Fuel and its Use in a Solar/Sawdust Crop Dryer*. Final Report, UNIDO Research Project No. UN-K 12624–380, Department of Mechanical Engineering, University of Sierra Leone, Freetown, Sierra Leone.

——— (1982). *Potential Use and Performance of Indirect Free Convective Solar Crop Dryers in Sierra Leone*. Final Report, IDRC Research Project No. 3, p-78–0013, Department of Mechanical Engineering, University of Sierra Leone, Freetown, Sierra Leone.

——— (1983a). 'The use of sawdust for small-scale energy applications', in Meyer, R. F. & Olson, J. C., eds, *The Future of Small Scale Energy Resources*. McGraw-Hill Inc., New York, Chapter 66.

——— (1983b). 'Characteristics of hole-through-sawdust type burners'. *International Journal of Ambient Energy*, Vol. 4, No. 1, pp. 39–46.

——— (1985). 'Performance of a solar steam cooker'. *African Journal of Science and Technology*, Vol. 4, No. 1, 1985.

——— (1987). 'Solar energy systems for rural development'. *Nigerian Journal of Solar Technology*, Vol. 6, pp. vii–xvi.

——— (1989a). 'Besoin en séchage: le point de vue des fermiers de Sierra Leone', in Parmentier, M. & Fouabi, K., eds, *Céréales en Regions Chaudes: Conservation et Transformation*. AUPELF/UREF, John Libbey Eurotext, Paris, pp. 57–69.

——— (1989b). 'Development and use of solar drying technologies'. To be published in *Nigerian Journal of Solar Energy*, Vol. 8.

Bassey, M. W. & Brown, B. H. (1982). *Performance of Solar Water Heaters Manufactured in Sierra Leone*. Final Report, ODA Research Project No. R 3039B, Department of Mechanical Engineering, University of Sierra Leone, Freetown, Sierra Leone.

Bassey, M. W. & Schmidt, O. G., eds. (1987). *Solar Drying in Africa*. International Development Research Centre, Ottawa (IDRC-255e).

Bookhaven National Laboratory. (1987). *Energy Needs, Uses and Resources in Developing Countries*. Upton, New York.

Chandra, M. & Oguntuase, O. (1986). 'A natural convection solar water heater for application in Nigerian buildings'. *Nigerian Journal of Solar Energy*, Vol. 5, pp. 151–61.

Chigbundu, C. N. (1986). 'Design and manufacture of a solar cooker'. *Nigerian Journal of Solar Energy*, Vol. 5, pp. 25–34.

Commonwealth Science Council. (1985). *Biomass Resources Assessment*. Proceedings of a Workshop on Biomass Resources Accounting Procedures, Arusha, Tanzania, 30 June – 5 July 1985. London.

——— (1986). *Renewable Energy Development in Africa*, Vols 1 and 2. London.

Davidson, O. R. (1985). *Energy Use Patterns in Sierra Leone*. IDRC Manuscript Report No. IDRC-MR103e, International Development Research Centre, Ottawa.

Ezekwe, C. I. & Ezeilo, C. C. O. (1981). 'Measured solar radiation in a Nigerian environment compared with predicted data'. *Solar Energy*, Vol. 28, pp. 181–6.

Energy Research Group. (1986). *Energy Research: Directions and Issues for Developing Countries*. International Development Research Centre, Ottawa.

Foell, W. K. (1985). 'Energy planning in developing countries'. *Energy Policy*, Vol. 13, No. 4, pp. 350–4.

Gnininvi, M. & Amouzou-Abiba, K. (1985). 'Experimentation d'un bassin solaire en Afrique de l'ouest', in *Compte Rendu du Seminaire Regional sur l'Energies Renouvelables*, 25–29 November 1985, Université du Benin, Lome, Togo.

Hagan, B. (1986). 'Pyrolysis of wood shavings and sawdust – a review of the demonstration project in Ghana'. *Renewable Energy Development in Africa*, Vol. 2. Commonwealth Science Council, London, pp 235–43.

International Development Research Centre. (1986).'Deep well solar pumping (Senegal)'. Project Summary No. 3 p-86-0152, International Development Research Centre, Ottawa.

Kapur, J. C. (1986). 'Solar energy – a diverse solution', in Bilgen, F. and Hollands, K. G. T., eds, *Intersol 85*. Proceedings of the Ninth Biennial Congress of the International Solar Energy Society, p. 32.

Khon Kaen University (1987). *Proceedings of the 1985 International Conference on Rapid Appraisal*. Rural Systems Research and Farming Systems Research Projects, Khon Kaen, Thailand.

Kpakote, K., Smith, H. & Smith, P. (1988). 'Études togolaises de stockage du mais en milieu rural', in Adjanaba, A. M., ed., *La Production Alimentaire et L'Agriculture en Afrique*. Foundation Publishing Company, Athens, pp. 210–37.

Massaquoi, J. G. M. (1985). 'Biomass resources assessment: a survey of Sierra Leone's Energy potential from agricultural and forestry wastes'. CSC Technical Publication Series, No. 160, Commonwealth Science Council, London.

Menanteau, P. & Peultier, P. (1985). 'Une experience villageoise de biogaz en Casamance (Senegal)'. *Environment Africa*, Vol. VI, 1–2, Nos 20-21-22, Dakar, Senegal.

National Academy of Sciences. (1976). *Energy for Rural Development: Renewable Resources and Alternative Technologies for Developing Countries*. National Academy of Sciences, Washington, DC.

Newell, R. E., Reichle, Jr. H. G. & Seiler, W. (1989). 'Carbon monoxide and the burning earth'. *Scientific American*, October 1989.

Oosthuizen, P. H. (1988). 'Modelling of an indirect natural convective solar rice dryer', in *Proceedings of the Ninth Symposium on Engineering Applications for Mechanics, 29–31 May 1988*, University of Western Ontario. London, Canada.

Oosthuizen, P. H. & Sheriff, A (1988).'Experimental study of a simulated indirect free convective solar rice dryer', in Murphy, L. M. & Mancini, T. R., eds, *Solar Engineering – 1988*, Proceedings of the Tenth Annual ASME Solar Energy Conference, Denver, Colorado, 10–14 April 1988. The American Society of Mechanical Engineers, New York.

Prasad, K. K. & Verhaart, P., eds. (1983). *Wood Heat for Cooking*. Indian Academy of Sciences, Bangalore, India.

Reddy, A. K. N., ed. (1980). *Rural Technology*. Indian Academy of Sciences, Bangalore, India.

Toure, I. & Niare, S. M. (1985). 'Étude de l'échauffement de la surface absorbante du capteur plan exposée au soleil par ciel clair'. *Compte Rendu du Seminaire Regional sur l'Energies Renouvelables*, 25–29 Novembre 1985, Université du Benin, Lome, Togo.

United Nations Environment Programme. (1984). *The Niaga Wolof Energy Centre*. Energy Report Series, ERS-12–85, UNEP, Nairobi, Kenya.

United Nations Economic and Social Council (1982). *International Directory of New and Renewable Energy Information Sources and Research Centres*. First edition, UNESCO, Paris.

United Nations Industrial Development Organization (1978). *Technology for Solar Energy Utilization*. Development and Transfer of Technology Series, No. 5, United Nations, New York.

United Nations Industrial Development Organization (1979). *Appropriate Industrial Technology for Energy for Rural Requirements*. Monographs on Appropriate Industrial Technology, No. 5, United Nations, New York.

Viaud, P. (1984). *Energie et Biomasse au Sahel*. École National Supérieure Universitaire de Technologie, Université de Dakar, Senegal.

Viaud, P. & Preveral, M. (1986). 'Adaptation of petrol engines to biogas', in *Renewable Energy Development in Africa*, Vol. 2. Commonweath Science Council, London, pp. 335–44.

Wereko–Brobby, C., ed. (1986). *Assessing Biomass Resources in Developing Countries*. CSC Technical Series No. 188, Commonwealth Science Council, London.

World Bank. (1980). *Energy in Developing Countries*. World Bank, Washington, DC.

Promoting Alternative Energy in Botswana: The Case for Subsidies

8

JOHN DIPHAHA

Botswana's Sixth National Development Plan (NDP VI) started in 1985 and finished in March 1991. This chapter examines the tasks that this Plan set itself, with special reference to rural energy. The policies that were formulated to guide the Plan are stated and its achievements are assessed in the light of these policies. The chapter proposes an approach which calls for a substantial and long-term governmental financial commitment to rural development.

Government Policies on Investment in Energy for Rural Development

Government recognizes that the majority of people (over 80%) in Botswana live in the rural areas and will continue to do so notwithstanding rapid urbanization, and that they are amongst the poorest in the society, with 'least access to public services and reliable sources of income' (Botswana Government, 1985). Strategies for rural development thus had the following objectives:

1 To achieve diversification of the rural economy for development of cash incomes and productive employment;
2 To develop a National Food Strategy, one of the aims being 'investment in the limited areas of the country that may prove suitable for irrigation or large-scale commercial crop production';
3 To improve national extension services which are considered 'crucial to the success of Government's rural development efforts' (Botswana Government, 1985).

Regarding energy for rural development, NDP VI recognized the overwhelming part played by woodfuel as an energy source in the rural areas, a source which was being depleted at 'high cost in terms of environmental degradation' (Botswana Government, 1985). The Plan's main rural energy sector policy objectives are:

1 To maintain and increase the sources of energy available to the majority of rural people and reduce the time and ecological damage involved in firewood collection.
2 To ensure that consumers, wherever feasible, are accountable for the cost of supply and that prices and tariffs properly reflect resource costs.

In pursuit of the above objectives, a number of rural energy initiatives were planned. Villages that were being served by isolated generators would be connected to the grid and thus removed from existing government subsidies. The Tuli Block farming area was to be electrified (UNDP/IBRD, 1987b). An investigation would be undertaken into the marketing and distribution of coal and coal consumption in households, industry and government institutions. If the investigation proved favourable, a distribution and sales network operating 'on a commercial basis' would be established (Botswana Government, 1985). Although no specific mention was made of the rural areas, the project subsequently included major villages (see Map 8.1).

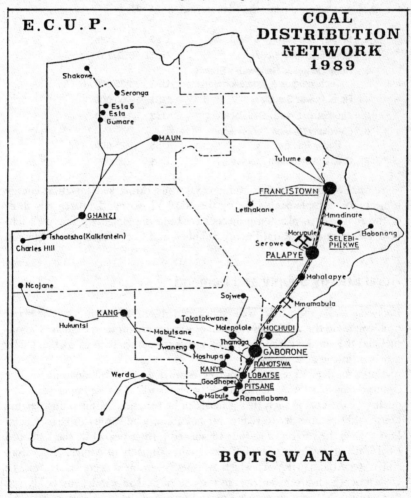

Map 8.1: Coal Distribution Network, Botswanal, 1989

NDP VI focused on 'increasing the supply of renewable energy and increasing the efficiency of energy use' (Botswana Government, 1985) in the rural areas in order to reduce the collection of firewood and the resultant environmental degradation. Metal stoves, retained heat cookers and small batch solar water heaters were to be introduced through organizations such as the Rural Industries Innovation Centre (RIIC) and the Botswana Technology Centre (BTC). The Ministry of Agriculture undertook to examine the possibility of initiating afforestation projects and programmes.

A number of projects to implement these programmes were formulated. The following energy projects, with estimates of the costs, were earmarked for implementation during the Plan period, 1985–91.

1.	Energy Technology Substitution	US$	700,000.
2.	Rural Energy Supplies	US$	650,000.
3.	Rural Domestic Renewable Energy Technologies & Extension Service	US$	235,000
4.	Rural Power Supplies	US$	1,500,000
5.	Alternative Energy Development	US$	176,000
6.	Electricity Service Connection Policy Review	US$	25,000
7.	Coal Development Studies	US$	200,000

A total of about US$3.5 million was thus earmarked for rural energy projects to be implemented during the NDP VI period. To date, only three of the above seven planned projects have been implemented: Energy Technology Substitution, Rural Energy Supplies, and Coal Development Studies.

Rural Energy Supply and Demand

Botswana is, on the whole, well endowed with energy resources. The major problem lies in the spatial distribution of some energy resources such as woodfuel and the conversion of the primary energy sources such as coal and solar radiation into usable forms.

Botswana has large coal resources estimated at 17 billion tonnes. The country's only coal mine at Morupule produces 612,800 tonnes per year. The quality of the coal is such that it needs to be beneficiated for industrial and household use in order to reduce air pollution. The supply of coal in rural Botswana is the subject of a study (discussed further below) by the Extended Coal Utilization Project (ECUP) under the Ministry of Mineral Resources and Water Affairs (MRWA), which oversees government energy activities. The government's desire to encourage the use of coal in rural households was dictated by the need to reduce demand on woodfuel use. Villages targeted for coal distribution are shown in Map 8.1. The exact demand for coal in rural households is not known, but the potential demand can be derived from the figures on woodfuel consumption, assuming total replacement of woodfuel by coal.

The total installed capacity in Botswana is 216 MW, plus 75 MW of power from the Republic of South Africa. There is a supply of 2MW from the Zambia/Botswana interconnector in the North. A World Bank study concluded that 'there is little need to worry about the effects of increased connections on power supply through the medium term' (UNDP/IBRD, 1987). In addition to the urban areas, most of the major villages in Eastern Botswana are connected to the national grid.

Demand for electricity in the country's 15 major villages, which house a large proportion of the rural population, has been estimated by the World Bank (UNDP/IBRD, 1987b). The study calculates that some 36,000 additional potential consumers existed in those villages in 1985. The estimate was based on the total number of occupied dwellings. The number of existing consumers in 1985 was only 1176, and not more than 3000 in 1990.

Using the existing population projections for 1981–2001 (Central Statistics Office, 1987) and assuming an average of five people per household, the estimated number of households or dwellings in 1991 and 2011 are, respectively, 48,658 and 97,388. These figures provide a rough estimate of the number of potential consumers of electricity in the 15 main villages during the years in question.

Taking the country as a whole, the supply of woodfuel in Botswana is in excess of the demand for it. The northern region is well endowed. The western region, except for the extreme south-west, is not under stress, largely because of the sparseness of the population. It has been noted that 'the sparse, low-density vegetation cover of the Kalahari cannot support any but a sparse low-density population' and that the 'over-provision of borehole water, food aid or employment in too few centres' (ERL, 1985) could lead to great environmental consequences.

The eastern region, which is the main concern of this chapter, presents a different picture. It is the most densely populated and is the centre of economic activity. The continued supply of woodfuel is thus a source of concern. A number of studies on the availability of woodfuel in the east have been undertaken and, as indicated by Arntzen and Veenendaal, there is a large variation in the figures for annual wood increments (Arntzen and Veenendaal, 1986). They state that 'Annual wood increments fluctuate between 0.5 and 1.04 tonnes/ha, with an average of 0.91 tonnes/ha. . . . The standing crop may vary [somewhat around] 0.60 tonnes/ha and annual increments from 0.66 – 1 tonnes/ha.' The production of woodfuel is adversely affected by drought, fires, felling of trees and livestock. Notwithstanding the lack of accurate figures on woodfuel production, there are indications that the supply is being depleted, especially in the vicinity of settlement. This is evidenced by the larger distances being travelled to collected firewood (Kgathi, 1987). The Energy Resources Limited (ERL) study has also revealed areas of shortage in the east.

Policy Issues and Action Proposals

With the economy in a buoyant state, the government has expressed the need for diversification of the rural economy to promote employment creation and income generation. The government has committed itself to investment in irrigation for food production and to strengthening the extension services in support of rural development programmes.

In pursuit of the above objectives, a number of studies on rural energy have been undertaken and more are planned. To reduce the pressure on wood energy resources, the provision of backbone electrification in major rural areas is being vigorously pursued and the government recognizes the need for the introduction of appropriate energy technologies in the rural areas. Thus it would seem that most parameters necessary for alternative energy use in rural areas are in place. Clearly the good intentions are there, yet progress has been painfully slow. Why?

As pointed out earlier, only a few of the rural energy projects have been implemented so far. It is understood that lack of implementation capacity is partly responsible for this. In addition, the impact on the country's rural inhabitants of implemented projects – such as the Coal Development Study, the Tuli Block Electrification and the Rural Power Supplies – has been minimal. The reasons for this are to be found in government financing and pricing policies. Consumers are directly accountable for the cost of energy supply and 'prices and tariffs "must" properly reflect the resource costs' (Botswana Government, 1985). To a rural consumer, this constitutes a major disincentive.

There is also the question of how 'resource costs' are interpreted. The current interpretation is based on short-term considerations such as payment of upfront cost of the electricity reticulation; or in the restricted sense that does not take into account the environmental implications of woodfuel use. Consequently, its relevance to rural development is limited. For alternative energy sources such as electricity, coal and solar energy to contribute effectively to rural development, and for them to reduce the 'ecological damage' caused by demand for woodfuel, a fresh approach is necessary. Three projects will be used to illustrate this new approach.

Rural Power Supplies

The country's 15 main villages were connected to the national grid under a rural electrification scheme funded by the Swedish government. More villages are to be connected. The objective was to provide mains electricity to government institutions. Provision was also made for private consumers to be connected. To assist private consumers, a Revolving Fund (RF) was set up with an initial sum of US$250,000. The idea was for an area to be connected to the grid using funds from the RF on the basis of potential consumers in that area. The RF would be replenished as the consumers paid for the full cost of the electricity supply (in line with government policy). The RF was a failure, mainly because the distribution and connection charges were prohibitive, and had to be paid in a lump sum up front.

A scheme to overcome this was proposed by the MRWA. This involved the concept of Specified Supply Areas (SSA). Within the SSA, the Power Corporation was to make available, without charge, an electricity supply line to the point of entry of a consumer's premises, and instal its meter there – provided that the consumer was within 20 metres of a distributing main. The SSA would broadly correspond to a band 100 metres wide on either side of the distributing main.

Where the distance from a distributing main exceeded 20 metres the cost of the additional supply line was to be met by the consumer. Where this cost exceeded P250 (US$1 = P2.) the BPC was to recover the amount in equal instalments over two years. Within the SSA, no domestic consumer was to be required to reimburse the Corporation for costs in respect of transformers.

In those cases where a commercial basis for electrification initially existed, but where investment was justified on development grounds, it was proposed that the initial funding required should be made available. It was recommended that the BPC should itself generate capital resources for funding such long-term investment and that, in the absence of such a reserve, it would be incumbent upon the central government to provide the initial working capital.

The rationale behind these proposals was that rural electrification should be seen as a long-term investment with a gestation period of between 10 to 20 years. It should be seen in the context of the damage to the environment caused by woodfuel collection and should be priced in a way that would eventually encourage switching away from woodfuel.

These proposals were rejected on the grounds that rural electrification would be a subsidy to the rich. In essence, the SSA would be in conflict with government policy, which is not supportive of subsidies and emphasizes the need for energy prices and tariffs to reflect the resource costs.

Coal Development Studies

In 1985, the Botswana government, with German aid, undertook a study 'to examine the economic and technical potential of the utilization of coal for domestic and small/medium industrial use' (ERL, 1985). The study found that in 1985 there was an estimated annual market for 134,800 tonnes of coal, out of which 90,000 tonnes would substitute domestic use of woodfuel. A follow-up to these findings was the commissioning in 1987 of the Extended Coal Utilization Project (ECUP) to examine the marketing and distribution of coal.

ECUP had two important objectives. The first was to study the potential for the dissemination of coal in the household sector while the second was to address 'strategic planning for future commercialization and distribution of coal throughout Botswana' (Rodeco, 1986). Another important aspect of ECUP activities was the development of a low-cost coal stove. ECUP focused its activities in areas where the demand for woodfuel is greatest – urban areas and major villages. There is now pressure for ECUP activities to be privatized on the grounds that the project has demonstrated commercial viability. In the short term, this pressure may be successfully resisted, because of aspects of coal use – such as air pollution and potential danger to household users – that need careful attention.

Compared to electricity, coal appears to have a greater potential for woodfuel substitution, especially in the poorest household categories. Bearing in mind the low incomes in the rural areas, and the higher costs associated with coal use in comparison with woodfuel, the success of this project will depend largely on government support. For that support to be forthcoming, as is the case with rural electrification, a departure from the existing rigid anti-subsidy stance will be required.

Renewable Energy Technologies

Under this project, research and development, together with the adaptation of technologies, were to be funded with a view to increasing 'the energy available to the majority of rural people'. Prime targets would be improving the efficiency of woodfuel use and the development of a low-cost solar water heater.

The development of renewable energy technologies for efficient woodfuel use was due to a recognition that substituting woodfuel with conventional energy sources such as coal and electricity would take a long time. Renewable energy technologies present an interim solution. To date, none of the targets mentioned above have been met. To proceed with these initiatives would provide a powerful tool for woodfuel substitution, provided they are seen as an integral part of rural development, with a long-term gestation period. Successful implementation of these projects would, however, require subsidization. The subsidy should take into account the following important factors:

- The damage to the environment inherent in current dependence on woodfuel.
- The opportunity cost of time spent on woodfuel collection – that time could be more profitably invested in other productive activities.
- The immediate benefits to the wealthier rural consumers could in the long term trickle down to the poorer members of the rural community through increased investment in the rural areas triggered or encouraged by availability of adequate energy supplies.

- The adverse effects of the rural–urban migration which is in part caused by unavailability of employment opportunities in the rural areas. Development of rural energy can contribute to rural employment creation.

Restricting the analysis to projected population totals in the 15 major villages, it is possible to provide estimates for the consumption of woodfuel, coal and electricity over the next 20 years. The results and underlying assumptions are shown in Table 8.1.

Table 8.1
Consumption of coal, electricity and wood by households

	1981	Year 1991	2011
Total households	32,600	48,660	97,400[1]
Coal (tonnes)	95,192	142,087	284,408
Electricity (MWh)	97.8	426.3	853.2
Woodfuel (tonnes)	122,250	182,475	36,5250
Woodfuel (above in ha)	110,025	164,227	32,8725

NOTE: 1. Population divided by 5.

ASSUMPTIONS

Coal consumption	=	8kg/household/day
Woodfuel consumption	=	75 tonnes/capita/year
Electricity consumption	=	250 KWh/month
Electricity charges	=	PO. 2236/KWh
Household size	=	5 people
1 cubic metre of wood	=	1.12 tonnes of wood
1 hectare yields	=	1.25m3 of firewood

A recent study (Sir M. Macdonald & Partners, 1988) estimates the cost of tree planting to be P1000/ha. The same study proposed a compensation alternative of P182/ha, the latter figure representing the loss to the community. From Table 8.1 it can be calculated that the amount of woodlots consumed between 1991 and 2011 would be 164498 ha. Applying the monetary figures quoted above, the value of this to the community would be P33 million. The cost of electrifying the 15 villages was estimated in 1985 at P25.5 million. At 1990 prices, assuming a 10% rate of inflation, the cost would be P41 million. These assets would still be'there in 2011, when the amount of woodfuel consumed would be valued at P33 million at today's prices. Looked at in this simplistic manner, an investment of P41 million now would be a saving of P33 million to the environment. Taking a hypothetical situation whereby government electrifies the 15 villages and puts up the money for a complete switch from woodfuel to electricity, the costs are as shown in Table 8.2.

Table 8.2
Cost of electrification of 15 major villages

Cost of distribution extension	P 41.0 million
Cost of service connection @ P390 per household	P 38.0 million
Cost of household wiring @ P200 per household	P 19.5 million
Cost of appliances (hot plate, pots) @ P180 per household	P 17.5 million
Total	P 116.0 million

If the wiring and the appliances (Table 8.2) are paid for by the consumers, then the actual cost to government would be P79 million. Subtracting the savings in woodfuel valued at P33 million the cost is P46 million. The monthly costs to the consumers (per household) are summarized in Table 8.3, assuming the cost of wiring and appliances is loaned to the household consumer.

Table 8.3
Monthly cost to consumers for electricity

Cost of wiring	P 1.60[1]
Cost of appliances	P .75[1]
Cost of bulbs	P 5.00[2]
Electricity charges	P55.90
Total	P63.25

NOTES:
1 The cost of internal wiring and appliances, totalling P37 million, is repaid to government free of interest over 20 years.
2 Five bulbs running for five hours a day at a charge of PO.2236/KWh.

The annual woodfuel consumption per household is 3.375 ha, valued at P675 or P56 per month. This is to be compared to the total cost of electrification to the consumer (Table 8.3). If the money is loaned to the consumers under the same conditions that government extends to parastatals (7.5% interest rate and 25 years repayment), the cost to the consumer would be P55.9 per month, about the same as for woodfuel. Thus a complete rural electrification scheme, requiring an outlay of P46 million by government, would not cost the consumer any more than woodfuel.

The government contribution would need to take into account other benefits such as the release of human labour from the drudgery of woodfuel collection and the availability of woodfuel land for productive activities. This would be meaningful only if rural electrification is part of an integrated rural development strategy which would ensure that the time available to the woodfuel collector is invested in other more useful undertakings, and that there are small-scale employment-generating industries that would utilize the electricity.

A study commissioned by the Southern African Development Coordination

Conference (SADCC) on woodfuel in Botswana has commented correctly that 'if government will only supply [electricity] at least cost, the implication is that switching to electricity is something that will occur gradually as wood becomes more and more expensive' (ETC Foundation, 1987). The study goes on to assert that the rural incomes are too small to produce a switch away from wood. Kgathi (1987) also stresses that without subsidies 'electricity is not likely to be adopted as a substitute for wood energy in rural Botswana'. The point this chapter attempts to develop is that the 'subsidies' may not be prohibitive if a long-term view of an integrated development strategy is adopted.

Government policies on rural development, rural energy and the environment are exemplary; its associated financing and pricing policies, however, are unsupportive. The result is a rural stalemate and continuing underdevelopment on the peripheries of urban affluence. Another attractive alternative involves wholesale introduction of coal and electricity at the same time: coal for cooking and space heating, electricity for lighting. In this case the hot plate is replaced by the coal stove (estimated cost P200) and the monthly electricity charges (for lighting only) are estimated on the basis of five 60 watt bulbs per household. The cost of coal is put at P150 per tonne (it sells for P130 in urban areas, near the rail line). Table 8.3 gives the monthly electricity charge for lighting only.

These simple calculations provide an illustration of the approach that could be adopted for development of energy resources in the rural areas. Using the same approach, renewable energies could be introduced to rural areas without backbone electrification and far removed from the rail line. It is realized that the problem is a great deal more complex than indicated here. But for a country like Botswana, with financial resources at its disposal, these illustrations suggest that government policies on rural development and rural energy supplies can be realized. There is a Chinese saying that 'a long journey starts with one step'.

REFERENCES

Arntzen, J. W. & Veenendaal, E. M. (1986). *A Profile of Environment and Development in Botswana.* IES, Free University/NIR, University of Botswana.

Bhalotra, Y. P. R. (1987). *Climate of Botswana, Part II: Elements of Climate.* Meteorological Services, Gaborone.

Botswana Government. (1985). *National Development Plan VI 1985–1991.* Government Printer, Gaborone.

Central Statistics Office. (1987). *Population Projections: 1981–2011.* Government Printer, Gaborone.

Energy Resources Ltd (ERL). (1985). *A Study of Energy Utilization and Requirements in the Rural Sector of Botswana.* Ministry of Mineral Resources and Water Affairs, Gaborone.

ETC Foundation. (1987). *SADCC Energy Development: Fuelwood Study.* Netherlands.

Kgathi, D. L. (1987). *Conventional Solutions Adopted to Alleviate the Rural Energy Problem: the Case of Botswana.* University of Botswana, Gaborone.

_____(1989). *A Critical Review of Socio–Economic Surveys on Fuelwood in Botswana.* University of Botswana, Gaborone.

Rodeco Consulting. (1986). *Coal Utilization Study*. Ministry of Mineral Resources and Water Affairs, Gaborone.

Sir M. Macdonald & Partners. (1988). *Metsemotlhaba Transfer Scheme – Environmental Impact Assessment*. Water Utilities Corporation, Gaborone.

UNDP/IBRD. (1987). *Electricity Service Connection Policy*. World Bank, Washington, DC.

———— (1987). *Tuli Block Farms Electrification Pre-Feasibility Study*. World Bank, Washington, DC.

9

Sudan's National Energy Research Council and Renewable Energy Technologies

HASSAN WARDI HASSAN

Energy Requirements and Sources for Rural Areas

In the rural areas of Sudan the main energy-consuming activities are:

1 Household activities, including cooking and lighting. Main fuels include firewood, charcoal, agricultural and animal residues, kerosene and dry cell batteries.
2 Institutional activities, such as education, health, village water supply and communication. Kerosene and diesel are used for lighting, refrigeration for vaccine storage, pumping systems and educational TV sets.
3 Productive activities, such as irrigation and other agricultural activities, crop processing and transport. Diesel and animal power are the main fuels.

All the above activities face difficulties in obtaining the necessary supplies of energy, either because of the high cost of imported petroleum products or because lack of transport makes fuels unavailable. Firewood is becoming more scarce and the consequent increasing dependence on agricultural and animal residues deprives the soil of valuable nutrients.

There is thus a need to develop other energy sources that are available in rural areas. Promising alternatives include solar power, wind, small-scale hydro-power and agricultural residues. Solar radiation is high, with an average intensity of about 1 KW per square metre and annual sunshine duration of more than 3600 hours in virtually all parts of the country. Wind speeds of more than three metres per second (the minimum speed required to exploit wind energy) are available in 80% of the country. Small and mini hydro-power potential is high along the Nile and its tributaries, and more abundant in the south, where solar and wind energy resources are less significant. Agricultural residues such as cotton stalks, bagasse and groundnut shells offer attractive energy options.

Renewable Energy Development

In line with the overall research policy of the National Council for Research, the Energy Research Council started a long-term research and development

119

programme for developing and adapting renewable technologies suitable for rural applications. These efforts extended from development and adaptation through to field testing, local manufacture and wide-scale commercialization. The energy technologies that have been introduced are discussed below.

Charcoal from agricultural residues

UNIDO provided support to develop cotton stalks as a source of energy. Every year, large quantities of cotton stalks (more than one million tons) are burned in the field to prevent the spread of diseases from one crop cycle to the next. Carbonized, these cotton stalks also provide a good source of energy. A joint project with the Netherlands-based Biomass Technology Group undertook laboratory testing and development of carbonization and briquetting technologies. This has now culminated in the construction of a factory to produce about 800 tons of charcoal in the form of briquetted cotton stalks.

Biogas

A number of biogas units of both Chinese and Indian types have been built by the ERC in different parts of the country. These vary from small individual household digesters to big institutional units. A number of technicians have been trained in building digesters and some private workshops are producing the requisite appliances.

Solar thermal technologies

Solar thermal conversion devices have been developed, adapted, tested and are being disseminated in rural areas. These include: solar water heaters for sterilization purposes, solar dryers for crops and brick making, and solar cookers.

Photovoltaic systems

The ERC's efforts in introducing PV technologies to rural areas include the promotion of the following energy systems:

1 Lighting systems that include individual portable PV lamps, groups of lanterns with central charging systems, and street lighting systems. These were introduced in cooperation with private distributors (as potential future suppliers) for use in village houses, clubs, schools and mosques.
2 A number of PV-powered pumps, of different capacities and including both submersible and floating types, have been installed to operate under actual field conditions for demonstrations and economic evaluation purposes. A comparative study is now underway to compare the performance

and economic viability of pumping systems that use diesel, wind and solar energy.

3 Use of PV vaccine storage started with the installation of five refrigerators in remote rural clinics. The results were so encouraging that the Ministry of Health's Extended Programme of Immunization decided to adopt the PV refrigerators as its main technology for building its 'cold chain' of vaccine storage in the rural areas. About 50 more have been installed and an additional 70 have been ordered.

4 About 12 PV-powered TV sets have been installed in a number of villages in one of the biggest agricultural schemes. The TV sets are used to screen special agricultural extension programmes. The administration of the scheme and the Tenants Union are working towards extending this project to cover other villages.

Wind energy project

A joint project of the ERC and the Netherlands-based CWD has installed about a dozen wind pumps on small private farms for field testing and evaluation of their performance. A local manufacturer has been granted a licence to produce them locally.

Improved charcoal production

Traditionally, charcoal is produced using earth kilns. It was thought that these kilns have a very low efficiency. Experimental work carried out by the ERC showed that the efficiency of these kilns was reasonably high and the introduction of new improved kilns was unnecessary.

On the other hand, studies showed that efforts should be directed towards the production of charcoal from trees being cleared in large mechanized farming. These are usually burnt in the field. Their use for charcoal production would provide an important additional source of energy.

Improved stoves

The burning of fuelwood can be made more efficient through the use of improved stoves. The ERC has developed, adapted and disseminated two designs of improved charcoal stoves. Though charcoal is mainly used in urban areas, the rural areas also benefit through the overall reduction of charcoal production. Similar projects on efficient rural woodstoves are now being undertaken.

Forest management and plantations

Forests, the most important sources of traditional energy, are disappearing at an alarming rate. In many cases, reforestation is left to the painfully slow process of regeneration. Millions of hectares have to be planted annually if the projected demand for fuelwood is to be satisfied.

The ERC has developed pilot plantation projects which include the establishment of nurseries; shelter belts and windbreaks; the introduction of trees into some agricultural schemes; and community-based afforestation with village woodlots.

Renewable Energy Development and Commercialization

The ERC stresses the need to ensure the commercialization of its research results. Need-driven ERC programmes and projects are designed to serve specific end-users. An integrated approach takes the technology from development and adaptation through field testing, demonstration and dissemination all the way to commercialization. This process is designed to be flexible, allowing for the necessary modifications.

The ERC aims to select technologies which – either wholly or partially – can be manufactured locally using local materials and skills. Therefore they should be simple and easy to install. The approach calls for active participation of manufacturers and users in technology development and in its final commercialization. It requires a multi-disciplinary team approach that includes technologists and socio-economists.

To ensure rapid commercialization, the ERC involves the private sector in decision-making. Other beneficiaries and users are also encouraged to participate at the relevant levels. In all its programmes and projects, the ERC considers the local production of technologies as an important component of any successful commercialization effort. Studies of the availability of skills, and the maximum use of locally available materials, are a prerequisite in renewable energy technologies.

ERC programmes and projects clearly define the roles of potential investors and manufacturers in technology development, manufacturing and commercialization. The ERC plays the role of coordinator in addition to providing the necessary technical assistance and, sometimes, limited financial support. – as with wind pumps, charcoal from cotton stalks, improved stoves and solar cookers projects.

A UNIDO initiative is also promoting the commercialization of renewable energy equipment. The project brings together a National Team composed of the ERC, the Sudanese Development Corporation and representatives of the Sudanese Industries Association. The first phase identified a number of technologies thought to be viable for wider application in the Sudan. These include wind pumps and generators, photovoltaic systems, gasifiers, and engines which can be modified for applications in producing gas, ethanol production, and solar thermal equipment (especially water heaters and dryers).

A report compiling project profiles, brief technical specifications, availability of materials and a list of interested investors and manufacturers has been prepared. This report has been distributed to different investors and manufacturers, and to potential external partners in a number of industrialized countries. The National Team is now in the process of matching the interests of prospective external partners to those of local investors.

The experience of the ERC clearly demonstrates that for renewable energy resources to play a significant role in the overall energy balance of the rural areas, special attention should be given to the local production of these technologies and the private sector should be encouraged to invest in them.

REFERENCES

Ali, Gaafar E. (1989). *Integrated Framework for Renewable Energy Technology Development and Commercialization: Sudan Case.* ITDG, Alexandria.

National Council for Research. (1981). *Programme of Building the Modern Science-based State, 1981–1990.* NCR, Sudan.

NRA. (1985). *The Sudan National Energy Plan.* NRA, Khartoum.

Scientific Conference. (1989). *Energy Research in the Sudan: Strategies, Policies and Programmes.* Scientific Conference, Khartoum.

Taha, Azmi & Wardi, Hassan. (1987). *Sudanese Experience in Promotion of Some PV Applications.* Islamabad.

UNDP/World Bank. (1983). *Sudan: Issues and Options in the Energy Sector.* UNDP/World Bank, Report No. 4511–sn.

Wardi, Hassan, Ali, Mubarak & Dooyweerd, E. (1988).*Programme for Identification and Promotion of Industrial Investment Projects for the Local Production of Renewable Energy Equipment.* Khartoum.

III NORTH AFRICA AND THE MIDDLE EAST

10 Renewable Energy Development in North Africa

ANHAR HEGAZI

The rural sector of most developing countries is characterized by its low use of commercial energy per capita and corresponding dependence on non-commercial sources of energy. The commercial energy used in agricultural production for mechanization, fertilization of the soil and agro-processing must in the future increase substantially. A shortage of rural energy supplies, compounded by generally low energy efficiency, reduces the ability to provide the necessities and amenities of life – food, shelter, clothing, communications, health care and transportation – and has a direct impact on morbidity and mortality rates. Rural energy development must be seen within the overall context of rural and national development objectives and constraints.

The North African countries have a population of 117 million and form a broadly homogeneous group in terms of prevailing climatic, geographical and cultural conditions. However, their energy resources vary enormously. Libya is a leading oil producer with almost no fuelwood, while Morocco imports oil but has substantial fuelwood and other biomass energy resources. Algeria, Egypt and Tunisia have a mixed supply of energy resources.

The objective of this chapter is to review the rural situation in the region within the overall energy and agricultural planning of the different countries. The chapter discusses country-specific energy sources, requirements for rural development, and current use of renewable energy resources. Finally, the chapter outlines an action plan for integrating renewable energy resources in the region's rural development.

Energy Resources: Supply/Demand in the North African Region

With the exception of Morocco, the countries of the region all export oil; Libya is one of the world's major exporters, while Algeria, Egypt and Tunisia are all middle-ranking producers. The average per capita energy consumption in the region reaches 4.83 barrels per year. The country-specific consumption ranges from 1.8 barrels per year in Morocco to 21 barrels per year in Libya due to the surplus availability of oil. In Algeria, Egypt and Tunisia consumption ranges from four to 6.9 barrels per year.

New and renewable energy resources, specifically wind, biomass and draught animal power, are available to varying degrees in most of the North African countries (Table 10.1). Morocco, Algeria and Tunisia have fuelwood and forested areas, but these are often far from population centres. However, deforestation will limit the ability of these countries to meet future energy requirements.

Table 10.2 shows the 1986 energy supply/demand pattern in Egypt and Morocco as an example of the variable conditions in the region. Agricultural energy ranges from 3% to 5% of total consumption. It is lower in Libya where farming activities are limited. The region's annual consumption of energy in agriculture has a range equivalent to 20–30 million barrels of oil.

In both urban and rural areas households consume more energy than any other economic sector: 30%–45% of the total. Rural households account for an average of 35% of total household consumption. Rural households thus account for about 10%–15% (equivalent to 60–90 million barrels of oil) of the region's total energy consumption. The energy consumed by the fertilizer industry is usually accounted for in the energy budget of the industrial sector, as is rural transport. Draught animal power is not included in the energy budget for agriculture. This can reduce estimates of the agricultural sector's energy consumption by about 40% to 50%. Efficient use of fertilizers is essential for agricultural development, together with increased utilization of mechanized techniques. Agricultural and rural activities may account for about 15%–25% (equivalent to 90–150 million barrels of oil) of the total energy consumption in the North African region.

Fuelwood, charcoal and other biomass sources account for almost 80% of the energy used by urban and rural households and by agriculture in Morocco, Algeria and Tunisia. Egypt and Libya depend mainly on electricity and petroleum products such as kerosene and Liquefied Petroleum Gas (LPG). These commercial household fuels account for over 60% of household and agricultural energy used in Egypt and for as much as 90% in Libya.

National agriculture and forestry institutions in the region usually develop their plans and projects independently of the energy sector. As a result, the information available does not constitute an adequate data base for assessing rural and agricultural energy resources and consumption patterns. There is an urgent need to incorporate energy issues and requirements into rural development planning, which, in turn, should be integrated into national energy plans.

Energy Requirement for Integrated Rural Development

Several studies have been carried out to estimate the energy requirement in developing countries. However, the studies generate figures varying widely from 8 MJ per capita per day upwards. In addition, very few data are available

Table 10.1
Energy resources and reserves in North African countries

Country	Conventional energy reserves[1]						Renewable energy resources					
	Oil mboe	Gas mboe	Heavy Oil BB	Oil Shale BB	Hydro[2] Mw	Coal[3] mtoe	Forestry & fuel 10⁴cm/y	Solar[5] Kwh/m2/d	Wind m/sec	Biomass[6] mtoe/y	Geo-thermal[7] mtoe/y	Draught animals million
Algeria	8,440	23,874	–	–	4,800	20G	3,563	5.4	–	–	–	–
Egypt	3,100	942	–	–	3,800	80G	–	6.0	3–9	5.6	LG	3.7
Libya	23,500	4,080	–	–	160	–	–	6.1	3–6	n.a.	n.a.	0.05
Morocco	–	–	1.0	0.59	975	96G	3,240	5.4	5–7	4.8	–	1–
Tunisia	700	1,488	–	–	29	–1,039	5.1	3–5	n.a.	–	n.a.	–

1. SOURCE: World Bank Report, 'Energy in Developing Countries'.

2. Includes all installed and installable capacity.

3. G = geological resources not yet recoverable; R = recoverable reserves (technologically and economically).

4. SOURCE: Fuelwood supplies in the Developing Countries (FAO Forestry Paper No. 42); UNDP/World Bank Energy Section Assessment Studies; National Reports.

5. Values given are the average annual global radiation. SOURCE: Country data and mission reports of the ESCWA Energy Regional Advisor.

6. Biomass resources include agricultural residues (animal waste), municipal solid waste and sewerage waste. Animal wastes are mostly used as fertilizers. SOURCE: 'Biomass energy in the Arab world', Consultancy Report prepared for UN ECWA, November 1980.

7. Geothermal resources are classified according to the temperature levels available. L = 50 to 80 degree centigrade, M = 80 to 150 degree centigrade, H = 150 degree centigrade, G = geological resources not yet used. One metric ton of biomass is 0.2 t.o.e.

Table 10.2
Energy supply/demand for selected North African countries, 1986

Supply/demand (sectoral)	1986 Supply/demand (10^3 t.o.e.)						
	Oil	Natural gas	Coal	Fuelwood & electricity	Biomass	Total	Sector %
Egypt TAS[1]	19,020	3,520	1,500	640	3,700	28,380	
NDC[2]	11,600	1,780	1,500	2,289[3]	3,700	20,869	
Agriculture	870	–	–	240	–	1,110	4.5
Household	4,592	80	–	430	3,000	8,102	33.3
Transport	3,077	–	–	30	–	3,107	12.7
Industry	4,247	1,700	1,500	1,390	700	9,537	39.2
Others	2,296	–	–	200	-2,496		10.3
Morocco TAS	4,344	64	397	254	2,725	7,784	
NDC	2,977	40	52	1,171	2,362	6,602	
Agriculture	143	–	–	61	–	204	3.1
Household	360	–	4	260	2,362	2,986	43.3
Transport	1,458	–	–	171	–	1,629	25.3
Industry	537	30	–	225	–	792	11.6
Others	473	10	48	454	–	985	14.7

1. Total available supply.
2. Net domestic consumption.
3. Includes TAS from 'hydro' and generation from fossil resources.

on rural and agricultural energy consumption patterns, particularly for households, agro-industries, transport and electrification. A set of well-defined guidelines should be formulated to identify appropriate methodologies for detailed assessment of energy resources and end-use utilization in rural areas. Such assessments would provide a base for integrated rural planning and policy formulation and implementation.

New and renewable sources of energy encompass a variety of energy forms, as well as a wide range of associated technologies at different levels of maturity. Rural planning should incorporate the choice of an appropriate combination of renewable technologies which can satisfy specific needs of rural development and compete with other energy technologies.

Household

Household activities are a major consumer of energy in the rural areas of the North African countries, accounting for 30%–35% of total consumption in Algeria, Egypt and Tunisia, and reaching over 45% in Morocco and Libya. The main household supplies in North Africa are non-commercial fuels, specifically fuelwood and charcoal. In 1986, rural households in Morocco consumed the equivalent of over 2000 tons of oil, about 80% of which consisted of fuelwood and charcoal. In Egypt and Libya, by contrast, LPG, kerosene and electricity are extensively used by rural households.

Agriculture and irrigation

Energy needs for pumping and distribution of irrigation water vary according to the depth of water, crop requirements and the techniques used. For a water depth of 20 metres, an installed pumping capacity of 0.5–1 KW/ha is needed which consumes 5–10 KWh/day. The total irrigated land in North Africa is almost 10 million ha, equivalent to 60% of the total cropped land in the region. No reliable data exist for energy consumption by pumping and irrigation. The prevailing fuel consumption rates for irrigation in the region are equivalent to about 440 kilogrammes of oil per hectare irrigated by groundwater, and 190 kilogrammes of oil per hectare for surface irrigation. On this basis, the present total energy consumption by pumping and irrigation in the region can be estimated as equivalent to about 3.2 million tons of oil.

In many cases, crops are fertilized with animal and crop residues, usually applied by hand. Mineral fertilizers, which require large amounts of primary energy for their production, are intensively used in most North African countries. In 1986, the total amount of mineral fertilizers consumed in the region reached 3.4 million metric tonnes. Algeria, Egypt and Morocco are producers of fertilizers.

Land preparation, harvesting and mechanization are major consumers of time and energy, depending on conditions such as climate, rainfall patterns, existing vegetation and types of crop planted. In the past, land preparation and harvesting used human and draught animal power. The use of agricultural machinery, introduced in the late 1960s, expanded rapidly in Egypt and Morocco, where the number of machines in service in 1986 reached 814,000 and 260,000 respectively.

Tractors and combine harvesters, with an average power of 45–60 horse power, are often used in agriculture. Improved maintenance, better matching of power units and equipment, and the use of reduced tillage, are some of the measures which could reduce energy consumption in mechanized agriculture.

The use of plastic material to cover greenhouses for horticulture is expanding rapidly in the region. This practice enhances productivity and allows off-season cropping. In Egypt, intensive efforts are directed towards cultivation in greenhouses, with solar energy being used directly to warm the greenhouse. In the warm summer climates of North Africa, the greenhouses need to be cooled and this is done by ventilation, shading or cooling. Energy-efficient, low-cost cooling/heating techniques for agricultural greenhouses are needed in the region.

Agro-industries

The amount of energy required by agro-industries depends on the product to be processed, the type of processing, temperature and climate. In general, the volume of agro-industries in rural areas is minimal except in Egypt, where agro-industries are growing rapidly. Efforts should be directed towards processing agricultural products within the rural communities themselves, using local energy resources to the maximum extent possible.

Crop drying is an important agro-processing activity which needs large amounts of energy determined by the crop moisture content, climate and required product quality. Artificial drying techniques are better than natural sun-assisted drying. A number of economically and technically viable solar-powered drying systems can be constructed in rural areas. The main crops which are traditionally dried in the region are grains, fruits, vegetables, herbs and medicinal plants.

The market value of processed milk (cheese, yoghurt, etc.) is much higher than that of raw milk. The potential for such processes in the region is substantial. Solar thermal systems, wind energy technologies and biogas produced from animal waste can be used for milk processing. The technical and economic feasibility of such systems is being examined in Egypt and pilot systems are being tested.

Poultry processing and chicken farms require energy to fuel processes such as slaughtering, scalding, rendering of ovals and cold storage. The energy required is mainly in the form of low pressure steam and electrical power. Solar thermal systems and waster-heat recovery techniques can help to reduce energy consumption. Chicken farms that consume energy for poultry space heating in winter could fuel biogas digesters with chicken manure, using the resultant gas for heating.

In many countries of the region, there are active rural and cottage industries. Among the cottage industries that consume significant amounts of energy are brick and tile making, potteries and ceramic studios, bakeries, tobacco curing and fish drying. Few data exist on the energy consumption of these activities. It is necessary to assess their energy requirements, develop more energy-efficient systems and, where possible, substitute fuelwood with other renewable energy sources.

Fisheries

Fishery activities are common to all North African countries. The major fishing areas are on the Atlantic (Morocco), the Mediterranean (Algeria, Libya, Tunisia) and the Red Sea (Egypt). Energy is needed to supply household requirements and cold storage. Low-power photovoltaic systems and biogas digesters (using spoiled fish and residues) could be of assistance in meeting these needs.

Rural transport

No reliable data are available on energy consumption or requirements for human transport or transport of agricultural products. An assessment is needed.

Water desalination

In spite of its long coastlines, most of the North African region lacks fresh water resources. As a result, desalination, which consumes energy in large quantities, is one of the urgent needs in the region. For large-scale production of fresh water, conventional thermal and reverse osmosis technologies are used. In the remote areas of the region, where water consumption is low, solar stills and solar or wind-driven reverse osmosis desalination plants are more appropriate.

Rural electrification

Integrated PV and wind-powered rural electrification presents an attractive alternative to conventional energy sources. PV systems range from one module for individual isolated homes to complete electricity generation and distribution systems (mini-utilities) for rural villages. Early sites in the region were typically rated at 2 KW or less, but more recent sites have up to 500 KW. Renewable energy rural electrification systems provide primary power for lighting, water pumping, communications and medical refrigeration for remote rural settlements, and power for small rural industries.

New and Renewable Energy for Rural Development in North Africa

The concept of new and renewable sources of energy encompasses a hetero-geneous range of energy forms, as well as a wide range of associated technologies at different levels of maturity. There are technologies that are proven and in operation and others that are at the frontier of scientific knowledge. The dynamic scientific and technological progress in the field, and the context of overall energy developments, are essential factors to be constantly studied in assessing the potential of new and renewable sources of energy. It is clear that the economic feasibility of energy applications is not universally fixed, but depends on a combination of site and non-site specific elements such as resource availability, costs, alternative fuel costs, energy pricing policies, lifespan and local economic indicators. At the same time, the applicability of these technologies also depends on non-pecuniary factors such as social benefits in the form of employment opportunities, health and sanitation aspects, national strategies for self-sufficiency and environmental criteria regarding pollution and sustainable development.

Table 10.3 shows the level of development of those new and renewable energy applications which appear to be most promising for the North African region. This information, together with national and site-specific considerations, needs to be considered when assessing the potential of energy options.

North African countries were amongst the earliest users of renewable energy, particularly in rural areas. Passive solar buildings were developed and built in ancient Egypt as well as the rest of North Africa during the Coptic and Islamic ages. Solar drying, cooking and the use of animal and agricultural waste are old practices in the region.

Modern renewable energy innovations have been under consideration in the region since the late 1950s. During the last decade, interest has intensified and several applications have been implemented. The current status of renewable energy use in the region reflects the experience gained through the different planning, demonstration and commercialization activities undertaken during the last two decades. The situation in each country is discussed below.

Algeria

In the early 1980s, the government established a Renewable Energy Directorate and its programme is now one of the most important achievements in the country. Algeria is a particularly sunny country especially in its Saharan part. It has an average of 2500 to 4000 hours of sunshine per year.

Solar water heaters were the first solar energy applications tried by the Renewable Energy Directorate. In 1983, four different types were produced and eventually one design was chosen for local production. Now, a joint venture between the National Plastics Agency and the Mechanical Division of the Directorate to produce 2000 solar water heaters is under way.

Since 1984, 100 units of simple solar stills have been made and installed in hospitals and remote southern areas of Algeria. Solar still units producing 50 litres per day are being used to produce enough water for 300 inhabitants in the village of Bishar.

There are more than 30 photovoltaic pumps around the country. A PV village electrification system at Batra village serves 11 houses. Each house has a television, a radio, a refrigerator and three electric lamps, which are run by a solar photovoltaic station. Three other villages use the solar PV station.

Several hundred solar refrigerators for medical establishments are in operation. Several telecommunication units are powered by solar energy in the centres of Aris and Adrar, and also in the provinces of Tamanrasset and Beshar. In addition, one of the most effective photovoltaic projects in Algeria is that of lighting the 670 km road which connects Reqan with Burg Baji Mukhtar.

Average wind speed varies from 2.8 to 4.1 metres per second, which is suitable for water pumping. Ten different machines have been installed in various parts of the country. Biogas systems are being utilized in agricultural areas to produce methane from animal refuse and decayed dates. Although

Table 10.3

Identification of new and renewable sources of energy application/level of technology and maturity

Applications	Solar energy						Wind			Biomass				Draught animal
	Dryers	Stills	Thermal	PV¹	PV/D²	Passive	Mechanical	Electricity	PV/W³	Direct combustion	Gas fire	Biogas	Compost	
1. Household														
Cooking			xb							x	xb	xa		
Water heating			xa							x	x	xa		
Lighting and appliances				xa	xa			xb			x	xb		
Space heating			xb			xa					x	xb		
2. Agriculture														
Pumping and irrigation		x	xb	xb		xa	xb	xb		xb		xa		
Fertilizing											xa	x	xa	
Earth preparation, harvesting and mechanization			xb	xb			xb				xb		xa	
3. Agro-industries														
Crop drying	xa		xb							x		xa		
Milk processing			xa											
Poultry processing												xb		
Chicken farms			x									xb		
Crop processing (grinding)			xb	xb		xa				xb	xb			

Table 10.3 (contd)
Identification of new and renewable sources of energy application/level of technology and maturity

	Energy resources/technology options												
	New and renewable resources												
	Solar energy						Wind			Biomass			
Applications	Dryers	Stills	Thermal	PV[1]	PV/D[2]	Passive	Mechanical	Electricity	PV/W[3]	Direct combustion	Gas fire	Biogas	Compost	Draught animal
4. Fisheries community														
Households	x	x	x	x	x	x	x	x	x			x	x	
Cold stores			xb	xa	xa			x	xb					
5. Others														
Water desalination			x	x	x		x	x						
Clinics														
Non-agricultural production (according to end-use identified)														
Telecommunications				x				x						

a = Mature
b = Maturing
1/PV   Photovoltaic Solar Systems
2/PV/D   Hybrid Photovoltaic systems
3/PV/W   Hybrid photovoltaic wind systems

Algeria is well-endowed with fuelwood supplies in comparison with other countries in the region, it has a deficit of over 12 million cubic metres of fuelwood per year.

Egypt

Egypt developed its renewable energy development strategy with the aim of saving 3% to 5% of its total primary energy resource by the years 2000–2005 (excluding mini-hydro resources and non-commercial fuels presently used). The New and Renewable Energy Authority of Egypt (NRE) is combining with other concerned institutions to develop renewable energy in rural and remote areas.

Solar insolation in Egypt varies betwen 5–9 KWh per square metre per day, with an average of more than 6 KWh. There are active programmes to develop, demonstrate and manufacture solar equipment in the country. Solar applications include water heating, industrial solar energy applications, desalination, drying and poultry processing.

As a result of intensive development, demonstration and marketing efforts, the solar water heater is today a fully commercialized product manufactured locally in Egypt. About 30,000 family-size heaters are in use; it is expected that over 700,000 will be installed by the year 2000.

Different types of small-scale solar dryers as well as semi-industrial crop drying have been developed and are being disseminated by agricultural and village development organizations. Solar water heating in poultry processing and waste treatment are typical examples. Solar water heaters and dryers are produced locally and a joint venture for the manufacture of desalination equipment will be established soon.

As Egypt suffers fresh water shortage in its coastal areas, several photovoltaic desalination units have been installed with capacities of up to 30 KW producing 70–100 cubic metres of fresh water every day. Several PV pumping systems have been installed either as stand-alone units or as an integrated part of PV village electrification systems such as in Ewinat in the south-west of the country or in Sadat City. Demonstration and testing of remote rural PV applications started as early as 1979. By the year 2000, the estimated PV pumping market is expected to total about 2 MWp, with an annual market volume of 1300 KWp. The market for PV lighting, refrigerators and telecommunications is expected to be about 2.8 MWp, with an annual market of 1600 KWp.

Wind energy has been used in Egypt for water pumping since the early 1960s. Lack of maintenance and extensive availability of diesel fuel stopped the commercialization of such technology. Since 1984, interest in wind energy utilization has increased, particularly after a wind resource assessment that showed average wind speeds between six and ten metres per second at the Red Sea coasts and about five metres per second along the north coast. Wind electric pumping systems with respective capacities of 50, 15 and 10 KW have been installed and tested at Ewinat, Abo Ghossoum and Sadat City. In addition, the wind farm concept has been introduced at Ras Ghareb with 400 KW capacity connected to the local grid. Other systems are being installed.

The New and Renewable Energy Authority and local industries have an aggressive programme, financed and supported by UNIDO/UNDP, for the manufacture of 100 KW electric wind turbines.

Currently, the substantial biomass resource in rural areas is utilized using low-efficiency traditional processes. Since the late 1970s, both the Agriculture Research Centre and the National Research Centre have been active in the area of biogas production. More than 150 family-size biogas units have been built, tested and developed locally. Large biogas units have been built for animal husbandry and chicken farms. A programme for the production of modular biogas units for rural areas is being financed by the Academy of Scientific Research and Technology and should be finalized by 1992. Recent market estimates show that the equivalent of 90 thousand tons of oil can be saved by the use of biogas in rural areas by the year 2000.

Libya

Libya has a mix of solar radiation, wind and limited geothermal resources. Due to its expansive desert areas, remote rural applications are perfect candidates for renewable energy use. Solar radiation is as high as 7 KWh per square metre per day. Solar applications such as water pumping and electricity generation in remote areas are increasingly common. Solar activities started in Libya in the mid-1970s and a well-equipped solar energy research and development centre has been established.

Several solar PV applications have been used by the telecommunications and petroleum companies in relay stations, electricity generation, cathodic protection, water pumping and TV transmission. The solar energy centre in Libya has carried out several studies on solar water heating, passive heating and cooling, solar buildings, solar energy storage, solar ponds and desalination. In addition, many academic establishments are involved in fundamental research into solar energy.

The potential of wind energy in Libya, where the average wind speed is 3.5 to 5.9 metres per second, is just as great as that of solar energy. In 1950, 249 wind machines were used for water pumping in Libya. Due to lack of maintenance, the falling water level in the wells and the availability of cheap diesel fuel, electric generators replaced wind pumps. Now several scientists are being trained abroad on wind energy utilization.

Morocco

The interest in renewable energy systems in Morocco is high, particularly for small PV and biomass applications in rural and remote areas. Information given here on renewable energy activities in the country has been provided by the Centre for the Development of Renewable Energy (CDRE).

Morocco has about 2800–3400 hours of sunshine per year and solar insolation of between 4.7 and 5.6 KWh per square metre per day. Solar applications include heating, cooling, desalination, power generation, pumping and greenhouses. PV applications such as pumping, rural electrification, lighting, telecommunications and medical refrigeration are almost fully commercialized.

About 150 PV pumping stations and several medical refrigerators have been installed in the country. The pumping station at Qujda and Beni Oukil consists of 2600 W PV cells with a pumping capacity of 116 cubic metres per day. Some of the medical refrigerators used in Sidi Moussa Medical Centre have a power capacity of 216 W and a cooling volume of 200 litres. Several schools in remote areas are powered by PV stations. A typical solar electricity generating station, with a capacity of 4320 W, is installed in the school of metallurgy in Marrakech. It is used for water pumping, cooling and lighting. The electricity is stored in lead-acid batteries and used during the night.

There is a growing market for PV lighting kits in Morocco. More than a thousand 200 W lighting systems are installed in rural homes. Preliminary estimates of PV market size by the year 2000 total about 130 MWp.

Solar thermal applications in Morocco include distillation and water heating. Many solar stills have been installed in villages around the country. The typical size of a solar still is about 1300 litres per day for domestic use. The solar water heater market in Morocco has great potential. The cost of delivered hot water from residential systems (100 to 250 litres per day) has been shown to be about half the cost of electric water heaters but more expensive by a factor of about 1.5 than butane gas heaters. Currently, there are five companies in Morocco which manufacture solar water heaters. It is reasonable to estimate that each company sells no more than 100 systems per year at an average price of 10,000 dirhams each (about US$1200). All the companies have their own installation crews and are operating well below their capacity. Given proper incentives, the Moroccan market could reach a sales volume of a few thousand systems per year within the next five to ten years.

Morocco has an average wind speed of 5.3 metres per second, and 5.5–8.3 metres per second across 90% of the country. Several wind machines have been installed in rural areas for pumping water or telecommunications purposes. Most are multi-blade types with a power rating of 1–5 KW. The main market for PV and wind pumps in Morocco is in the supply of potable water. Currently, there are about 1000–1500 mechanical windmills operating in the country.

There is also a small market for wind-powered battery chargers: 400 to 500 systems (100 to 200 W) have been installed. Preliminary estimates of market size to the year 2000 range from 3.0 MWp for domestic systems to 0.8 MWp for public and commercial systems.

Morocco has wide experience in the field of biogas which is used for cooking and lighting. More than 60 biogas units have been built in different locations, 80% of the Chinese type with a typical volume of 10–20 cubic metres and a daily biogas production of 1–5 cubic metres.

Tunisia

Tunisia has about 2700–3600 hours of sunshine per year. The country's solar energy programme undertakes research in thermal, chemical and PV conversion as well as some demonstration projects. In Sidria Tower three solar laboratories have been established. The first deals with PV technology and houses a small production unit. The second concentrates on thermal applications and, in particular, on the production and testing of solar water heaters. The third is concerned with water desalination and has built models based on simple stills and various other technologies: multi-stage flash, reverse osmosis and electro-dialysis.

Several companies are producing solar energy equipment. At present, Tunisia produces about 8000 solar water heaters per year. A few large-scale water desalination plants are in use in the central and southern regions.

A 29 KWp PV station has been installed at the solar village of Hamam Beyatha which houses 22 families. It has a school for 400 students, a mosque, a health centre and several shops. The health centre has a solar water heater of 300 litres capacity. The village uses wind energy for water pumping and all houses are designed to reduce energy consumption. There are numerous PV pumping station in Tunisia. For example, two PV pumping stations (600 W and 1600 W respectively) have been installed on the Hindi Al-Zaiton farm.

Tunisia has utilized wind energy for over 200 years. During the early part of this century, more than 10,000 wind units were in use. This was the case until 1960, when diesel and electric generators replaced most of these wind machines. Recently, the government has taken the initiative of developing several wind machines for pumping and electricity generation. One of these projects is the Al-Hawaria project for lighting, with a power capacity of 21 KW. Several wind machines for pumping have been produced locally and are in use in central Tunisia.

Actions for the Promotion of Renewable Energy Use in Rural Development

Energy assessment and planning

Energy plans in many of the countries of the region are not based on an adequate assessment of the energy requirements and resources, particularly for rural energy. It is recommended that governments of the region develop plans and policies based on country-specific energy resources and requirements. To realize this, the following steps need to be undertaken:

- Incorporate rural energy planning as an integral part of rural and agricultural development plans, in particular, and of national economic and energy planning, in general.
- Develop a mechanism for the implementation of rural energy strategies

and programmes in their countries, with the role of coordinating all activities related to rural energy.
- Promote more efficient use of the limited supply of available energy resources, particularly for household appliances, irrigation, transportation and general farming.
- Direct energy policies towards reducing dependence on imported conventional fuels, and give high priority to investment in reforestation and energy plantations. In this context, revise fuelwood prices and mechanisms for generating extra funds to expand investment in forestry projects.
- Carry out surveys on the energy consumption patterns of households, mechanized operations and small agro-processes, and develop credit and marketing systems designed to promote the use of promising new and renewable sources of energy. In addition, an assessment of new economic activity options for rural communities, including identification of their energy resources and requirements, should be carried out.
- Ensure the necessary access to energy supplies of nomadic and fishing communities, usually small and remote and lacking adequate energy services. Establish settlements using renewable energy and provide suitable household energy systems as well as facilities suited to the prevailing economic activities. This requires appropriate research and demonstration programmes for the development of renewable energy packages designed to suit the needs of such communities.
- Establish realistic prices and revise subsidy policies for conventional energy resources as a means of promoting their rational use in industry and transport without adversely affecting the basic energy needs of the rural population.
- Launch cooperative activities at regional and sub-regional levels that tap the considerable experience found in the region.

Training and information dissemination

In order to strengthen existing institutions specializing in rural and energy development, the following training initiatives are recommended:
- Develop training programmes for policy makers, economists and engineers in the economic analysis of energy projects and feasibility studies with special emphasis on renewable energy systems.
- Establish specialized units within the rural development agencies to provide technical assistance on energy-related activities and issues.
- Disseminate information to farmers and the rural population in general on energy options and opportunities for raising productivity and improving living conditions.
- Intensify training programmes on the construction, installation, operation and maintenance of rural energy technologies.

Technologies and local industries

Local manufacture of proven and natural renewable energy technologies should be a priority of energy development in the region.

For solar energy, the following steps need to be undertaken:
- Develop modular designs for greenhouses to optimize the use of solar energy and reduce costs of production and operation of horticultural techniques, particularly in countries with extensive desert areas. Experiences in Algeria, Egypt, Jordan and Tunisia should be utilized.
- Develop modular and low-cost solar water heaters and crop dryers that can be manufactured and maintained by rural households and can be used in agro-industries.
- Incorporate the passive use of solar energy in building designs to reduce energy consumption on air conditioning.

For wind energy, the following measure is a priority:
- Promote the use of wind mechanical systems for water pumping. Utilize the experience gained in the region and recommission existing systems in areas which have average annual wind speeds of over three metres per second, such as the coastal areas of Egypt, Libya and Morocco.

For biomass energy, implement the following measures:
- Develop modular designs for poly-fuel burners and stoves which can be constructed in rural areas at low cost. The exchange of information and experience in this area is of particular importance.
- Promote the utilization of organic matter through recycling in order to reduce the demand for mineral fertilizers.

For draught animal power, there is one main task:
- Upgrade the role of draught animal power. Although commonly used in most of the countries of the region for agriculture and transport, this form of energy currently has an efficiency rating as low as 10%. This will require improvement of draught animal stock, better feeding, enhanced veterinary care and improved equipment.

Priorities

In summary, the development of renewable energy resources in the region will require intensive efforts aimed at:

- Assessing solar, wind, biomass and draught animal power resources in the region, as adequate data are not available in most countries. A review of the shortcomings of current systems of collection and processing of data is needed.
- Developing industrial capabilities in the region for the manufacture of renewable energy equipment. National and regional organizations should assess relevant industries, resources and technological capabilities, and identify ways of strengthening their potential. Regional manufacturing

standards and specifications should be developed.
* Encouraging research and development programmes to promote local design, improve efficiency and reduce production costs of renewable energy technologies.

REFERENCES

Aboushihada, A. (1986). *The Role of OAPEC in New and Renewable Resources in the Arab Countries.*
Al Rifai, M. *et al.* (1987). *Renewable Energy in the Arab States: A Regional Outlook.*
ESCWA. (1986a). *Solar and Combined Solar/Wind Energy for Rural and Remote Areas in ESCWA Region.* ESCWA publication No. NR/86/1/6.
────── (1986b). *Wind Energy for Rural and Remote Areas in ESCWA Region.* ESCWA publication No. NR/86/2/6.
Fakahany, A. *Biogas in Morocco.*
FAO. *Fuelwood Supplies in the Developing Countries.* Forestry Paper No. 24.
────── *Fuelwood Supplies in the Developing Countries.* Animal Production and Health Paper No. 39.
────── (1987). *Energy for Rural and Agricultural Development in the Near East.* Report No. NERC/88/4.
Hegazi, A. *et al.* (1985). *Solar Crop Drying.*
────── (1986). *Potential Market for Solar Water Heaters in ESCWA Region: The Case of Egypt.*
Organization of Arab Petroleum Exporting Countries (OAPEC). (1986). *The Secretary General's Thirteenth Annual Statistical Report. OAPEC Publications.*
OAPEC. (1985). *Proceedings of the Arab Experts Meeting on the Renewable Energy Field.* OAPEC Publications.
────── *Wind Energy in Libya.* OAPEC Publications.
────── *National Paper on Tunisia.* OAPEC Publications.
UNDP/World Bank. (1984a). *Morocco: Issues and Options in the Energy Sector.* Report No. 4157.
────── (1984b). *Energy Issues and Options in Thirty Developing Countries.* Report No. 5230.
UNEP. (1985). *Energy Supply/Demand in Rural Areas in Developing Countries.* Report No. ERS-11-84.

The Potential for Biogas Development in Yemen

11

MAHMOUD A. SALEH

Energy Supply and Demand in Rural Areas of the ESCWA Region

The issue of energy supply and demand in rural areas of developing countries has been discussed intensively and a vast number of research papers, studies and books have been published on this topic. However, very little work seems to have been done on the quantification of the energy demand for the different activities of each of the four major economic sectors (household, agriculture, small industries and transport) in the rural areas of the ESCWA (United Nations Economic and Social Commission for Western Asia) region.[1] The estimation of energy demand for each rural activity is not an easy task. It requires intensive surveys and the analysis of a large amount of data; the information is gathered from rural people who, in most cases, cannot estimate the quantities of traditional fuel consumed for each activity; and in many cases the researcher is measuring the consumption of commodities (non-commercial fuels) which are not exchanged through the market.

Demand

Rural areas can be divided into four sectors: households, agriculture, small industries and transport. The household sector is and will continue to be the major consumer of energy in rural areas of the ESCWA region, even with the introduction of mechanization in agriculture and some cottage industries in the villages. The transport sector relies mainly on human and animal power and, to a lesser extent, on liquid fuel (petrol and diesel oil).

On the demand side, the main energy-consuming activities in the household sector are cooking, baking, water heating, lighting, radio, TV, water lifting, space heating, ventilation and refrigeration.

The highest energy-consuming activities are those using energy in the form of heat. A survey undertaken on a small village located in the Nile Delta in Egypt[2] revealed that the utilized heat energy in households is about 1.24 GJ/capita/year which is generated from 35.5 litres of kerosene, 300 kg of agricultural residues and 100 kg of animal manure of about 7 GJ of heat equivalent. The heat energy consumed in the household sector represents more than 80% of the total energy consumed in the different sectors in the village.

The main activities in agriculture which require appreciable amounts of energy are land preparation (ploughing, etc.), irrigation, harvesting and post-harvest processing. The energy required to perform these activities is mainly in the form of mechanical energy, usually supplied by human power, animal power and/or internal combustion engines (diesel or petrol engines).

In the village survey it was not easy to differentiate the energy provided by humans and animals in the different agricultural activities. However, an assessment was made of the amounts of diesel oil consumed by engines (driving tractors, water pumps, etc.) in performing these activities. The results are summarized in Table 11.1.

Table 11.1
Energy consumption in MJ/acre/year

Crop	Land preparation	Irrigation	Harvesting & post-harvesting	Total
Wheat	123	820	615	1558
Clover	123	1435	–	1558
Rice	246	2050	410	2706
Corn	246	1435	–	1681
Cotton	492	1435	–	1927
Vegetables	246	1845	–	2091

Transportation inside the villages of the ESCWA countries is largely confined to animals. However, inter-village transport depends to a limited extent on vehicles. The energy consumption in this sector is either difficult to quantify (when animals are used) or relatively negligible.

The cottage industries are activities such as dairy products, weaving, food preservation and handicrafts. Such small industries add to the household energy demand a certain small percentage. The value of this addition will depend on the type and size of the activity undertaken.

Supply

The energy supply for rural areas of ESCWA countries can be classified in four categories: traditional energy sources, liquid and gaseous petroleum products, electricity from the grid and renewable sources of energy. Traditional fuels, it may be argued, fall in the category of renewable sources. In this chapter, however, traditional fuels are categorized with renewable sources of energy if, and only if, they are not converted to heat energy using direct burning in traditional stoves and ovens.

Traditional energy sources are used extensively in rural areas. These sources include fuelwood, agricultural residues, animal dung, animal power and human power. Charcoal and coal are rarely used in the rural areas of the ESCWA region. Fuelwood, dry agricultural residues and dry dung cakes are burnt directly in simple stoves and ovens to provide thermal energy to households for cooking, baking, water heating and space heating. Health hazards and environmental pollution associated with these fuels are a major source of concern. In addition, a considerable proportion of these fuels is wasted due to the low level of efficiency (5%–10%) of conversion devices. New stove and oven designs can increase the efficiency of fuel utilization, though the new stoves may be unacceptable under the prevailing socio-economic conditions of rural communities in some ESCWA countries. Factors explaining this rejection include comparatively higher cost and the reliance of rural people on the waste heat from traditional stoves and ovens to provide warmth, and on the smoke produced to keep the household free of parasitic insects.

The use of human energy in different agricultural activities is diminishing. Animals are still used in some rural communities as an energy source in land preparation, water lifting, harvesting and post-harvesting processes. They are also the most common transportation mode in the villages.

Kerosene is widely used for cooking and water heating in households in the rural areas of the ESCWA region. It is rarely used for baking and space heating. The data collected on energy indicators in the village study revealed that the per capita consumption of kerosene is 35.5 litres per year for cooking and water heating only. If kerosene is the only fuel supplying all heat energy requirements, the per capita consumption rises to 65 litres per year. The figures on kerosene consumption are relatively high, mainly due to the cheap price of kerosene which is subsidized by the government. High-income groups in rural areas of some ESCWA countries are now using liquefied petroleum gas (LPG) as a substitute for kerosene, but no reliable data are currently available.

Diesel oil is now replacing animal and human power in many agricultural activities. Water pumping for irrigation is the main consumer. Diesel sets are used by some high-income households to generate electricity for lighting, refrigerators and ventilation. Petrol does not play an important role in rural energy supply; it is mainly used for transportation between villages or between the villages and the urban areas.

Rural electrification has been promoted in many ESCWA countries as a solution to energy problems. In certain cases, it has lead to modernization of the life style of some rural people, particularly the high-income group. However, electrification alone has not and will not lead to real socio-economic development of rural areas since it cannot meet all the energy demand. Electricity is not the most suitable form of energy for meeting basic rural energy needs such as cooking, baking and water heating. For such activities, electricity is beyond the purchasing power of most rural households.

Renewable Energy Sources and the Rural Areas

The main renewable sources of energy available in rural areas of the ESCWA region are solar energy, wind energy and biogas generated from an anaerobic fermentation of biomass (animal manure, human waste and/or agricultural residues). These sources are expected to play a predominant role in the energy supply to rural areas in the ESCWA region. At present, one cannot claim that any of the renewable energy technologies have been commercialized, with the exception of a limited number of solar water heaters which are produced commercially in some villages in Egypt, Jordan, Syria and Yemen.

The ESCWA secretariat and a number of other international and regional organizations and national institutions are directing efforts towards the promotion of small-scale solar, wind and biogas technologies for utilization in rural areas. In this respect, the ESCWA secretariat has organized technical meetings, a study tour and training workshops, prepared several studies, established an information network and implemented several demonstration projects. It has also included in its regular work programme and its operational activities for the next two years a number of renewable energy projects with special emphasis on rural areas.

The ESCWA secretariat is fully aware that any serious implementation of a strategy for rural development and for the supply of energy must take into account the central role of women as major suppliers and users of energy. The efforts expended by women in these activities consume a large proportion of their time and any policy for alleviating the hardship experienced by women is, therefore, contributing to the development of rural women.

When planning a renewable energy activity, the ESCWA Secretariat takes into consideration the following:

- The selected technology should be mature and commercially proven.
- The technology must be able to compete in the marketplace with technologies using conventional fuels.
- The renewable energy technology should be introduced within an integrated programme of socio-economic development for the village.
- The chosen technology should satisfy a clearly defined demand.
- Local skills and local material should be used as much as possible in constructing renewable energy systems.
- Local people should be trained in design, construction, operation and maintenance of the different components of the systems introduced.
- Local user groups should participate in the project design, implementation and management, since acceptance by local users contributes substantially to the success of the project.
- Projects should have other outputs in addition to energy generation, such as reduction of air pollution and health hazards.

With these considerations in mind, the ESCWA secretariat initiated a series of operational projects in Democratic Yemen with the long-term objective of diffusing biogas technology in rural areas. A review of the projects follows.

Diffusion of Biogas Technology in Yemen

The first project implemented by ESCWA in Democratic Yemen (PDRY) and funded by the United Nations Development Fund for Women (UNIFEM) was a study of the technical, economic and social aspects of the introduction of biogas use in Yemen.

The study found that about 75% of the population are considered rural and nomadic. Rural women are involved in the various farming activities. However, their main responsibility other than housework is animal husbandry. Women are responsible for cleaning the animal shed, collecting fodder, grazing and milking animals. The sheds are cleaned once or twice a day depending on the animals' daily pattern. Cows are milked twice a day. Women are also responsible for herding, fetching water and collecting fuelwood, activities which occupy more than a third of their time. Women leave their homes early in the morning to collect wood weighing as much as 10–15 kg, carrying it for an average distance of three or more kilometres.[3]

Other tasks which women perform include caring for children, preparing meals, baking bread, cleaning the house, washing, sewing and mending clothes. Fresh bread is prepared two times a day. Women indicated that they disliked the baking process because it involves a high risk of burning their hands because the mud stoves used for cooking and baking are open and have no chimney. The combustion in these stoves is incomplete. Harmful smoke containing a considerable amount of toxic carbon monoxide is released and the resultant indoor air pollution is harmful to women and children. The efficiency of stoves of the type used in Yemen is only 5%–10%, which means extensive energy losses.

Gathered fuelwood and agricultural residues are burnt directly to produce heat for cooking, baking and other domestic functions. In addition, some of the fuelwood is purchased to supplement the gathered twigs and agricultural waste. This increases the demand, which in turn leads to higher prices. Many rural households cannot afford to purchase fuelwood and the increased cost has added to the financial burden of the poor rural community.

Huge piles of refuse containing animal dung are deposited next to the houses waiting for the rainfall to sweep them away. These piles attract flies and insects. Manual handling of the manure and the refuse piles poses serious health risks to women and children. The health situation is further aggravated by milking cows in unpaved sheds which cannot be kept free of dung.

In the villages which are not connected to the water supply network, women are responsible for fetching water. They handlift water from wells with depths ranging from 20 to 40 metres using ropes and rubber pails. At least two women are needed to lift one pail of water – an arduous and time-consuming activity. Waste water collects around houses in small stagnant ponds, thus creating an additional health hazard.

The pattern of sanitary disposal in the villages of Yemen constitutes an important health hazard. Most of the latrines in the villages are connected to a central pit which is about 15 metres deep. At this depth, part of the liquid waste penetrates the soil and pollutes the wells that supply water to the households.

The study concluded that introducing biogas technology (BGT) would help to relieve women of the burden of collecting fuelwood or agricultural residues and handling animal manure; it would also reduce exposure to unhealthy smoke levels generated by direct burning of organic materials. Using BGT will also improve the sanitary and health conditions of the household and the general environmental conditions of the villages, including the purity of the drinking water supply.

BGT can provide the village with a cheap energy resource which can meet about 70%–80% of the energy requirements of the household. Electric well pumps could be installed. In addition, the digested sludge obtained through anaerobic fermentation of animal, human and agricultural waste provides a clean, germ-free and seedless fertilizer with a high nitrogen content.

The second project tested different designs of biogas plants and convened a national seminar to discuss the different aspects of BGT. Three demonstration digester plants – an Egyptian-Chinese type, a Borda type and a typical Indian type – were constructed; the Egyptian-Chinese model proved to be the most appropriate for the local conditions of rural Yemen and could be constructed by skilled labour available in the villages.

The findings of the case study on BGT in Yemen, the successful operation of the three biogas plants and the enthusiasm of the villagers, moved the government to request ESCWA to pursue this activity further by implementing a pilot project for demonstrating the economic viability and social acceptability of BGT, and its social and environmental impact.

In January 1989 ESCWA, with financial support from UNIFEM, initiated the third project, 'Diffusion of BGT in Yemen: Development of Women in Al-Habeel Village'. This project installed a pilot BGT system in Al-Habeel, about 40 km from Aden and about 10 km from El-hota. The proximity to El-hota, the capital city of Lahaj, made it easier to monitor and supervise the project. The village consists of scattered groups of houses, distributed in such a way that there are large spaces sufficient for constructing biogas units all around. Open animal sheds are located near the houses. Three biogas plants were already in operation.

Key activities of the third project include:

- Formation of the village committee consisting of representatives of the Governorate, the Local Defence Committee, the local General Union of Yemeni Women, Federation of Democratic Yemeni Peasants, Federation of Yemeni Youth and three villagers (including one woman) selected by the community. This committee is responsible for (1) promotion of the objectives and activities of the project in the community; (2) participation in formulation of a detailed workplan of activities at the village level; (3) participation in site selection for biogas plants, beneficiaries and the labour force; (4) monitoring implementation of the extension programmes; and (5) ensuring the provision of the necessary requirements from the village for the construction of biogas plants.

- A pre-project survey of the socio-economic conditions of the village.
- Construction of 12 complete biogas systems (including digesters of volumes ranging between 3 and 6 cubic metres, each producing 1–2 cubic metres of biogas per day), animal sheds, latrines, waste water treatment plants, stoves and ovens. These systems serve 16 families. Figure 11.1 is a block diagram of the biogas system.
- Training six women extension workers and relevant local personnel in the design, construction, operation, maintenance and repair of biogas systems.
- Implementing an extension programme involving over 50 rural women.

ESCWA experts visited the village at the end of 1989. The positive impacts of the project on the village were clear. The piles of animal waste and the pools of stagnant water had completely disappeared. Kitchens were much cleaner. The effluent produced by the digesters and the treated waste water were being used as fertilizer. The land around the houses had become green areas. Biogas effluent is also taken to the agricultural fields, substantially reducing the need for expensive chemical fertilizer. Women have stopped collecting firewood, while cooking and baking take much less time. Women have more time to take care of their children and are not exposed to indoor air pollution from wood-fired stoves and ovens.

Biogas, solar and wind energy can play a key role in the rural energy supply in the ESCWA region provided that the selected technology satisfies a clearly defined demand. This technology should be proven commercially and appropriate for the local conditions. It should be introduced within an integrated programme for socio-economic development of the village and the end-users should participate in the different phases of project implementation.

NOTES

1. The ESCWA region consists of the following countries covered by the United Nations Economic and Social Commission for Western Asia (UNESCWA): Bahrain, Democratic Yemen, Egypt, Iraq, Jordan, Kuwait, Lebanon, Oman, Qatar, Saudi Arabia, Syrian Arab Republic, United Arab Emirates and Yemen Arab Republic.
2. This village is a prototype for 40,000 other villages in Egypt. It includes 19 households totalling 189 persons and 58 acres of cultivated land.
3. 'Introduction of biogas technology in PDRY: case study'. UNESCWA Document No. E/ESCWA/SDP/87/5/Rev.1, August 1987

REFERENCES

El-Mahgary, Y. & Biswass, A. K., eds. (1985). *Integrated Rural Energy Planning*. Butterworths.
Hamad, M. A. (1987). 'Biomass as a renewable source of energy for rural areas' (in Arabic). Proceedings of Seminar on Biomass Utilization in the Arab World, Riyadh, Saudi Arabia.
Olende, S. A. (1989).'Rural energy strategies'. *Natural Resources Forum*, February 1989.
Waddle, D.B., Perlack, R. D. & Jones, H. M. (1989). 'Renewable energy projects – lessons from the past and directions for the future'. *Natural Resources Forum*, November 1989.

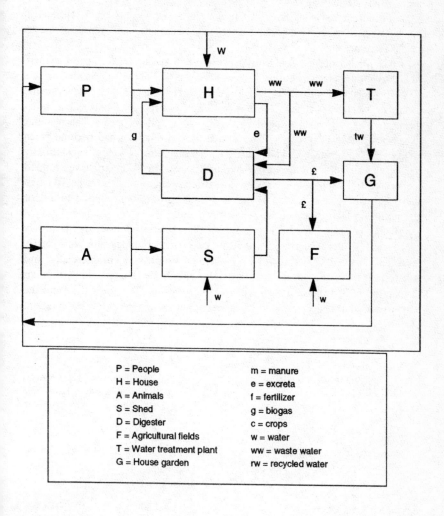

Figure 11.1
Biogas systems in Al-Habeel village

IV

ASIA

12 The Role of Renewable Energy in Rural Development in China: Achievements & Prospects

DA XIONG QUI

Rural Development and Energy Consumption

China is a large country and accounts for one-fifth of the world's population. The rural population stood at 662.88 million, representing 63.4% of the national total in 1985, declining to 577.11 million, or 53.4% of the total in 1987. Administratively, the rural area in a given province consists of villages, towns and townships, and counties. The rural population (excluding towns) dropped rapidly due to an administrative change in 1984 which broadened the definition of a town. If those living in towns were included in the rural population, then the 1985 rural total would be 844.2 million, forming 190.8 million households. For the purposes of rural energy demand projection, town dwellers will be included in the rural population.

Great changes have taken places in rural China in recent years (1980–7).

1 Total social output value, including agriculture, industry, construction, transportation and commerce, increased rapidly from 279.3 billion yuan to 694.4 billion yuan (1980 constant value); however, the agricultural share of total social output value decreased from 68.9% to 49.6%.

2 The proportion of the labour force engaged in agricultural production decreased from 68.8% to 60%. Ten million rural workers were employed in non-agricultural production in cities and towns, representing 16% of total new urban employment.

3 The rural standard of living also improved: the average annual income per capita increased from 191 to 323 yuan (1980 constant value), while housing area per capita increased from 9.4 to 16 square metres.

Agriculture, so important in China, witnessed growth in recent years. Its total output value grew 1.62 times from 1980 to 1987, from 192.3 to 311.5 billion yuan (1980 constant value), an annual average growth rate of 7.1%. Grain yields increased 1.26 times, from 320.56 to 424.73 million tons. Unit grain yield increased 1.32 times from 2.745 to 3.63 tons/ha. Figure 12.1 gives the mix of total social output value in rural areas and agricultural output value.

All of these changes have resulted in changes in rural energy consumption. Rural energy is used for agricultural production, township–village enterprises (industry, construction, transportation, commerce and services) and peasant households in rural areas. As shown in Table 12.1, total rural energy consumption increased 1.6 times from 1980 to 1987. Due to the rapid increase of small town industries, the share of production in total rural energy consumption increased from 22% to 32.8%, while the proportion of commercial energy increased from 28.1% to 46.2%. Commercial energy consumed in rural households also increased (Figure 12.2), though non-commercial energy – in the form of biomass – is still the main source used by peasant households.

The rural share in total energy consumption in China increased from 39.57% in 1980 to 45.94% in 1987, while the share of commercial energy consumption increased from 16.5% to 28.2% during the same period. Wide-scale rural electrification has been introduced: more than 92% of townships, 82% of villages and 73% of peasant households have electricity. Electricity consumed in rural areas increased from 48 KWh in 1980 to 78.6 KWh in 1987, 15.7% of total electricity consumption (500 KWh) in 1987. Table 12.2 gives the consumption mix of electricity in rural areas in 1985.

Energy shortage and backward technology remain the major problems of energy consumption in rural areas. Supply shortfalls in oil have restricted agricultural production in rural areas for a long time: 70% of oil-powered agricultural machines can work only 160 hours per year due to the shortage.

Table 12.1
Energy consumption in rural areas in China (1980–7)

	1980		1987	
	Million tce	%	Million tce	%
Total energy consumption	319.5	100	524.4	100
Commercial energy	89.5	28.1	242.4	46.2
Non-commercial energy	230	71.9	282.0	53.8
Energy consumption in production	67.8	22.0	177.8	32.8
in livelihood	251.7	78.0	346.6	67.2

tce = tonnes of coal equivalent

Table 12.3 shows the faltering oil supply to agro-machines in recent years, when two-thirds of farm work was done by human and animal power.

The shortfall in electricity supply has often led to power cuts; even though most of the villages have been electrified, they have often had no electricity. Small-town industries receive only 40% of demand and farming work is sometimes affected during busy seasons.

Biomass is the main fuel used for cooking and heating in peasant households. Total consumption of biomass in rural areas in 1987 was 282 million tons of coal equivalent (mtce), of which 150 mtce was from straw and stalks and 132 mtce from firewood. Since traditional low-efficiency energy conversion facilities are still used by most peasant households, the average amount of energy used by a peasant household daily was estimated at only 3500–3700 kilocalories, 20% less than the minimum energy requirement for cooking.

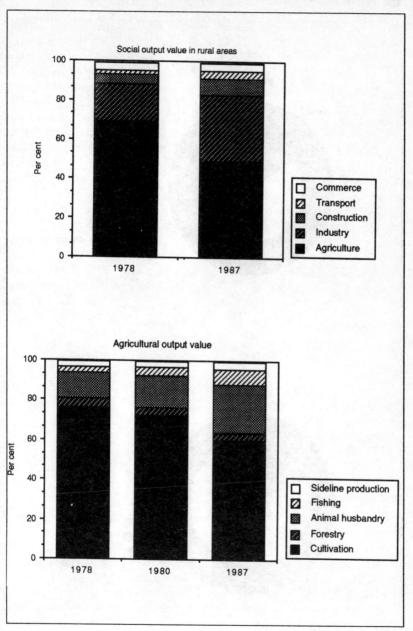

Figure 12.1
Social output value in rural areas and agricultural output value.

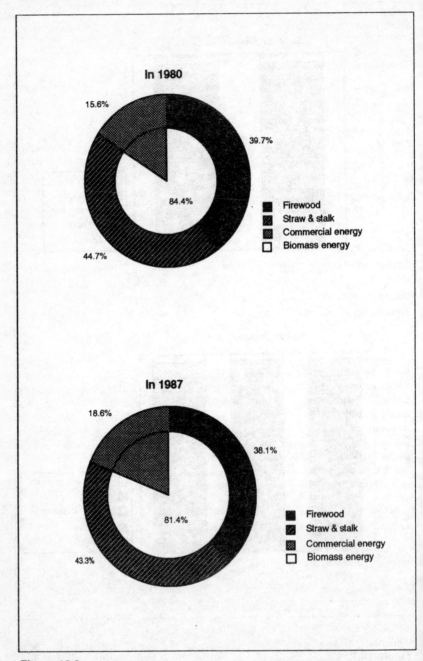

Figure 12.2
Structure of energy consumption in rural livelihood (in percentage)

Table 12.2
Rural electricity consumption, 1985

	Billion KW	%
Total rural electricity consumption	60.01	100
Irrigation	12.72	21.1
Agro-processing	11.16	18.5
Township–village enterprises	17.73	29.4
Household lighting	9.05	15
Others	9.35	15.5

Table 12.3
Utilization of farm machinery and impact of oil supply

	1980	1982	1983	1984	1985
Total power of farm machinery (mill. hp)	200	226	245	265	284
Total power of oil farm machinery (mill. hp)	130	150	160	180	200
Oil supply (million tons)	8.78	7.18	7.34	7.45	7.55
Unit oil consumption (g/hp.hr)	245	245	245	240	240
Annual working time (hrs)	276	217	185	174	101

The development of township-village industries is a constructive way to solve the problem of the surplus labour force in rural areas and diversify the rural economy. However, these industries have led to a rapid increase in rural energy consumption, absorbing 80% of the commercial energy used in rural areas. Table 12.4 gives the pattern of energy consumption in rural industry in recent years. Owing to backward technologies, low-efficiency devices, the low level of management, etc., unit energy consumption in rural industry is much higher than the nation's average. The rapid development of rural energy has led to competition for raw materials and energy with large industry. It is, therefore, necessary to readjust the development of rural industry.

Demand and Supply in the Future

Demand analysis

Rural energy is used in three sectors: rural households, agricultural production and township-village enterprises.

ENERGY DEMAND PROJECTION IN RURAL HOUSEHOLDS
According to the population forecast, there will be 1.25 billion people in China by 2000; it is estimated that they will form 220 million households. The daily energy used by a peasant family will include the minimum cooking energy

Table 12.4
Energy consumption of township-village industry (million tce)

	1980	1982	1983	1984	1985
1. Metallurgy	1.18	1.62	2.19	3.05	5.26
2. Coal	1.18	1.81	2.05	2.36	2.71
3. Chemical industry	1.60	2.14	2.06	3.09	4.26
4. Mechanical industry	6.90	8.61	9.74	11.67	16.64
5. Building material	26.58	37.82	40.98	47.94	50.93
6. Food	2.75	4.16	4.58	5.34	6.78
7. Textile	1.88	2.83	3.54	4.60	6.64
8. Total	42.07	58.99	65.14	78.05	93.22

Table 12.5
Energy input, output and output/input ratio in agricultural field in different regions with different yield levels (1979)

	Yields	Total energy input	Organic energy input	Non-organic energy input	Total energy output	Energy output of grain	Energy output/ input ratio	Organic-non-organic input ratio
	kg/hect	GJ per hect.	GJ per hect.	GJ per hect.	GJ per hect.	GJ per hect.		
Region with high yields > 6000 kg/hect.	10142	124.4	86.2	38.2	301.1	162.4	2.43	2.59
Region with medium yields 4125–6000 kg/hect.	4992	76.5	56.1	20.4	147.3	79.9	1.95	3.18
Region with medium-low yields 3000–4125 kg/hect.	3376	54.6	42.2	12.1	99.6	54.0	1.83	3.73
Region with low yields <3000 kg/hect.	2016	40.1	34.8	5.4	59.3	32.5	1.43	6.44
Average in China								
1979:	4275	64.3	49.6	14.7	126.1	68.6	1.96	3.37
1965:	2160	38.1	36.2	2.0	63.7	34.6	1.67	18.1
1952:	1648	30.1	30.1	0.06	449.7	26.9	1.65	501.7

requirement of 4500 kcal. The average efficiency of the cooking stove is expected to increase to 20%, since a number of improved stoves will be disseminated. The total energy demand for rural households will thus be 320–335 mtce, and the proportion of commercial energy will increase to between 20% and 25%. It is estimated that 90% of rural households will have electricity and that electricity use per capita will increase from the current 15 KWh to 40 KWh annually. Total electricity consumption will thus increase from 12.5 billion KWh annually to 33 billion KWh by 2000.

DEMAND ANALYSIS FOR AGRICULTURAL PRODUCTION

The encroachment of housing and industry will reduce the total area of cultivated land slightly. The demand for crops will grow and increasing the yields per unit of sown area will be the main way of expanding crop production to meet demand. More energy will thus be required for both agro-machines and fertilizer (chemical and organic). Table 12.5 shows the energy input in agriculture in different regions with different yield levels. As can be seen from the table, high-yield areas need much more energy input (especially non-organic energy) than low-yield ones. It is estimated that the demand for petroleum products will increase by a factor of three, given the need to improve the efficiency of farm machinery. In addition, energy consumption for other applications – breeding, raising seedlings, drying, etc. – is expected to increase with yields. Electricity consumption for agricultural production was 31.5 KWh in 1987; the demand is estimated at about 60 KWh by 2000. The total energy demand for agricultural production is thus expected to double to 60–70 mtce.

ENERGY DEMAND FOR RURAL ENTERPRISES (TOWNSHIP–VILLAGE INDUSTRY, TRANSPORTATION, COMMERCE AND SERVICES)

The annual growth rate of rural enterprises during the 1980–7 period was 23.5%, from 86.96 to 382.89 billion yuan (1980 constant value). It is, however, estimated that the growth rate will drop to 8%–10% annually. In addition, the energy saving rate will average 2%–3% annually. The estimated energy demand for rural enterprises will be 300 mtce. Most of this will be met by coal. Electricity consumption for rural enterprises was 34.6 KWh in 1987. The rate of growth of electricity use, closely tied to the growth rate of output value, is expected to expand demand to 94 KWh in 2000.

In summary, the total rural energy demand by 2000 will be between 650 and 700 mtce, 60% of which will be for commercial energy, and the electricity demand will be 186.4 KWh. Table 12.6 gives the estimated figures.

RURAL ENERGY RESOURCES AND SUPPLY

Rural energy resources include a type of biomass from forest resources; straw and animal excrement; electricity from small hydro-power stations; coal from small rural collectively owned coal mines; and wind power, solar energy, geothermal energy and other locally situated sources. Rural energy supply

Table 12.6

	Total energy demand MTce	Commercial energy				Non-commercial energy			
		Sum MTce	Coal MT/MTce	Oil MT/MTce	Electricity Twh/MTce	Sum MTce	Firewood MT/MTce	Straw MT/MTce	Manure MT/MTce
Total energy demand	670–700	430	415.3/296.8	41.3/58.9	186.4/0.746	2.40			
For rural livelihood	320–350	80	93.5/66.8		33.0/0.132	2.40			
For agricultural production	68	68	16.8/12	22.7/32.4	59.4/0.238				
Township-village enterprises	282	282	305/218	18.6/26.5	94.0/0.376				

includes not only the energy exploited from local resources but also conventional energy imported from outside the region.

Small coal mines: China's proven coal reserves of more than 800 billion metric tonnes are the largest in the world. Economically recoverable reserves are sufficient to meet the country's projected demand for well over 100 years. However, the coal-bearing areas are not situated near the major consumption centres. Nevertheless, more than half of the 2300 counties and cities in China have coal resources.

Recent years have witnessed the growth of small coal mines owned by collectives and individuals in small towns and townships, especially following the deregulation of coal prices in 1984. Between 1978 and 1985, production from small coal mines increased from 100 to 228 million tonnes, while production from larger state or locally owned mines increased from 618 to 872 million tonnes during the same period. Table 12.7 shows that 60% of coal supplied in the rural areas now comes from small coal mines.

Biomass: Biomass resources are closely linked to afforestation and agricultural production. Forest energy resources include woody plants that provide fuel. From north to south, China traverses four climatic zones with high mountains in the south-west and little precipitation in the north-west. The same variety of forest, growing in different climatic zones, or with different soil conditions, shows great diversity in growth rate and amount of biomass to a unit area.

By the end of 1988, 5.6 million hectares of fast-growing fuel forest were afforested; this would produce 47.6 mtce of firewood. Firewood produced from other types of forest was estimated at about 36.6 mtce. The total fuelwood supply of 84.2 mtce was, however, less than the total consumption. More fast-growing fuel forests are planned. By 2000, if the fuel forest area could be developed to 10 million hectares, 85–90 mtce could be supplied; other types of forest are expected to produce 50 mtce, giving a total of 135–140 mtce.

Crop residue resources depend on crop yields. Grain yields could be increased to 500 million tons, and nearly the same amount of residue (500 mtce) could be obtained. Assuming that 40% of the straw could be used as fuel, more than 100 mtce of straw could thus be obtained. On these figures, a target for total biomass fuel production of between 230 and 240 mtce by the year 2000 would not be unrealistic..

In China, a small hydro-electric station (SHP) is defined as one with a total installed capacity of under 12,000 KW, a single-machine capacity of under 6000 KW and a small power grid. Potential small hydro-power resources are estimated at 150 GW, of which 70 GW are exploitable and could generate 200–250 KWh annually. The exploitable potential is distributed in the country as follows: 1100 out of the 2300 counties have more than 10,000 KW; 470 counties have 10,000–30,000 KW; 500 counties have 30,000–100,000 KW; and 134 counties have in excess of 1,000,000 KW.

Table 12.7
Coal supply and consumption (million tce)

		1979	1980	1982	1987
Supply from:	**a** State	39.42	48.69	50.22	60
	b Small coal pits	42.02	42.69	81.60	122.5
Consumption for:	**a** Production	35.81	39.10	76.05	112.9
	b Household	45.63	51.88	55.77	69.6

By the end of 1988, a total capacity of 12,000 MW had been installed, generating 30 billion KWh and supplying more than one-third of the electricity used in rural areas. Rural grids have developed rapidly, as local or regional grids were well adapted to utilizing SHP capacity. In south China, where hydro resources are most abundant, rural electrification has come about through the linking of individual stations to small local grids which then grew into large regional grids. The development of SHP will be continued; it is estimated that a further 8,000 MW will be installed by the year 2000, enlarging total capacity to 20,000 MW.

Solar energy: Solar energy resources in China are abundant. About two-thirds of the regions in China have total annual radiation intensity in excess of 120 Kcal/sq.cm (502 KJ/sq .cm.) with 2200 hours of radiation time in the average year. The classification of solar energy resources has been carried out on the basis of abundance or scarcity, effect of climatic conditions and seasonal variations, and regularity of insolation distribution during the day.

By the end of 1988, a capacity of 600,000 square metres had been installed as solar heaters, 100,000 square metres as solar stoves, and 170,000 square metres as passive solar buildings. Solar driers utilized several thousand square metres in rural areas and there were also some solar photovoltaic stations including one in a village in Gansu province with a capacity of 10 KW that is able to supply electricity to 200 peasant households. Further development of solar energy equipment is envisaged in the future.

Wind energy: It is estimated that wind energy resources in China amount to 1 billion KW from a minimum average wind speed greater than three metres per second, of which 10%, or 100 million KW, could be harnessed. The evaluation has been carried out on the basis of the effective density and annual cumulative hours of wind energy.

China was one of the earliest users of wind energy. The vertical sail windmill was used for many centuries. A series of windmill, wind pump and windpower generation systems have been developed in China. Mini-windmills of 50W and 100W developed in the Inner Mongolia pastoral districts have been well received by the herdsmen. By the end of 1988, there were 70,000 wind machines of the type developed in Inner Mongolia, with a total capacity of 4700 KW, constituting 48% of total wind power capacity in China. Other models of wind machine (1 KW, 50 KW, 80 KW, 100 KW, etc.) are also under development. The number of mini-windmills is expected to double in the next five year plan.

Other renewable resources: Geothermal energy, tidal energy and wave energy are also being developed in China, where these resources are abundant. There are 345,000 square metres of greenhouses utilizing geothermal energy. Some geothermal power generation stations have been constructed, the biggest one (13 MW) in Tibet. In the coastal regions, both tidal and wave power are being developed. Annual generation from tidal power stations is almost 20 million KWh, of which 6 million KWh is generated at the 3,000 Jiangxia tidal power plant in Zhejiang province. China's first wave power station is being built on the Pearl River estuary, Guangdong province.

Technological, Socio-cultural and Environmental Issues in Rural Energy

Technological options

The thermal efficiency of traditional stoves for cooking and water heating is quite low (Table 12.8). Efficiency is of the order of 10%–12% for straw and stalk, 12%–15% for firewood, 18% for scattered coal and 25%–30% for honeycomb bridge. Improved stoves could increase efficiency by as much as 60%–100%.

The average oil consumption in agricultural machines is 240 gallons per horsepower hour; this could be reduced to 200 gallons through improved efficiency. The high energy loss of farm tools could also be decreased by 20%, and the efficiency of irrigation machines increased by 10%–20%. It is estimated that average water leakage in irrigation canals is as high as 50%. The potential for saving both water and energy is thus high.

Primitive technology and the low level of technical and management skills in township–village enterprises have resulted in low efficiency of energy production and use. Per unit energy consumption is 20% higher than the national average in China (15%–20% for electricity and 20%–25% for oil).

Table 12.8
The heat conversion efficiency of various rural energy resources in China

Resource	Heat value kcal/kg	Conversion efficiency of:		Remarks
		a old type stove	b improved stove	
Coal	5000	18	30	Stove for household
Straw	3400	10–12	15–20	Dry material, traditional stove
Firewood	4000	12–15	20–25	Dry material, traditional stove
Dung (dry)	4250	18		Firing directly, the percentage of dry substance in fresh dung for various animals: pig 20%, cow 18%; sheep 40%; horse 25%; human 13%
Biogas	5000	30		

Socio-economic considerations

The issues of dissemination and utilization of rural energy technologies involve not only technological but also socio-economic aspects. The different users in rural areas should play an important role in addressing these issues and should participate in the formulation and implementation of new plans and projects in order to ensure their successful implementation. The experience of dissemination of improved fuel stoves is a good example. A county in northern China introduced an improved stove which had been disseminated in southern China, but dissimilar socio-economic situations undermined the success of the project. Nevertheless, the dissemination of improved stoves in China as a whole, introduced in 1983, has been successful. By the end of 1988, there were 90 million such stoves, accounting for 45% of the total rural household use. Table 12.9 shows the number of improved stoves installed between 1983 and 1988, while Table 12.10 gives comparative figures in selected developing countries.

Experience has shown that, in diffusing a technology, it should be considered not only as hardware but also as a system. The framework of the system is shown in Figure 12.3, while Figure 12.4 shows how the different actors play their parts during the diffusing process.

Environmental issues

Faced with a fuel shortage, the peasants have to use whatever they can find for cooking. Straw and stalk used for cooking account for 69% of the national total; this represents a substantial loss of organic matter from the fields. In the last few decades, the amount of organic matter in the soil of the great north-east plain has declined from 5%–9% to 2%. More trees are being felled for fuel by peasants than are planted or grown. The result is that national forest cover has declined to a mere 12.8%, much less than the world average of 22%. Consequently, soil erosion occurs, leading to a yearly loss of 5 billion tons of topsoil and 5 million tons of fertilizer. The yearly loss of nitrogenous fertilizer is equivalent to the country's annual national production. The area of land affected by soil erosion has expanded from 1.16 million square kilometres in the 1950s to 1.5 million square kilometres in the 1980s. The desert area has also increased, from 106 to 127 million hectares. This all illustrates the serious disruption of ecological equilibrium in China.

On another ecological front, the utilization of large quantities of chemical fertilizer and pesticide in agricultural production, and the increase in commercial energy consumption in township–village industries, have caused environmental pollution in rural areas. Water pollution in rural areas is serious; nearly 60% of the water source areas are polluted. It is estimated that more than 100 million people drink water with an oxygen content which exceeds the sanitary standard.

The following measures are being taken to protect the environment:

Table 12.9
Number of improved firewood stoves set up from 1983 to 1988

	No. of pilot counties*	No. of households using improved stoves in said year		Sum of no. of households using improved stoves at the end of the year	
		No. of household	No. from pilot counties	Sum of the no.	Sum of the no. from pilot counties
1983	90	6641	2615	6641	2615
1984	200	20719	11034	27360	13649
1985	100	17876	8368	45236	22017
1986	97	18402	9896	63638	31913
1987	101	18034	8924	81672	40837
1988	96	17491	10009	99163	50846
Total	684			99163	50846

* Pilot counties are the counties which have signed the contract with Ministry of Agriculture for diffusing improved firewood stoves.

Table 12.10
The dissemination of improved fuel stoves in several developing countries in 1985

Country	Rural population (million)	Number of rural households (million)	Number of improved fuel stoves (million)	Number of rural households per improved stove
China*	811.4	163.3	83.7	2
India	573.8	114.75	3	38
Indonesia	121.65	24.33	0.025	973
Nepal	15.34	2.5	0.030	83
Sri Lanka	12.48	2.49	0.119	21
Guatemala	3.28	0.66	<0.01	66

* Number of improved fuel stoves in 1987

1 A nation-wide campaign of afforestation has produced positive results. To date, 30.6 million hectares of artificial forest have been developed, accounting for 26% of the total forest area in China. Another policy measure is the closing-off of mountains and other areas to allow the natural regeneration of tree cover.

2 Some shelter-forest programmes have been or are being undertaken, like the large-scale programme in the Yangzi River valley recently approved by the State Council. The drainage area of the Yangzi River is the most extensive in China, covering a fifth of the total territory of China and containing a third of the population. However, since 1950

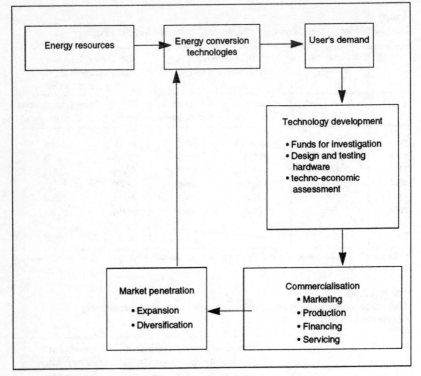

Figure 12.3
Framework of a rural energy technology system

about 31.1% of this area (360,000–560,000 square kilometres) has suffered serious ecological deterioration. The first project programme was to increase the forest area from the current 6.7 million hectares to 13.3 million hectares; forest cover in the area will thus increase from 19.1% to 39% and this is expected to control water loss and soil erosion across 74,000 square kilometres in the next 15 years.

3 The development of ecological agriculture is being encouraged, taking biogas digesters as a vital link in the eco-agricultural system. The biogas digester programme has been quite successful. Five million family-size digesters have been disseminated, to supply not only biogas for energy use but also organic fertilizer, fodder, etc.

4 Energy conservation programmes in township–village industries are being expanded.

Energy Investment and Pricing Policies

The investment policy for rural energy development is that the funding of energy construction should be raised mainly from local sources. The state

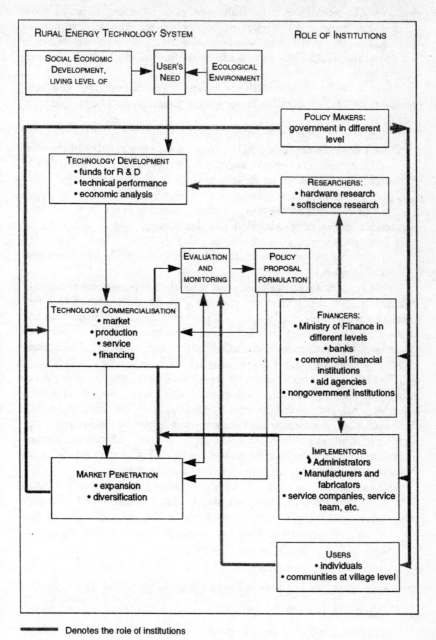

——————— Denotes the role of institutions

Figure 12.4. Rural energy technology system and role of institutions

will only give subsidies or support through loans, often long-term, with low interest. For instance, the investment ratio as between state, local authorities and local people in the programme for diffusing improved fuel stoves is 1:8:140. Table 12.11 gives an example of the investment ratio in one pilot county for its improved stoves diffusion projects.

There is also a policy ('self-construction, self-management and self-consumption') for small hydro-power station construction. The key points of this policy are:

1 Funding the SHP construction;
2 After commissioning, the SHP station is the responsibility of the local authority and local people, and should not be taken over by the state, even when connected to the state grid;
3 The power generated is to be used to meet local demand – any excess can be sold to the state grid at a price favourable to the local authority, taking into account national and local interests;
4 Profits from generation should be ploughed back to build more SHP stations; tariffs can be increased within reasonable limits to assist capital accumulation.

Three types of fuel price are in use: normal, negotiation and regulation. Normal price is allocated in the state plan. Negotiation price is that fuel produced above a specified quota by a producer, but still brought into line in the state plan. Regulation price is that of fuel produced above a specified quota but which the producer can sell directly to the consumers. The average differential between these three prices is 1:1.6-2:2.5-3.0.

The fuel price has been kept stable for several decades, but there is evidence of a slight rise in recent years. Electricity tariffs for agricultural consumers are lower than for urban consumers. For areas with abundant small-scale hydro subsidies, domestic prices during the wet season are used to encourage a policy of substituting fuelwood by electricity. In areas with energy shortage, electricity tariffs for the rural household are much higher than for the urban household, but the tariff for agricultural production is lower.

Multilateral and bilateral assistance programmes have played a positive role. The assistance is greatly appreciated by the government of China. Past and current programmes include assistance in the fields of research and development of advanced technologies, training, demonstration projects on integrated rural energy planning, and construction.

Actions to Promote Renewable Energy Sources for Rural and Agricultural Development

The basic principle for rural energy development, the so called 'Sixteen Words Principle', is quite successfully practised in China. This principle has emphasized adaptation to local conditions, mutual support between different energy sources, multi-purpose utilization and pursuit of real economic benefits.

Table 12.11

Fund source and expenditure for diffusion improved fuel stove in Jiangjin county, Sichuan province in thousand yuan

Fund source	Fund raising				Fund disbursement												
					1986				1987				1988			
	1986	1987	1988	Sum	research	training	propa-ganda	con-struction	research	training	propa-ganda	con-struction	research	training	propa-ganda	con-struction
Nation	11	14		25	2.0	3.0	4.0	2	2.0	3.0	2.0	7.0			2.0	7.0
County	18.2	5	15	38.2	1.0	8.2	2.0	15	1.0	1.0	1.0	2.0	2.0	4.0	2.0	14
Village collectives	50	40	24	114	7.0	20.0	8.0	15	50	18	5	20	1.0	7.0	2.0	14
Users	2100	2352	2226	6678.5		40		2060	40			2312	257			220.08
Sum	2179.2	2411	2265	6855.7	10	71.2	14	2077	8	54	8	2341	3	367	4	222.18

NOTE:
1. Total number of improved stoves: 279 000
   in which: no. of new improved stoves: 50 000
             no. of reformed old stoves: 229 000
2. Average cost for one new improved stove: 79.35 yuan
   Average cost for one reformed old stove: 11.7 yuan
3. Total investment: 6.86 million yuan
   Net revenue from fuel saving and labour force saving: 52.17 million yuan
4. Ratio of nation/local authorities and users: 1 : 6 : 267

Within this framework, the policy guidelines for alternative energy sources include active development of fast-growing forests, widespread popularization of improved fuel stoves, steady development of biogas, development of small hydro or small thermal plants and small coal mines where local conditions permit, and utilization of solar, wind and geothermal energy at pilot sites. A number of projects are under consideration for the development of these technologies by the year 2000.

Integrated rural energy planning is important for the implementation of the basic principle. 'Integrated' means that:

1 Rural energy planning should be integrated in accordance with the local energy resources and other possibilities of commercial energy supply from outside the region to satisfy the energy demand;

2 Rural energy planning should be comprehensive, covering all aspects of social and economic development and the environment. A framework of integrated rural energy planning at county level has been developed in China which provides a useful platform for future rural energy planning.

A series of administrative agencies on rural energy management have been organized from central government to county level, as shown in Figure 12.5.

It is necessary to create industrial systems for the development and diffusion of rural energy technologies. A common market will be set up; it will include a supply system of material and accessories, factories for device production, special companies of construction and service teams, etc. In addition to these, relevant education and research institutions will be developed. However, all of this needs to be supported by the public and private sectors. More than 3000 units of companies and factories, around which rural energy development has been organized, are run by the provinces, counties, townships and villages. Further development is contemplated.

The policy of disseminating new and renewable sources of energy technologies for integrated rural development in China has been quite successful. This involved 589 pilot counties for diffusing improved fuel stoves, 100 counties for SHP, 70 counties for biogas digesters, 60 counties for energy conservation in production, 18 counties for integrated rural energy construction, and several counties for solar, wind, and geothermal energy technologies. This policy should be continued.

Some research studies should be undertaken, such as:

1 Technologies for converting biomass to high-quality fuel, including:
   a. high-efficiency gas-powered generation apparatus;
   b. liquefaction technology for biomass; and
   c. energy recovery of organic waste.

2 Solar energy:
   a. high-efficiency (30%) photovoltaic technique and necessary accessories for its application;
   b. an optimized design for passive solar building.

3 Wind energy:
   a. wind generator of 100 KW capacity and demonstration wind field;

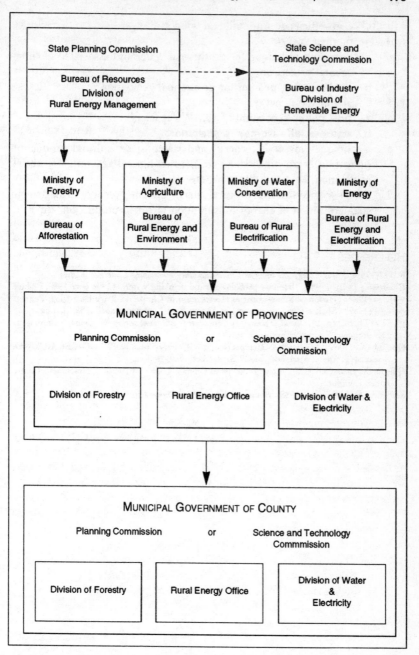

Figure 12.5
Chart of administrative organisation for rural energy in China

    b.   high–efficiency windmill and wind sail.
4 Geothermal energy:
    a.   recycling technique for geothermal water and associated environ-
        mental protection;
    b.   dual working medium for geothermal generation.
5 Tidal and wave energy:
    a.   tidal power generation of 10MW capacity;
    b.   series set of wave-power generation;
6 Techniques for saving energy and water in agricultural production
    (irrigation, agro-processing, etc.), township–village industry (brick
    production, etc.) and transport, etc.
7 Social science research on rural energy planning, energy management,
    standardization of energy consumption factor in production, etc.

REFERENCES

FAO. (1985). *Rural Energy Planning in China and other Developing Countries in Asia.*

Guangming Daily. (1989). 'Sanitary problem of rural drinking water'. 12 October 1989, Beijing.

—— (1989). 'Historical achievement of afforestation in China'. 15 September 1989, Beijing.

—— (1989). 'Shelter forest programme at Yangzi River'. 20 September 1989, Beijing.

INET/ITESA. (n.d.). *Rural Technology Assessment and Innovation in China.* International Development Research Centre, Ottawa.

Qui, D. X. (1989). 'Technological aspects of rural energy planning'. FAO/ESCAP/UNDP Regional Training Workshop, 21–27 September 1989, Beijing.

Qui, D. X. *et al.* (n.d.). 'Food energy nexus in China'. Asian and Pacific Development Centre, Kuala Lumpur.

Statistical State Bureau. (1988). *Statistical Yearbook of China.* China Statistical Press.

13 Bio-Energy in India: Potential and Prospects

C. V. SESHADRI

In India, energy cost is often treated as a significant parameter that could affect the overall performance of the economy, but this is considered strictly true only for what are called 'commercial sources of energy'. The other sources, 'non-commercial sources of energy' as they are termed, are derived from biomass and, as such, are not assigned proper value in the economy. In the developed countries, rising economic costs of energy led to the development of conservation strategies in energy utilization. But the lack of proper quantification of the value of biomass sources in general has been responsible for the absence of viable conservation strategies in biomass energy utilization in India.[1]

That the ultimate source of economic value was in natural resources had been the basic tenet of one school of economic thought (the Physiocrats) in the eighteenth century (Christensen, 1989). In the nineteenth century, Jevons, an English economist, emphasized the crucial role played by the availability of coal in making Britain the leading economic power of the day, and cautioned that too rapid a rate of exploitation of that resource might have disastrous consequences for the pre-eminent economic position of England. At the turn of this century there were several others, mainly scientists rather than economists, who repeatedly emphasized the role of energy availability and its utilization in the development and progress of national economies, or even 'civilizations'.

Attention was gradually diverted from this approach to economics after the late 1950s, when two new arguments were advanced. The first, exemplified in Barnett and Morse (1963), was based on the observation of time series decreases in the quantity of labour and capital required to 'harvest' natural resources. On this basis, it was argued that the interrelationship between energy cost, or the cost of natural resources, and overall economic growth could be decoupled over the coming years. The other argument, fully developed in Solow (1974), is based on the belief in the complete substitutability of energy by capital and labour.

Among economists, Georgescu-Roegen (1971) has contested the notion of full substitutability of fuels/resources by labour and capital. His point is that the generation of capital goods, such as machinery, itself requires use of a natural resource: capital cannot create the resource out of which it is made.

175

Thus, there obtains a new relationship between resource and capital, leading to the view that a resource is not like any other commodity governed by or subject to the action of market forces.

The nature of the energy basis of the substitution process has been brought out by Tyner *et al.* (1988) who considered the following example: when the price of oil in the USA was $10 per barrel, it was said that if the oil price increased, shale oil ($30 per barrel) would become competitive when the oil price reached $30 per barrel. However, even when this price level was reached, shale oil had not become competitive; this was because the hidden cost of the requirement of three barrels of oil in the extraction of one barrel of shale oil had been overlooked.

In a proper determination of the value of energy available from a conversion process or source, the framework developed by Odum (1988) is likely to be useful. Odum's approach consists in viewing any energy source as transformed solar energy. The value of energy derived from a source is thus estimated as the value of solar energy which it took to 'embody' the source. Such estimations can be carried out using the solar transformity ratios reported by Odum (1988). The principal advantage in the use of this framework is that energy derived from the biosphere (e.g., fuelwood) and fossil fuels could be compared on a unified basis; the extent of depletion that the use of a given process may cause can also be estimated.

The Value of Energy: the Importance of Evolving a Common Methodology and Conventions

Over the last 15 years, Energy Analysis (IFIAS, 1974), or Net Energy Analysis, as it is called in the USA, has gained currency as a viable method of estimating energy requirements in the supply of goods and services to the economy. It has been applied to the dynamics of attaining self-sufficiency in rural systems with reference to India (Slesser *et al.*, 1982). The emergence of an analysis based on the Second Law of Thermodynamics (Wall, 1986) is important in applying process analysis to the conservation of energy.

But these concepts and methods have not been used adequately in energy surveys in India. The lack of a common methodology, an agreed set of conventions and standard units makes comparisons futile and is an obstacle to integrated energy–economics planning. For example, in a recently completed rural energy survey of Wardha District in the state of Maharashtra (Table 13.1), the aggregate energy demand is reported in megawatt-hours rather than in joules (there were errors in calculation in the original report which have been corrected in Table 13.1). But a more serious lapse is the lack of a commonly accepted set of calorific values, in particular for biomass fuels, and device efficiency factors. It would be helpful if a suitable government department would undertake to gather experts who would evolve detailed methodologies and conventions and standardize the relevant input values.

Table 13.1
Decentralized rural energy plan

Sl	Energy source	Unit	Total per annum
1	Firewood	1000 tons	299.58
2	Crop residue	1000 tons	153.42
3	Dung cakes	1000 tons	59.97
4	Electricity	kWh	4102005
5	Kerosene	kilo litre	5512.3
6	Diesel	kilo litre	2220.428
7	Petrol	kilo litre	98.00
8	Coal	1000 tons	2.147
9	Human power	Person days	55972236
10	Animal power	Pair of Bullock days	8367710

Sl	Recalculated	Percentage share
1	1642697	54.3
2	626465	20.7
3	170994	5.6
4	4102	0.1
5	54965	1.8
6	23164	0.7
7	875	0.0
8	14810	0.4
9	130602	4.3
10	359254	11.5
Totals	3027928	100

SOURCES: Department of Non-conventional Energy Sources, Government of India.
Recalculated table from 'Decentralized rural energy plan, Wardha District' (Operations Research Group, Baroda), p. 25, Table 8.

Energy Flow in an Indian District: a Case Analysis

Preliminary results of an energy survey of the Nilgiris District in the state of Tamil Nadu will now be considered. The principal flows of energy into and out of the district are shown in Table 13.2. The broad results of the survey are presented in terms of the storage or flow of solar energy, using the concepts developed by Odum (1988). Use of such values enables accounting of ecological contributions (e.g., rainwater-based hydel generation, biomass from primary production) in the energy flow.

In Table 13.2, a '+' sign indicates imports or receipts, and a '-' sign, exports. The main storage points of solar energy are rainwater and primary production (terrestrial); of these, rainwater leaves the district (rivers) with a fraction of the kinetic energy of flow being used to generate electricity (the

Table 13. 2
Flow and storage of solar energy in the Nilgiris District (annual)
(in 10^{18} solar emjoules)*

Flow/storage systems	+/-	Embodied solar energy
Global solar radiation	+	20
Rainfall	+	400
Rivers	-	$250^a + 100^b$
Primary production	+	200^c
Petroleum products	+	60
Coal/lignite	+	4.2
Electricity	-	60
Fertilizers	+	0.25
Fuelwood	-	80
Food (mostly imported)	+	320
Plantation crops	-	0.1
Vegetable & horticultural products	-	0.1
Timber	-	5

NOTES

The values are derived from a preliminary survey by the MCRC. Data on the gross features (solar insolation, rainfall, river flow/storage, hydel generation, forest cover, etc.) have been derived from the information available from the Department of Statistics, Government of Tamil Nadu. The remainder of the data, except where indicated, have been derived from the survey.

* See Odum (1988) for solar transformity ratios.
a Based on chemical energy of pure water.
b Due to kinetic energy flow.
c Based on a value of 40 kg/m²/year for rainfed forests (Leith, 1975).

largest proportion of hydel generation in the state takes place in this district) which is mostly supplied to other parts of the state. Food, fertilizers, petroleum products and coal are imported, while timber and horticultural products (tea, vegetables and fruit) are exported. The overall balance between these sources of energy is positive, implying that the district is a net importer of energy or transformed solar energy. An energy plan for this district will have to take into account the plentiful contributions from ecological processes to energy storage in the district and use them, at least in part, to relieve the stress on the production of mature biomass.

Energy in India: a Flow Chart of Energy Use

We shall use the notion of flow of energy from a source to a use–sector in an analysis of the energy scene in India. Only the primary sources of energy will be counted as sources; electricity is treated as a secondary source. On the basis of statistics compiled from various sources (ABE, 1984, Satish Chandran, 1983, Pendse, 1988; Government of India, 1986) a flow–chart of energy use in India has been developed for the year 1982/3 as shown in Table 13.3. The year 1983 was chosen because reliable biomass data are not available after this period.

The following inferences may be drawn from Table 13.3:

1 The contribution of electricity to total useful energy in India is very small (3%); its contribution to the domestic sector, the largest use-sector, is extremely small (less than 1%).

2 Biomass sources of energy contribute over 50% of total useful energy. This proportion has been somewhat stable since the 1970s (Henderson, 1980), by which time it had declined from a value of 68% in 1953/4.

Table 13.3
A flow-chart of energy use in India, 1982/83

Units: Petajoules	Total	Electricity	Industry	Agriculture	Domestic & others	Transport	Energy sector own use
A Oil	4737	343	880	231	905	2188	190
B Hydel	411	411	—	—	—	—	—
C Nuclear	27	27	—	—	—	—	—
D Lignite	67	52	—	—	—	—	—
E Coal	2593	944	1273	—	55	231	90
F Gas	126	17	—	—	109	—	—
(a) Total (A1+B1+C1+D1+E1+F1)	7961	1794	2153	231	1069	2419	295
G Veg/agri waste	1407	—	100	—	1307	—	—
H Dung	770	—	—	—	770	—	—
J Fuelwood	4585	—	—	—	4585	—	—
(b) Total (G1+H1+J1)	6762	—	100	6662	—	—	—
K Gross Total (a1+b1)	14723	(470)	2253	231	7731	2419	295
L Electricity		382	222	64	43	10	43
M Net total	13309		2475	295	7774	2429	338
N % net	100%		18.6%	2.2%	58.4%	18.3%	2.5%

Judging from this, it is reasonable to infer that biomass sources will remain the most significant source of energy in the decades to come.

But the economic planning does not reflect this realization. During the VII Plan (1985–90), the allocation to the power sector was Rs320 billion (US$20 billion) out of a total allocation of approximately Rs1600 billion (US$100 billion), whereas development of biomass received less than Rs20 billion (about US$1.3 billion). This is an outcome of planning premised solely upon the economic value of energy conversion processes. This requires immediate correction in the years to come, in view of the possibility of designing biomass resources development to contribute to prevention of environmental degradation.

Energy in Indian Agriculture

Agriculture in India makes a significant contribution to the flow of useful energy by way of agricultural residues. In 1982/3 this contribution was about 10% of the total useful energy flow in the country and was available to both the domestic and the industrial sectors (Table 13.3). Bagasse from sugar cane crushing is a fuel in sugar refineries and it has been suggested that it is possible to produce a power supply of 70 MW per million tonnes of sugar cane through co-generation in sugar refineries using bagasse as fuel (Reddy, 1988). Given that the total annual production of sugar cane in India is not less than 150 million tonnes, and that about 50% of it reaches sugar refineries, potential for power production with bagasse as fuel is 5000 MW.

Thus, agriculture in India is not only a source of metabolic energy but is a source of fuel energy as well. But over the period 1951–87, agriculture in India has declined in output/input energy efficiency (output measured only with respect to the edible portion) from about 4.0 in 1951 to about 1.25 in 1987 (Figure 13.1). This is because the input of energy in the form of petroleum products, electricity and fertilizer has increased by over 900% in this period, while the grain output has increased by only about 300%. In estimating the input energy in Indian agriculture, electrical energy is computed in terms of coal replacement while the embodied energy in fertilizers is computed using published values (Slesser & Lewis, 1979). It may also be mentioned here that the fertilizer industry in India is one of the largest 'sinks' of useful energy, accounting for nearly 25% of the energy consumption in the industrial sector.

The increase in the energy requirement in Indian agriculture needs to be viewed with caution. If the present trend were to continue, the capacity of agriculture to contribute to energy flow in India might decline in the years to come.

Conservation through Process Integration

Conservation of energy has been advanced as a way of curbing energy demand, in addition to resorting to administration of prices. The latter approach in India

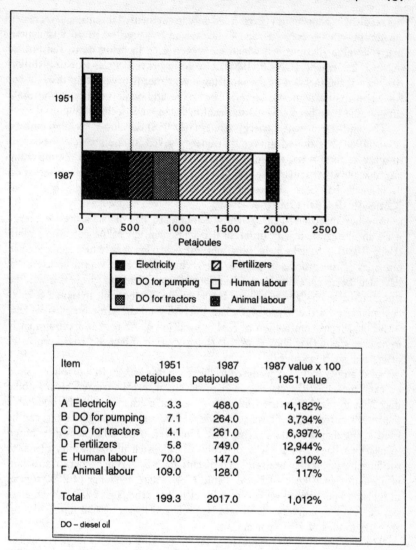

Figure 13.1
Energy consumption in Indian agriculture, 1951 and 1987

has resulted in anomalous effects: it led only to augmented revenue and increased consumption of energy sources. Conservation has been taken up seriously in many developed countries, which have been able to bring down the rate of increase in demand (UNEP, 1986). Use of improved *chulas* (cooking stoves) has been recommended as the most important means of reducing demand for fuelwood in the domestic sector. The scope and achievements of the *chula* programme have been covered in detail in Pachauri & Joshi (1989).

The end-use oriented energy strategy (EOES) developed by Goldemberg *et al.* (1988) has the advantage that energy saved in one sector can be used in other sectors. It has the further advantage of identification of the matching end use for a particular resource. Use of such an approach for conservation of biomass has been suggested in an energy plan for the Indian state of Karnataka (Reddy, 1988).

Another approach to energy conservation is to view it as a source of energy itself and integrate it with different uses. The concept of 'process integration' (Berg, 1980) is based on the possibility of using low-grade heat generated in one step of the process in another step where such heat would be useful; it has also been generalized to situations where different processes can be integrated along a chain of rejects. For example, it is possible to have a coking-coal plant and a thermal power plant operating on the same quantity of coal – the heat from combustion of coal is used in coking coal and subsequently in making steam (Velikhov *et al.*, 1987). Integration of biomass-based processes offers one such possibility.

An example will be considered to illustrate this aspect. In a distillery based on cane molasses, the effluent, a high-pollutant, can be treated by anaerobic digestion to yield methane (minimum yield of methane would be one cubic metre per cubic metre of waste per day). The methane so generated can be used in the distillery, thus saving coal. However, if the effluent is distributed to nearby villages, where it is anaerobically digested in community plants to produce biogas, it may be useful in replacing fuelwood. A hypothetical situation is presented in Figure 13.2 and Table 13.4, where a savings of 2500 tonnes of fuelwood per annum is possible with effluent at the rate of 750 cubic metres per day from a distillery. This is to be preferred to saving 600 tonnes of coal and 105 tonnes of HSD per annum.

The rationale here is that fuelwood for the cooking stove is a more immediate need than saving energy for the plant by reclamation of energy from effluent. Another factor to be considered is that for a C_4-plant like sugar cane, the CO_2 in the atmosphere may be fixed faster; hence a cycle that generates as much CO_2 as can be fixed locally can lead to alleviation of the Greenhouse Effect.

Conclusions

There is need for Third World countries to decide on a uniform methodology for inclusion of commercial as well as non-commercial sources of energy in their plan strategies.

Table 13. 4
Energy yields from effluents*

I Assumptions and norms

Ethanol output from distillery (cane molasses-based)	: 106 litres/year
Operational days	: 200/year
Daily effluent output (Indian conditions)	: 750 m^3
Methane production rate (minimum)	: 1m3/m^3 effluent/day
Methane requirement per average family (5 persons) per day (cooking only)	: 0.75 m^3

II If effluent were distributed (by trucks) to rural areas nearby distillery

No. of daily trips (10 m3 effluent per trip)	: 75
Distance per trip (average)	: 50 km
HSD required per trip	: 10 l
Annual requirement of HSD	: 150, 000 l (105 tonnes)
Methane available per day	: 750 m^3
No. of beneficiary families	: 750/0.75=1000

SAVINGS

Biomass requirements for 1000 average rural families over a year	: 3500 tonnes
Of this, fuelwood requirement	: 2500 tonnes

III If the methane generated is used within the distillery:

Annual production of methane	: 0.15 x 106m^3
Coal replacement (1 million m^3 methane = 4000 tonnes coal replacement)	: 600 tonnes

IV a) Total Fuel Expenditure (annual).

Coal	: 600 tonnes
HSD	: 105 tonnes
b) Total savings	
fuelwood	: 2500 tonnes
dung and residues	: 1000 tonnes.

---

* See Figure 13.2

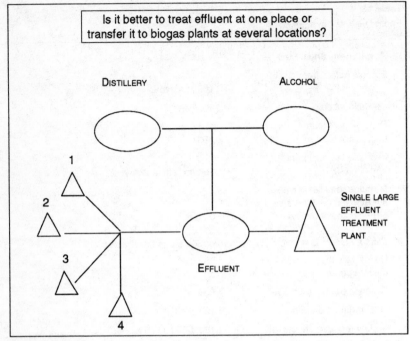

Figure 13.2
Energy conservation through microbial cycles – process integration

There is need to recognize that for several more years to come domestic energy demands will be the major demand and this will be met substantially from biomass sources.

District level energy surveys even in biomass-rich districts seem to lead to the conclusion that expenditure on new biomass plantations is not proportionate to its harvest.

Process integration using microbial is an efficient way of sequestering and using energy. In tropical countries the use of carbohydrate waste for domestic cooking and heating seems to be the most fruitful pathway.

NOTE
1 The introductory section of this chapter draws extensively on Balaji (1989).

REFERENCES
ABE (Advisory Board on Energy). (1984). *A Perspective on Demand for Energy in India up to 2004–05*. ABE, Government of India, New Delhi.
———— (1986). *Energy Conservation: Challenges and Opportunities*. ABE, Government of India, New Delhi.

Balaji, V. (1989). 'Microbial energy production: process integration of microbial energy cycles'. Ph.D. thesis submitted to the University of Madras.

Barnett, H. J. & Morse, C. (1963). *Scarcity and Growth: The Economics of Natural Resource Availability.* Johns Hopkins University Press, Baltimore.

Berg, C. A. (1980). 'Process integration and the second law of thermodynamics: future possibilities'. *Energy,* 5, pp. 733–41.

Christensen, P. O. (1989). 'Historical roots for ecological economics – biophysical versus allocative approaches'. *Ecological Economics,* 1, pp. 17–36.

Georgescu-Roegen, N. (1971). *The Entropy Law and the Economic Process.* Harvard University Press, Cambridge, USA.

Goldemberg, J., Johansson, T. B., Reddy, A. K. N. & Williams, R. H. (1988). *Energy for a Sustainable World.* Wiley-Eastern, New Delhi.

Government of India. (1986). *Statistical Abstract 1986.* Central Statistical Organization, Government of India.

Henderson, P. D. (1980). 'Energy resources, consumption, and supply in India', in eds Smil, V. and Knowland, W. E., *Energy in the Developing World: the Real Energy Crisis.* Oxford University Press, New York, pp. 172–93.

IFIAS (International Federation for the Institutes of Advanced Study). (1974). *Energy Analysis Workshop Report No. 6* (ed. Slesser, M.) Solna, Sweden.

Lieth, H. (1975). 'Primary productivity of the major vegetation units of the world', in eds Lieth, H. & Whittaker, R. H., *Primary Productivity of the Biosphere.* Springer-Verlag, Berlin, pp. 203–15.

Odum, H. T. (1988). 'Self-organization, transformity, and information'. *Science,* 242, pp. 1132–9.

Pachauri, R. K. & Joshi, L., eds. (1989). *Energy Policy Issues,* Vol. 4. Tata Energy Research Institute, New Delhi.

Pendse, D. R. (1988). *Statistical Outline of India 1987–88.* Tata Services, Bombay.

Planning Commission. (1987). *Seventh Five-Year Plan: A Mid-term Appraisal.* New Delhi.

Reddy, A. K. N. (1988). 'A development-focused end-use oriented energy plan for Karnataka', in *Perspective Plan 2001.* Karnataka, Chapter 5.

Satish Chandran, T. R. (1983). 'National energy balances of India'. Paper presented at the Twelfth Congress of the World Energy Conference, New Delhi.

Seshadri, C. V. (1989). 'Energy in Indian agriculture' in *Review of Agriculture. The Hindu,* Madras.

Slesser, M., Lewis, C. W., Hounam, I., Seshadri, C. V., Roy, R. N., Jeejibai, N., Keshavaraj, N.,. Manoharan, R., Raja, G., Subramani,V., Thomas, S. & Venkataramani, G. (1982). 'Biomass assessment in third world villages via a systems methodology'. *Biomass,* 2, pp. 57–74.

Slesser, M. & Lewis, C. (1979). *Biological Energy Sources.* E & F. N. Spon, London.

Solow, R. M. (1974). 'The economics of resources or the resources of economics?'. *American Economic Review,* Vol. 64, No. 2, pp. 1–14.

Tyner, G., Costanza, R. & Fowler, R. G. (1988). 'The net energy yield of nuclear power'. *Energy,* 13, pp. 73–81.

UNEP (United Nations Environment Programme). (1986). *Energy Conservation in Developing Countries.* UNEP, Nairobi.

Vatsala, T. M. (1989). 'Augmentation of biogas from distillery effluent using c. freundii'. Project report submitted to the Department of Non-Conventional Energy Sources, Government of India from MCRC, Madras.

Velikhov, E.P., Mastennikov, V. M., Shendlin, A. E., Shpilrain, E. E. & Shtrenberg, V. Ya. (1987). 'Integrated and industrial processing as a method of energy conservation'. *Energy,* 12, pp. 1083–95.

Wall, G. (1986). *Energy – a Useful Concept.* Chalmers University of Technology, Goteborg, Sweden.

Renewable Energy in India: Present Situation and Future Plans

14

MAHESHWAR DAYAL

In India, the provision of energy has been considered a priority area since Five Year Plans were started in 1950/1, but government investment has been restricted largely to augmenting the supply of commercial energy through centralized facilities. In recent years, however, the tremendous potential of new and renewable sources of energy has been recognized and significant progress has been made in the development and utilization of the appropriate technologies, some of which are now serving millions of families, especially in the rural areas where most Indians live. Indeed, it is now clear that rural and agricultural energy needs can be met most suitably by renewable sources of energy. Moreover, these sources can supply many development objectives (including education and health) quickly; they can also help preserve the environment and improve the welfare of women and children. For these reasons, developments in India may be of widespread interest to other developing countries.

Commercial energy (coal, oil, gas, hydro and nuclear power) accounts for about 60% of the total primary energy supply in India, with the balance coming from non-commercial energy such as firewood and agricultural or animal wastes. The growth of commercial supply has been 5.3% per annum compared to 1.7%–2.5% for non-commercial energy. The percentage contributions of the various energy sources to sectoral consumption for the year 1982/3 are shown in Table 14.1. Even in the domestic sector there has been a great disparity between the rural and urban areas in the source of energy consumed. The share of non-commercial fuels is 80% in rural areas and only 51% in urban areas. Further, the figures make it clear that in the rural sector cooking is the main object of energy consumption, both for the households of the landless poor and for cultivators' families (Table 14.2). The other major energy needs in the rural and agricultural sectors are transport, lighting, water pumping, electricity for radio, television, communication and medical facilities, and power for rural and agricultural industries.

The Need for Renewable Sources of Energy

Like India, many developing countries are faced with a dual crisis – arising out of scarce oil resources, on the one hand, and caused by firewood scarcity

Table 14.1
Energy shares in total sectoral energy consumption
(percentage) as measured in terms of MICR Units

Sector	Oil	Coal	Electricity	Natural gas	Non-commercial fuels	Total
Industry	27.88	32.6	36.44	3.07	-	31.14
Transport	89.00	8.93	2.07	-	-	22.52
Domestic	18.85	2.76	4.65	-	73.74	41.54
Agriculture	18.77	-	91.23	-	-	3.07
Final consumption	36.86	13.31	18.82	0.95	30.95	100.00

MTCE: Million Tonnes Coal Equivalent

Table 14.2
Domestic Energy Use in Rural Areas in Gujarat State,
in Kcal(*) per household per month

Activity	Landless households	2ha	2.4ha	4.10ha	10ha	Common source
Cooking						
a Fuel	551,000	657,000	619,000	804,000	871,000	wood, crop residue
b Manual energy in cooking	4,257	4,257	4,644	–	4,385	manual
c Manual energy in fetching fuel	2,773	–	–	–	–	manual
Lighting (**)	19,987	19,276	18,665	21,253	28,124	kerosene
Water requirements	2,808	2,808	2,808	3,120	3,900	manual
Water heating	8,500	45,543	49,980	65,410	8,006	
Total	589,325	728,884	695,097	893,783	915,415	

* : Kcal = Thousand Calories

**: Electricity consumption for lighting is not included.

Source: Gujarat Energy Development Agency. 'Executive Summary of Rural Energy Survey of 50 Villages in Gujarat'.

and deforestation, on the other. Their rising energy requirements and expectations in the quest for higher economic development have come at a time when conventional energy systems are proving more and more difficult to supply; furthermore, the adverse environmental consequences of fossil fuels and of excessive tree cutting are increasingly realized. There is, therefore, a great need for a transition from present energy systems, heavily dependent on hydrocarbons, to a non-depletable, more sustainable mix of energy sources that relies increasingly on new and renewable sources of energy that provide clean energy and help to preserve the environment and the ecology. The issues of global warming, ozone layer depletion, global climatic change and deforestation make this an object of both international and national concern.

According to estimates made by the National Commission on Agriculture, the population of India is likely to increase from 650 million in 1980/1 to about 935 million in 2000/01, a 44% increase. The estimated total food grain requirement at this future date will be about 225 million tonnes, an increase of 59%. Since the per capita availability of usable land is likely to decrease from 0.29 ha. in 1971 to 0.17 ha. in 2000, the only alternative is to increase productivity per unit of land.

India has a total forest area of about 75 million ha. which forms only 22.8% of the total geographical area of the country. Much of this is also now denuded and the real forest cover is as low as 11% according to some estimates. The estimated total requirement of fuelwood is 133 million tonnes per annum, whereas estimated annual availability is only 39 million tonnes. As a consequence, agricultural residues and animal dung which otherwise would have been used for replenishment of soil fertility are burnt for fuel needs, while soil erosion, floods, siltation and desertification follow the depletion of the forests, further devastating the fertility of the soil. The large-scale development of other non-conventional, renewable sources of energy to meet the cooking energy requirements of rural communities is, therefore, vital.

Biogas

In India, we have started giving attention to the integrated energy and food-energy approach. A specific application of this is the biogas programme. Each biogas unit produces methane gas which is a clean fuel used for cooking and lighting, as well as an effluent and residue which can act as good organic nitrogenous fertilizer. Put back on the field, it creates additional crops which, in part, are eaten by cattle who produce the waste, thus closing the cycle. In this simple example, one attempts to increase food production by producing fertilizer from the biogas plant while, at the same time, contributing towards energy requirements through the production of methane. Already, within a few years of taking up biogas as a national programme, 1.2 million biogas plants have been set up in the country. Their popularity and rate of installation overtake planning targets as fast as they can be set. Already they are saving an estimated 4.24 million tonnes of firewood equivalent, valued at Rs1697 million (more than US$100 million) per year. Besides, 20.4 million tonnes of enriched manure is produced every year which is valued at Rs1689 million, giving a total annual benefit of Rs3386 million (US$200 million). The entire investment pays for itself in less than two and a half years.

Improved Cookstoves

The support of women has made the National Programme of Improved Chulhas another popular success, in both rural and urban areas. Fifty different models of improved and efficient stoves have been developed for large-scale utilization, offering a choice of models to suit local food habits and household requirements. A new scheme has involved self-employed workers in constructing and maintaining about 300 *chulhas* a year, receiving Rs10 per stove (Rs15 in hill areas and North-Eastern Region states) from the government for providing follow-up maintenance services. A massive Women's Education Programme on Improved Stoves has also been launched. As in the national programme on biogas, a combination of technical, administrative, financial and infrastructural measures have been adopted which have brought rapid progress in dissemination and use of the improved smokeless woodstoves. Within a few years over 6.3 million have been set up, saving an estimated 4 million tonnes of firewood equivalent per year – an annual benefit of Rs1484 million (US$95 million).

Solar Thermal Programme

Successfully commercialized low-grade solar thermal devices include water and air heating systems, dryers, timber kilns, desalination systems, domestic hot water systems and cookers. In 1984, a scheme of cost sharing for the purchase of these devices, which require a comparatively high initial investment, brought a marked increase in demand. The devices are distributed by the state's nodal implementing agencies under the extension programme. Water heating systems are particularly popular: large numbers have been installed, with capacities ranging from 200 to 120,000 litres per day for temperature applications of 60°–80° Celsius. When regularly used, solar cookers can save between 30% and 50% of the conventional fuel. Cookers for community use, such as in hostels and midday meal schemes, have also been developed and are being made available under the extension programme. In all, solar thermal devices are estimated to be producing or saving 300 million KWh of thermal energy per year.

Solar Photovoltaic Programme

Solar cells are made in India from single crystal silicon wafers produced locally, connected in strings of 33 or 66 cells and encapsulated to form a module. The modules supply the power required for driving electrical devices and appliances. The electrical energy generated can also be stored in batteries for use at night time or on a cloudy day. Today, three companies in the public sector are manufacturing solar cells, modules and systems. Some industries in the private sector have also been licensed and a few of them have started pilot production. Solar photovoltaic systems, now used in 6000 villages, can be installed easily and require very little maintenance. The modularity of the technology permits flexibility in power from a few watts to a few megawatts.

Wind Energy

Individual wind generators can produce several KW of electricity and feed the power to existing grids. The first 'wind farm' project, grouping several generators at the same location, became operational in 1985–6. Now there are seven projects with an aggregate capacity of 10 MW working in Gujarat, Maharashtra, Tamilnadu, Orissa and Karnataka. Over 22 million units of power have been supplied to the respective state grids. Most wind farms employ 55 KW machines, while recently commissioned projects in Tamilnadu and Karnataka use 90–110 KW generators and a pilot project for installing six 90 KW models at six different locations has been completed. Further expansion will increase aggregate capacity to more than 34 MW by 1990. Wind battery chargers up to a unit size of 4 KW and stand-alone wind systems (10–25 KW) are also being demonstrated in several states.

Producing Gas from Biomass

Gasification is one of the efficient ways of utilizing biomass. The conversion takes place in gasifier units which can be linked to engines for power generation or water pumping, achieving a diesel replacement of 65%–70%. Under its demonstration programme, the Department of Non-conventional Energy Sources (DNES) has so far supplied about 370 systems ranging from 5–10 HP for mechanical application and 700–800 KW for power generation. The performance of these systems is being carefully monitored. Site-specific problems have been experienced with about 50 systems.

Measures have been taken to improve the implementation strategy and the pre- and post-installation operations. Six manufacturers are producing pilot gasifier systems based on indigenous research and development, aiming to ensure quality and reduce cost. Among the concepts introduced recently is the use of a sterling engine which is an externally fired biomass engine. The design and development of fluidized bed and rice husk combustors have been supported.

Integrated Rural Energy Supply Systems

DNES is implementing a programme for village-level integrated energy projects called 'Urjagrams' (energy villages). The programme aims at achieving cost-effective energy self-sufficiency by using a combination of non-conventional energy sources. The system configuration is finalized on the basis of surveys of the consumption patterns, energy needs and local energy resources in individual villages. The Urjagrams take into account energy requirements not only for basic minimum needs but also for agricultural, cottage industry and community facilities.

A large number of energy surveys have been sponsored by DNES in different parts of the country to develop an extensive data base for planning and implementation of rural energy systems. So far, 1,075 energy surveys have been completed in 19 states and Union Territories; 861 more surveys are in progress. As the first step in implementing the programme, it was decided to establish at least one Urjagram project in every parliamentary constituency: 352 villages have so far been identified as suitable, 321 of these have been surveyed, and detailed plans for the installation of different systems and devices have been made for 175 villages. Already, 85 Urjagrams have been completed and a total of 181 projects are in various stages of implementation. During 1989–90 it is proposed to carry out energy surveys in 200 villages and take up 75 Urjagram projects.

The Plan Targets

It is proposed to achieve an annual energy generation and savings of about 250 mtce through non-conventional energy sources by the year 2001. The Plan targets for non-conventional energy generation and savings over the period 1985–2000 are shown in Table 14.3.

It is expected that a number of consumer applications in renewable energy will be developed as a result of research and development in different areas. DNES is sponsoring research and development into alternative fuels for the transport sector (e.g. electric vehicles, alcohol-fuelled vehicles). The government of India is sponsoring research and development in hydrogen fuel cells, ocean energy systems, macro-hydro dynamics (MHD), etc.

REFERENCES

DNES. (1987). *Energy – 2001 Perspective Plan Non-Conventional Energy Sources.* DNES, Ministry of Energy, New Delhi.

ICAR. (1989). Annual Report, Scheme on Renewable Sources of Energy for Agriculture and Agro-based Industries. Central Institute of Agricultural Engineering, Bhopal.

Dayal, M. (1984). 'Food–energy nexus – activities in India'. Paper presented at International Seminar on Ecosystems, Food and Energy, Brasilia, Brazil.

——— (1986). 'Development and energy'. Lecture at Osmania University, Hyderabad.

——— (1989). *Renewable Energy Environment and Development.* Konark Publishers, New Delhi.

Table 14.3
Five Year Plan targets for energy generation/savings from non-conventional
energy sources during the VII, VIII and IX Plans

Source	1985–90	1990–5	1995–2000	Total
Power from biomass	100 MW	1200 MW	4700MW	6000MW
Power from wind	140 MW	1000 MW	3860MW	5000MW
Power from solar system	60 MW	440 MW	1500MW	2000MW
Power from small hydro	200 MW	600 MW	1200MW	2000MW
Improved *chulas* (number)	15 m	30 m	55m	100m
Biogas plants (numbers)	1 m	4 m	7m	12m
Energy plantation (ha)	0.25m	0.75 m	1.5m	2.5m
Sewage sludge	5 MW	15 MW	30MW	50MW
Solar thermal systems	2 mtce	6 mtce	12mtce	20mtce
Photovoltaic pumps	1.5 MW	4.5MW	9MW	15MW
Windpumps	5 MW	15MW	30MW	50MW
Small battery chargers and stand-alone systems	1MW	3MW	6MW	10MW
Energy from distillery	14	40	86	140
Energy from municipal solid waste	16MW	48MW	96MW	160MW

15 Integrated Rural Energy Programme in Sri Lanka: Approach and Institutions

B. P. SEPALAGE

A Background to the Rural and Energy Sectors

The rural sector in Sri Lanka is similar in many ways to those of other developing countries in the region. It holds a high percentage of the total population (76% according to recent studies) and agriculture is the main source of income and employment. In demographic and related studies the rural population is further divided into the rural and estate sub-sectors; in the 1981 census they held 86% and 14% respectively of the rural total. The rural-estate distinction refers to the type of employment or economic activity patterns and also to socio-cultural factors. Sri Lanka has a well-established tree crop agriculture sector with tea, rubber and coconut as the main plantations. The plantation workers with their families generally constitute what is identified as the estate population. The main economic activity in the rural sub-sector is agriculture for food production. This difference in economic activity becomes important when undertaking any rural development project as there could be distinct energy consumption patterns demanding different planning approaches.

The village and/or the Gramasevaka division is the smallest unit in the administrative set-up. A Gramasevaka (GS) division has about 200 households and some large villages are divided into two or more GS divisions. A number of villages/GS divisions constitute an Assistant Government Agent (AGA) division which is also the smallest political unit or electoral division. Several AGA divisions constitute one of Sri Lanka's 24 districts. Districts are grouped into nine provinces which are being developed as politically independent administrative units responsible to the central government. In the Sri Lankan context the village is an administrative demarcation rather than an aggregation of households. Most of the households are distributed unevenly within the village area with households located in individual home gardens. This spatial distribution often makes infrastructural development an expensive undertaking.

The rural Sri Lankan population is supported by agriculture (both food production and commercial agriculture), fisheries, forestry and mining. In 1984 the agriculture sector's contribution to the GNP was 22.5% compared to the 1970 figure of 28.8% – a declining, but still major, share.

Population studies of the composition of the rural and urban populations over the period 1946–71 show that the rural population declined to 77.6% in 1971 from 84.6% in 1946. However, the rural population has shown an increasing trend in the period 1971–81, reaching 78.5% in 1981. As there have not been any major differences in the population growth rates between the urban and rural sectors during this period, the increasing trend of rural population growth could be attributed to a reversal in rural–urban migration which could be a positive result of some recent rural development efforts.

The energy sector has been the most critical area of the Sri Lankan economy over the last 15 years. The value of petroleum imports reached a total of Rs11.5 billion in 1985, 32% of total income from exports. Petroleum imports absorbed 67% of earnings from non-petroleum exports in 1982. At present, petroleum imports amount to Rs8.7 billion (current), 16% of export earnings.

The principal sources of energy in Sri Lanka's economy are locally available fuelwood and agricultural residues, fossil fuels (all imported, including a relatively small quantity of coal) and electricity derived from indigenous hydro resources and from fossil fuels. In 1987, Sri Lanka's total estimated energy consumption was equivalent to 6.536 million tons of oil, of which 70.4% came from fuelwood and agricultural residues, 19.6% from petroleum products and 9.9% from hydro-electricity. Table 15.1 shows energy supply by the different types of fuels for 1987 and their percentage shares.

The principal sectors of energy consumption in Sri Lanka's economy are industry, household, agriculture, transport and commercial (Table 15.2). The sectoral energy consumption patterns indicate that half of the commercial energy in Sri Lanka is consumed in the transport sector, which takes more that 50% of the petroleum fuel supply. Industry is the next highest consumer of commercial energy and the main consumer of electricity. The household and agricultural sectors together account for the largest share of total energy consumption (70%). Most rural industries – brick and tile manufacture, bakeries, distilleries, desiccated coconut and coconut oil mills, smoked rubber making, drying and curing of tea and tobacco, lime kilns, sugar, juggary (unrefined sugar) and treacle making, parboiling of rice – are dependent on fuelwood and agricultural residues. As Table 15.3 shows, agriculture uses less commercial energy than any other sector, relying mainly on animal and human power and other non-commercial energy sources.

The main features of the national energy scene are:

1 The predominance of traditional energy sources (fuelwood and agro-residues, increasingly in demand).
2 The major role played by traditional fuels, even in the industrial sector (particularly in the agricultural and rural manufacturing industries).
3 The low level of energy use in the agriculture sector and the pre-dominance of animal and human power. Recent studies, however, show a trend towards modernization and mechanization, and the sector's consumption could shift towards commercial energy.
4 The high and increasing demand for commercial energy (petroleum fuels) in the transport sector.

Table 15.1
Energy supply 1987 (1000 toe*)

	Energy supply	Percentage of total energy
Petroleum fuels	1,197	18.4
Electricity	649	9.9
Coal	87	1.3
Fuelwood and agro-residues	4,603	70.4
Total commercial	1,933	–
Total non-commercial	4,603	–
Total	13,072	100.0

* Toe: Tonnes of oil equivalent

Table 15.2
Sectoral consumption of energy 1987 (1000 toe)

	Commercial fuels					
	Coal	Petroleum	Electricity	Total consumption	Fuelwood	Total
1. Industry	86.7	163.1	74.6	324.4	753.4	1077.7
2. Household & agriculture		199.9	32.9	232.8	3699.0	3931.8
3. Transport	0.5	684.2	–	684.7	–	684.7
4. Commercial	–	3.6	86.3	89.9	81.5	171.4

Rural Energy Supply and Consumption

The principal sources of energy in the rural sector are biomass fuels including fuelwood and agro-residues, used essentially for cooking and in some rural industries; kerosene, used mainly for lighting; and human and animal power, used in transport, agriculture and some cottage industries. Electricity is used for lighting in the households and for some rural industries, but only in villages linked to the rural electrification schemes. The supply of energy from other renewable sources such as solar power, wind and biogas remains very limited.

Biomass fuels

Firewood and agricultural residues constitute a major resource both in the

Table 15.3
Percentage share of commercial energy in agriculture and its contribution to GDP.

Year	Percentage share of commercial energy input	Percentage share of GDP
1975	3.64	30.35
1976	3.51	29.01
1977	3.39	30.69
1978	2.86	30.49
1979	2.91	26.94
1980	2.85	27.55
1981	2.82	27.70
1982	2.39	27.45
1983	2.23	27.13

national context and more so in the rural context. Biomass fuels are mainly derived from the following sources.

1 Rubber plantations, yielding an estimated 1.5 million tons annually. Tree trunks and branches in log form are mostly marketed in urban centres and for industry, while the roots, small branches, twigs and dead branches from existing plantations find their way into the rural energy supply.

2 Waste from coconut cultivation and tea plantations, and other residue such as rice husk, sawdust, bagasse and cinnamon sticks, are estimated to provide 3.5 million tons annually. Except for a small quantity of coconut shells and husks, cinnamon sticks and sawdust, this source is not marketed.

3 Clearing of jungles in Mahaweli Development Areas, estimated to yield about 0.25 million tons annually. As the Mahaweli Development Project is now nearing completion, this is a diminishing source.

4 Pruning of forests within ecologically sustainable limits – estimated to yield about 0.5 million tons annually.

5 Unidentified sources, such as home gardens or hedges –but possibly including irrational exploitation of jungles. As the present annual demand for biomass fuels is around 9 million tons, about 3.25 million tons probably comes from these sources.

Biomass fuel supply in Sri Lanka is not yet in crisis, although in certain rural areas fuelwood shortages are being experienced. Fuelwood prices in the urban markets have shown a sharp rise in the recent past, indicative of diminishing supplies and rising transport costs. The main issues are:

1 Rapid denudation of the forest cover. During the last two decades the forest cover has been halved. It is estimated that around 30,000 – 40,000 hectares of forest land are being cleared annually. Reforestation, however, is costly and long-term. At present, it is not being undertaken on an

adequate scale, nor is it articulated with the country's fuelwood requirements, according to a UNDP/World Bank study.

2 About 94% of the rural population in Sri Lanka uses biomass fuels for cooking. They use the three-stone hearth or the semi-enclosed mud hearth, both inefficient in fuel usage.

3 Per capita fuelwood consumption in Sri Lanka averages about 1.43 kg/day, a level significantly higher than in other countries of the region.

4 The demand for fuelwood and biomass fuels is increasing steadily because of the population increase and because some economic activities and industries have switched to biomass fuels in the recent past.

5 Fuelwood made available from jungle clearings under the Mahaweli Development Project temporarily eased the problem in recent years, but as the project nears completion the loss of this source could cause major distortions in the fuelwood market.

6 To take advantage of the temporary glut during the Mahaweli Project, some fuelwood was converted to charcoal and an effort was made to develop a charcoal market. The size of this market, how it would behave and its interactions with the fuelwood economy after Mahaweli, are yet to be studied.

7 Timber is in growing demand, both for local use and for export. Rubber tree trunks, which hitherto were being used as fuelwood, are now also being used as structural timbers.

Petroleum

The common petroleum fuel in the rural area is kerosene, used by more that 80% of the rural population for lighting and, to some extent, for water pumping in agriculture. The price of kerosene is kept low by the government to help the rural population, while a stamp scheme helps the poorest to procure a certain quota. It is not a popular fuel for cooking in rural areas. Diesel oil is being used in the rural areas for water pumping, driving tractors and powering fishing craft, and as motive power in some industries. Use of other petroleum fuels is very limited.

The main features of the petroleum fuel supply are as follows:

1 Sri Lanka has no known indigenous resources of petroleum and other fossil fuels; they are all imported at a considerable foreign exchange cost.

2 More than 50% of the population is dependent on kerosene stamps and this continuing subsidy is a major financial burden.

3 Heavy demand for middle distillates (kerosene and diesel oil) leads to over-production of other products in refinery operations.

4 In rural households kerosene is used in open wick bottle lamps for lighting which is inefficient and a hazard to health and safety.

5 In remote areas kerosene is sold at a price higher than the controlled one and is often sold short of measure.

Rural electrification

Sri Lanka's programme of rural electrification, pursued since the early 1960s, has so far benefited 20%–30% of rural households. The problems are:

1 The high cost of equipment and materials for extending the grid.
2 Technically and economically it is not feasible to extend electric lines to all households in a typically dispersed Sri Lankan village. Thus, even in electrified villages only about 30% of the households have any reasonable access to electricity.
3 Inability to pay the capital and recurrent costs.
4 Poor financial returns on investment and high cost of maintenance.

Development and Utilization of New and Renewable Sources of Energy

There is growing awareness of the potential of new and renewable sources of energy in the rural context. Solar energy for improved drying, for hot water and for small-scale electricity generation in remote areas, wind energy for water pumping and for shaft power, small hydro-power for electricity, shaft power and gravity irrigation, improved use of agricultural residues and industrial wastes with such technologies as better furnaces, gasifiers and biogas digestion – these are only some of the interesting opportunities for providing energy for rural development.

The current use of new and renewable sources of energy in the rural areas is quite insignificant compared to its potential. Solar photovoltaic panels for rural household lighting and operating TVs and radios have now been installed in 3000 households, particularly among the rural rich. Three villages have been electrified on the basis of a central battery-charging solar PV array. About 50 rural community centres are provided with solar-powered TV receivers. A few rural hospitals and some schools have been provided with solar PV electricity systems. There are some experimental solar grain dryers and a commercial wood-seasoning facility.

A programme for the development and dissemination of water-pumping windmills has been operating for the past eight years. About 200 units have been disseminated during the first two phases of the project. Under the third phase, carried out with technical support from The Netherlands government, an improved version has been developed and is being evaluated before dissemination. Small battery-charging windmills are under development and evaluation by research institutions such as the Industrial Development Board (IDB) and the National Engineering Research and Development (NERD) Centre.

From the geo-climatic characteristics of Sri Lanka, it is evident that there is considerable small hydro-power potential, particularly in the rural hill country. Before the advent of generators driven by fossil fuel or electricity, most of the tea and rubber factories derived their motive power from small hydro-power units. The ongoing small hydro-power development is limited mostly to the rehabilitation of abandoned small hydro-power facilities in tea and rubber estates, in view of their high techno-economic viability. Although these small hydro-power units are located in rural areas, their benefits are not directly enjoyed by the rural population.

Large quantities of agricultural residues and industrial wastes such as coir dust, rice husk and sawdust are available in rural areas, with a large potential for application as substitutes for commercial as well as traditional fuels. Currently, the Commission of European Communities is assisting a programme for the conversion of coir dust and rice husk into substitute fuels for industrial and domestic applications. Several gasifier and furnace designs for the use of biomass residues are under development and evaluation by the IDB, NERD Centre and the Alternative Energy Development (AED) Division of the Ceylon Electricity Board (CEB).

The Ministry of Power and Energy has launched a national programme for the conservation of fuelwood and has given high priority to the dissemination of improved wood-burning stoves in the household sector. The programme is being implemented by the AED Division of the CEB in collaboration with both government and non-governmental agencies such as the Ceylon Institute of Scientific Industry Research (CISIR), Sarvodaya Sangamaya of Sri Lanka and others. The programme is being supported by several bilateral donor agencies (including The Netherlands and UK government agencies, NORAD and SIDA) and forms an important component in Integrated Rural Development Projects (IRDP), implemented in a number of districts with foreign assistance. Since the launching of the project in 1984, about 200,000 stoves have been disseminated in rural areas. The urban project has achieved local manufacturing capability and a substantial market presence of about 100,000 improved stoves per year.

The use of biogas has, in the main, been limited to those cattle owners who could afford the high initial cost. The National Livestock Board, the AED Division of the CEB, the NERD Centre and the private sector are working on various aspects of biogas technology – research, development, dissemination, training and commercialization. Another example worth noting is the use of biogas for electrification of a village with 25 households, using a biogas-fuelled engine generator. The system is operated and maintained by the villagers themselves.

The Pattiyapola village Rural Energy Center is an important development in the introduction of new and renewable energy technologies in a rural setting. The project was established under the aegis of the United Nations Environment Programme in 1978. It currently provides electricity to about 100 households in the village, using a combination of wind, solar, biogas and biomass (producer gas) resources in an integrated manner. The project has provided many useful insights concerning social, technical, economic and environmental issues in the introduction of renewable technologies to rural settings.

Integrated Rural Energy Planning and Development

In 1989 the government launched a major initiative towards the development and implementation of an Integrated Rural Energy Development Plan (IREDP) with the Ministry of Power and Energy as the focal organization responsible for planning and coordination.

Though Sri Lanka has been pursuing a programme of rural electrification for three decades, electricity has reached only a small fraction of the rural population. Under the present circumstances of resource constraints and the poor economic standards of the rural population, it is not viable to make grid-based electricity available to most households in the country. There is, therefore, a strong case for improving opportunities for income-generating activities, integrating these efforts with energy development.

The high cost of development and distribution of electricity, the continuing subsidy on kerosene and the problems of distributing fuel to remote areas on one hand, and the restrictions in the supply of traditional sources of energy on the other, place a high emphasis on the development and utilization of indigenous new and renewable sources of energy. Such a strategy could pave the way towards reducing the dependence on imported sources of energy, while avoiding an exposure of the people to the negative effects of international energy price changes.

There is increasing concern about the environmental consequences resulting from the development and utilization of various forms of energy, particularly those resulting from commercial energy activities. The development of renewable energy sources within an integrated rural energy development programme can minimize environmental damage. Further, renewable energy activities often offer multiple functions, providing not only energy but also other benefits. For example, biogas technology provides energy for cooking and lighting while simultaneously generating environmentally benign organic fertilizer.

Policy guidelines and priorities

Uniform guidelines are essential for the development and implementation of integrated rural energy programmes. Such guidelines are also important if the planning process is to take place in a 'bottom up' fashion, in which the micro level plans developed in the regions will be combined to give the macro plan at the national level. In developing policy guidelines, the following should be kept in view:

1   Satisfying basic energy needs.
2   Need-based planning and meeting energy demand arising from the rural development effort. Among the priorities should be energy for agricultural production, rural industry, food processing and conservation, and health care.
3   Choosing the optimum mix of energy resources and technologies to

    meet energy requirements at minimum cost to the user and the country.

4 Reducing dependence on imported fuels by optimum development of indigenous resources.

5 Reducing energy waste and improving the efficiency of energy use.

6 Proper development and management of forest and non-forest biomass resources.

7 Continuity of supply, price stability and sustainable development through private sector participation; commercialization; motivation through profits, incentives and equitable sharing of benefits; suitable pricing and taxation policies; standardization and certification; regular monitoring and follow-up; research and development support for product improvement and cost reduction; market development and exploration; and publicity, promotion and training.

Energy resource and technology orientation

The IREDP will focus its attention on both the commercial sources of energy and the NRSE technologies. Such an emphasis is justified as the energy requirements arising from the rural development effort are to be satisfied through seeking the best match between sources, needs and technologies while giving adequate weight to indigenous new and renewable sources on the grounds of energy independence and sustainability.

NRSE and alternative technology options are classified into six categories according to their level of maturity and potential for application: (1) already commercialized; (2) ready for commercialization and promotion; (3) ready for demonstration; (4) ready for field evaluation; (5) ready for development and adaptation; and (6) at the research stage. Individual technologies falling within each of the above categories are identified in Annex 15.1.

Structure of the Integrated Rural Energy Development Plan

Annex 15.2 depicts graphically the key activities, programmes and plans perceived as essential components of the core programme of the IREDP. This core programme incorporates ten plans: (1) institutional, (2) logistics, (3) resource assessment, (4) energy needs assessment, (5) research and development, (6) financial, (7) resource development, (8) sensitization and demonstration, (9) publicity and promotion, and (10) commercial.

The IREDP has got under way with the establishment of the institutional infrastructure, including staffing at the various levels called for by the institutional plan. This plan highlights the structure required at the Ministry of Power and Energy and the linkages at various levels for plan implementation and coordination (Annex 15.3). The Ministry of Power and Energy is mainly responsible for programme coordination and the Ceylon Electricity Board for implementation aspects. Consultative committees are being organized at the national, provincial, district and AGA levels for the initial planning activity.

The logistic plan will identify the desired logistics at both the national and provincial levels for development and implementation of the plan. The needs assessment and resource assessment plans will jointly generate the required data base information; currently questionnaires structured for different levels are being developed and tested before the island-wide enumeration. Data and information have been gathered on various technologies for effective technology matching and scenario development, to be carried out at the next stage. This evaluation will also identify requirements for the research and development plan. The identification of projects and programmes will be carried out jointly by the centre, the regions and the sub-regions to provide planning capability at the micro level. Projects identified as viable after the evaluation stage will be incorporated in programmes which could be at national, provincial or sub-provincial level, depending on significance, implementation scenarios, resource endowment, etc.

Resource mobilization and identification of strategies will follow, together with their associated plans on resource development, finance, sensitization, demonstration, publicity and promotion, etc. Already key areas for training and familiarization have been identified, and some of the ongoing renewable energy programmes have been expanded to incorporate additional training requirements. Sensitization workshops and seminars are being organized for provincial level officials as well as for politicians.

The next stage of field activity will commence with the establishment of pilot village projects which will demonstrate the practical application of technology while validating assumptions and concepts; the pilot projects will also throw light on policy areas and on deficiencies in the project planning implementation and management. Proven technology options will be taken up for widespread dissemination through appropriate policy mechanisms, which will also lead to commercialization of some of the technologies. The plan will be looped back through a monitoring process, so that improvements to the plan can be effected as the implementation is carried forward.

Conclusions

Unless correct policy initiatives are deployed, adequate energy supply to the overall economy in general and to the rural economy in particular will continue to be a major problem. Most of the rural energy planning and development approaches carried out so far have focused on meeting the energy requirement for subsistence. It is essential to focus instead on the energy requirements arising out of the imperatives of overall socio-economic development in the rural areas.

Policy initiatives should endeavour to create the necessary planning background covering all relevant sectors and not just the energy supply institutions. Energy users, as well as those concerned with development fields such as agriculture and rural industry, should be brought into the process which addresses problems in an overall perspective and avoids tackling individual issues in an ad hoc way. The policy should also guarantee participation at all levels so that contributions can be expected in all aspects of planning, implementation and management.

As well as all-round participation, micro-level planning in the regions and sub-regions demands the necessary planning know-how and an environment which integrates various contributions to the planning process. There is thus an urgent need to provide the necessary training and familiarization to relevant personnel, particularly at the micro level. Modern approaches to planning with micro-computer support need to be introduced wherever necessary and there should be an adequate flow of know-how and assistance both vertically, between developed and developing countries, and horizontally, between developing countries themselves.

In the Integrated Rural Energy Development Plan, new and renewable sources of energy have an important role to play. However, the planning process should include commercial and traditional forms of energy, as well as conservation technologies, if energy is to be delivered in an optimum manner. An equally important priority in the strategy is the sustainability of energy delivery and the development process. Special policy attention should be given to realizing this objective.

Annex 15.1.
Classification of NRSE and alternative technologies

1. TECHNOLOGIES ALREADY COMMERCIALIZED
   - Solar Photovoltaic Technology
     - **a** Household lighting
     - **b** Operation of TV and radio receivers at households and community centres
     - **c** Village electrification
   - Solar Thermal Energy Technologies
     - **a** Provision of potable and distilled water by solar stills
     - **b** Improved drying using hot boxes, solar dyers
   - Wind Mills
     - **a** Water pumping in agricultural applications
   - Biomass Technologies/Activities
     - **a** Improved stoves–urban household sector
     - **b** Improved stoves–rural household sector
     - **c** Generation of biogas from animal residue
   - Small Hydro Power Technologies/Activities
     - **a** Rehabilitation of small hydro power facilities in tea and rubber factories
   - Energy Conservation and Demand Management Options
     - **a** Conservation in energy supply and consumption sectors

2. TECHNOLOGIES READY FOR COMMERCIALIZATION AND PROMOTION
   - Solar Photo-Voltaic Technology
     - **a** Communication facilities

- Wind Mills
    - **a** Water pumping in industrial and commercial applications
- Biomass Technologies/Activities
    - **a** Pyrolytic conversion of coconut shells to charcoal and gas
    - **b** Development of bio fertilizer
- Small Hydro Power Technologies/Activities

3. TECHNOLOGIES READY FOR DEMONSTRATION
- Wind Mills
    - **a** Generation of electricity for decentralized applications
- Biomass Technologies/Activities.
    - **a** Improved fuel wood furnaces in industrial and commercial sectors
    - **b** Provision of hot air for industrial and agricultural applications using solar collectors

4. TECHNOLOGIES FOR FIELD EVALUATION
- SolarThermal Energy Technologies
    - **a** Provision of hot water for industrial, commercial, agricultural and domestic applications with flat plate collectors
    - **b** Provision of hot air for industrial and agricultural applications using solar collectors
- Wind Mills
    - **a** Water pumping and aeration in fish and shrimp farms
    - **b** Pumping of sea water for small-scale salt production
- Biomass Technologies/Activities
    - **a** Gasifiers for water pumping
    - **b** Establishment of fuel wood plantations
    - **c** Efficient charcoal production
    - **d** Evaluation of Stirling engines for water pumping generation of power
- Small Hydro Power Technologies/Activities
    - **a** Development of small hydro power sites for rural electrification
    - **b** Development of small hydro power based battery charging centres

5. TECHNOLOGIES FOR DEVELOPMENT AND ADAPTATION
- Biomass Technologies/Activities
    - **a** Low density briquetting of coir dust
    - **b** Use of agricultural residues as an industrial fuel
    - **c** Generation of biogas from biomass sources
- Small Hydro Power Technologies/Activities
    - **a** Establishment of small hydro power units for industrial applications

6. TECHNOLOGIES AT RESEARCH STAGE
- Solar Thermal Energy Technologies
    - **a** Establishment of pilot solar ponds for thermal power applications
- Wind Mills
    - **a** Assessment of the wind energy resource potential for large-scale power generation in Sri Lanka
    - **b** Wind/diesel oil hybrid power systems for village electrification and small industry

- Biomass Technologies/Activities
    - **a** Improvements to biomass fueled heat exchangers in industry
    - **b** High density briquetting of agro-residues
    - **c** Anaerobic digestion of industrial residues
    - **d** City refuse incineration for heat and power
    - **e** Gasifiers for power generation
    - **f** Gasifiers for transport vehicles
- Ocean Energy Technologies/Activities
    - **a** Assessment of the ocean thermal energy resource potential at selected sites.
    - **b** Assessment of the wave power potential at selected sites
    - **c** Feasibility study of sea water pumping using wave power

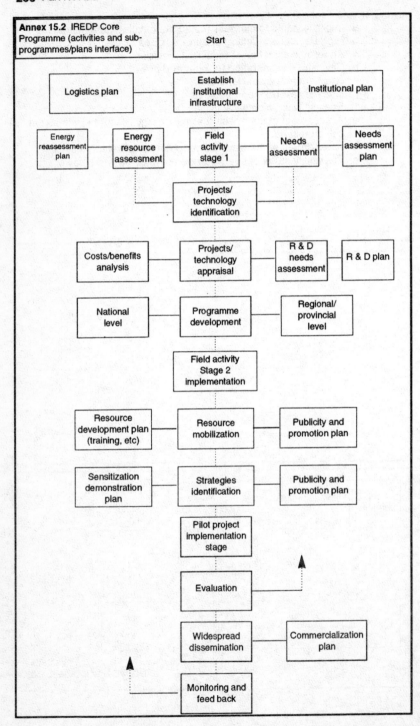

Annex 15.2 IREDP Core Programme (activities and sub-programmes/plans interface)

Annex 15.3
Planning and implementation institutional framework of the IREDP

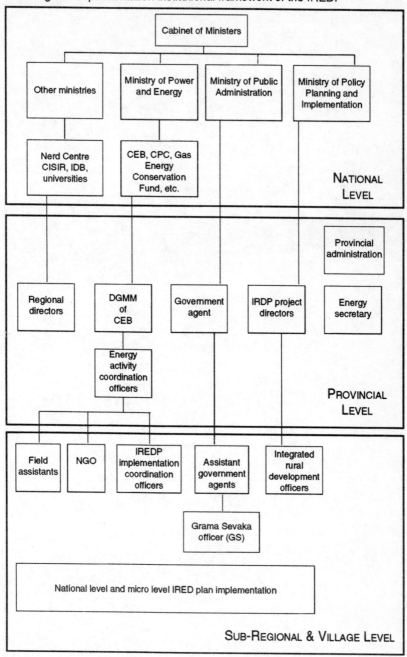

V LATIN AMERICA AND THE CARIBBEAN

16 The Potential of Renewable Energy in the Caribbean

DENNIS MINOTT

Energy Requirements and Supplies for Rural Development

With the exception of Trinidad (oil producer/exporter) and Haiti (very minimal industrial activity), energy-use patterns in Caribbean countries show remarkable similarities, especially in rural areas. In unique ways, the command economy in Cuba somewhat changes the rural energy consumption pattern, but generally, options for applying renewable energy to rural development need neither be many nor very country-specific among the states of the region.

In the Caribbean context, the pervasive assumption that rural areas are more amenable to supply by small renewable sources than are urban areas, is open to question. Notably, whenever centralized supplies of electrical power or petroleum products are significantly disrupted many households in urban Caribbean areas readily make the temporary change to renewable sources of energy for domestic purposes. The phenomenon serves to indicate a major potential for renewables linked to small appliances to play an important role even in the urban centres of this humid tropical region.

In any event, there are many opportunities for applying renewables to urban areas because (1) most urban dwellings have only one floor, and thus have direct rooftop access to sunlight for all occupants; (2) most urban dwellings occupy less than 40% of the property on which they are located; (3) more than 25% of the urban yard spaces in the region are covered by lawn grass (a renewable biomass resource); and (4) most urban domestic energy applications do not require high enthalpy energy sources.

Although, on balance, the rural areas offer the best opportunities for applying renewables, the potential in urban areas should not be ignored.

In a major UNDP/CARICOM Secretariat study on the feasibility of establishing a Caribbean Regional Renewable Energy Development Station (RREDS), Minott et al. (1985) carried out comprehensive sub-sector level projections of renewables market potential and annual US dollar savings possible over a 30-year period in the Caribbean region, based on extrapolations from analyses of the enthalpies and quantities of commercial energy usage in Jamaica at the start of the last decade. Table 16.1 is a summary of these projections for both urban and rural areas of the Caribbean (excluding Cuba).

In 1984, the primary demand for rural energy was for agricultural production, sugar processing, cooking, lighting, refrigeration and transportation. An estimate of the BOE demand may be made by extrapolating from the data given in Table 16.1.

The Energy Issues in the Caribbean

The industrial world of the late nineteenth and the twentieth centuries initially designed its industries around non-renewable fossil fuels: oil, gas and coal. As the enterprises expanded, their demand for these dwindling resources precipitated a large international trading activity involving the purchase of fossil fuel from the resources of the developing world at prices well below those that would be appropriate if rational marginal costings were applied.

The countries of the Caribbean group, in trying to improve the quality of life for their citizens, have increasingly adopted the lifestyles of the industrialized world, including heavy dependency on fossil fuels. But among the stark differences between this group and the industrialized country models which it seeks to emulate are (1) the availability of capital; (2) political power and international influence; (3) technological prowess related to the harnessing of the factors of production within the context of the Caribbean environment; (4) experience in implementing policies of self-reliance without disrupting the social order; (5) experience in commercializing local innovation by private and public concern; and (6) the relative availabilities of alternatives to fossil fuels.

In the critical field of energy, the Caribbean, which in past centuries was completely reliant on renewables, almost completely discarded its heritage. This was not necessary for industrialization. In developing countries such as the People's Republic of China, fuel and energy production benefited considerably from the wholesale adherence to the continued but modernized use of renewables, especially in rural areas by way of small hydro-power, biogas and woodfuel in conjunction with necessary use of available non-renewables.

There is an assumption that increased fuel and energy use per capita is essential to economic growth. While this may be so in some cases it is surely not so in the majority of cases. The problem is that we have almost invariably equated energy with high-grade fuels and electricity. In order to accomplish work in a 'modern' way we have forgotten or ignored equally simple ways to perform work without electricity. As the volume of work to be done increases with population, consumption of electrical power and petroleum fuels increases disproportionately to the actual end uses. Consequently, the volume of high-grade fuels that has to be wasted in order to provide electrical power at 15% to 30% efficiency climbs at a greater than linear rate. To put it bluntly, the shallow economic dictum that equates growth with energy consumption per capita results from a failure to understand the second law of thermodynamics and the degree to which electrical energy is abused due to ignorance about the options for performing work economically.

Table 16.1

Renewable and fossil fuels endowment and potentially exploitable resources for sustained energy production in the Caribbean group

Country	Direct solar thermal	Petroleum oil/gas	Small hydro-power	Conventional hydro-power	Existing natural forests biomass	Existing sugar cane biomass	Existing rice biomass	Potential for Leuc-aera biomass	Potential for cane & grass biomass	Lignite peat, coal	Geothermal energy	OTEC	Wind energy	Wave energy	Tidal energy
Antigua,	SS	O	O	O	SS	S	O	SSS	S	O	O	S	S	SS	O
Bahamas	SS	O	O	O	SS	O	O	SS	SS	O	O	S	SSS	O	O
Barbados	SS	S	O	O	O	SSS	O	SSS	SSS	O	O	O	SSS	SS	O
Belize	SS	O	SSS	SSS	SSS	SSS	SS	SSS	SSS	S	S	O	O	O	O
Cayenne	SS	O	SSS	SSS	SSS	SSS	SS	SSS	SSS	O	O	SS	O	O	O
Cuba	SS	S	S	SS	SS	SSS	S	SSS	SSS	O	S	SS	S	S	O
Dominica	SS	O	SSS	S	SSS	O	O	S	O	O	SS	S	S	S	O
Dominica Rep.	SS	O	SS	SS	SS	SS	SS	SSS	SSS	S	SS	S	S	S	O
Grenada	SS	O	SS	O	S	O	O	S	S	O	SS	O	S	S	O
Guyana	SS	S	SSS	SSS	SSS	SSS	SSS	SSS	SSS	S	O	S	S	S	SSS
Haiti	SS	O	SS	SS	O	S	S	SSS	SSS	SSS	SS	S	O	O	O
Jamaica	SS	O	SS	SS	S	S	O	S	SSS	SSS	S	SS	O	S	O
Montserrat	SS	O	S	O	S	O	O	S	O	O	S		SSS	SS	O
St Kitts/Nevis	SS	O	O	O	S	SSS	O	SS	SSS	O	SSS	SS	SSS	SS	O
St Lucia	SS	O	S	S	S	O	O	SS	SS	O	SSS	SS	SS	S	O
St Vincent	SS	O	SS	S	S	O	O	SS	S	O	SSS	O	SS	S	O
Surinam	SS	O	SSS	SSS	SSS	SSS	SSS	SSS	SSS	O	O	O	O	O	SSS
Trinidad & Tobago	SS	SSS	O	O	S	SSS	SS	SS	SSS	O	SS	O	S	S	SS

Key:
O not significant
S minor source
SS significant source
SSS major source

For the Caribbean, with the exception of Trinidad, the only options are the renewables. Their abundance is such that we are well placed to be among the first beneficiaries of the non-nuclear energy options which the entire planet will have to rely upon in the foreseeable future. What abounds in the region by way of year-round sunlight, land and aquatic resources in the continental countries, wind energy in the eastern states and relatively reliable rainfall are the 'raw materials' on which the world's new options must invariably be based.

Even in the cases of Trinidad and Tobago and Barbados, which produce fossil oil and gas, it is advisable that these non-renewable but valuable assets be husbanded for use in (1) meeting necessary present energy needs conservatively; (2) generating investment capital to provide alternatives for their replacement in the future; (3) manufacturing 'nobler' products which will be more resilient in sustaining economic well-being than fossil products can ever be; (4) building up energy reserves for meeting emergency needs for high-grade fossil fuels in national crises within the future of renewables; and (5) directly assisting the transition to biomass and other solar technologies on a phased basis by providing materials such as fertilizers, plastics, etc.

The Caribbean's bequest of renewable energy resources is such that the region can, in a generation, be living off its own natural energy income rather than continuing to exist on 'oil credits' generously provided by Venezuela, Mexico, Nigeria, and Trinidad and Tobago. Indeed, it is a commendable feature of the credit facilities offered under these oil supply agreements that capital investments in new sources of energy in the consuming countries may, to an appreciable extent, be offset against due repayments. Unfortunately, however, these facilities for renewable energy development remain, for the most part, under- or unutilized because there is no viable local capacity to effect a meaningful programme of renewable energy development in the region despite the many (but woefully fragmented) efforts of the agencies.

Of course, there is yet another awkward non-economic factor contributing to world-wide tardiness in large-scale development of renewables, especially in the Third World. Renewables are, by their very nature, anti-monopolistic, more democratic and less amenable to centralized control. This has its political implications. At the working level, there tends to be an incestuous institutional relationship between second-level policy makers, regulatory bodies, executing organizations and implementing agencies, largely brought about by the scarcity of available technical personnel to staff the various agencies. Consequently, these 'old boy' relationships work against diversity in thinking, reinforce non-innovative, non-critical conformity and perpetuate increased reliance on fossil fuels and electrical energy within large, highly centralized systems vulnerable to undemocratic manipulation.

The argument that the economies of scale of large power supply systems makes them more suitable to meeting national energy demand is of questionable validity. When one examines the distribution of electrical power in relatively industrialized Jamaica and Trinidad, compared to far less industrialized Haiti, the most striking similarity is the small proportion of the consumers' tariff dollar which is actually paid for energy. So much of the residential tariffs are to pay for (1) transmission and distribution losses plus power station losses; (2) subsidizing industrial and agricultural power supply; (3) paying for energy waste at levels which would not be typical if smaller, more efficient renewable systems were doing the same work; (4) maintaining idle reserves; (5) paying for new capital equipment which will reduce jobs and trap large amounts of capital, thus directing investment away from other critical targets for the development efforts; and (6) the negative effects of mis-timed demand forecasts, interest, escalations, strikes, administration and competition for foreign exchange to purchase fossil fuels from overseas.

Inevitably, we have to confront the fact that probably no more than about 12% of electricity use in the Caribbean really requires energy in the electromagnetic form. However, one hastens to add that where the potential for cheap hydro-electric power exists, this form of energy should be exploited fully since the development process can only benefit from this. Dominica, Cayenne, Suriname, Guyana, Haiti, Belize and St Vincent could well rationalize their industrial potential for producing high-grade power in the form of electricity from hydro resources.

Trinidad and Barbados, despite their hydrocarbon resources and relatively dense levels of population, may need to concentrate on those technologies and industries which can begin the process of exploiting their renewable resources in the forms of direct solar power, biomass and wind. In similar fashion, Jamaica, Antigua, the Bahamas, Belize, the Dominican Republic and most of the Windward Islands have the options of direct solar, biomass and, in the case of the eastern states, wind energy.

In the Caribbean context, ocean energy and geothermal resources, though promising, are inherently disposed to trapping large blocks of capital into low levels of economic production for too long. Furthermore, ocean thermal and geothermal sources do not create any significant employment and are not as environmentally benign as might at first appear.

So, what must be done regionally? Briefly, these countries need to set out together to develop small energy systems based on their affordable and sustainable renewables. But this must be done incrementally – first, by supplementing existing systems, then by deliberately allowing renewables to supplant existing systems. The approach needs to be structured, conducted by a comprehensively endowed body of experts in collaboration with existing institutions. The proposed programme would ensure the thorough public education and democratic and commercial participation of the Caribbean peoples whose lives will be affected by the development of new energy alternatives.

Research and Development in Rural Energy Supplies

Table 16.1 lists the types of renewable and fossil resources on a country-by-country basis and gives an approximate picture of the distribution of energy resources in the sub-region. Research and development should be designed to service the technology needs of each country according to its indigenous energy resources. The particular choices of technology are recommended on the perceived distribution of exploitable resources and on the demonstrable nature and magnitude of energy demands for each country.

In terms of renewable resources already being or likely to be exploited, Table 16.1 indicates the following order of technological priorities: (1) forestry/silvicultural biomass, including natural wood sources and cultivated wood and foliage sources for fermentation to fuels, etc.; (2) sugar cane and grasses biomass from existing plantations and from cultivation of enhanced varieties and species for alcohol, fuel gases and solid fuels; (3) direct solar for low enthalpy heat production and also for high temperature and electrical purposes; (4) small hydro-power (below 5 MW) and conventional hydro-power; (5) wind energy; (6) geothermal energy (not truly a renewable technology); (7) rice-derived fuels; (8) wave energy; (9) tidal energy; and (10) ocean thermal energy conversion.

This ordering of the technology priorities must be matched by:

1   Complementary facilities for technological developments in the uses of immediate by-products of the energy processes specific to the priorities determined above. These facilities must, in general, serve to promote the extraction of maximum economic and commercial benefits from the indigenous energy resources in an environmentally benign way;

2   Provision for a Regional Renewables Research Station to play a strong role in promoting and facilitating thrifty and efficient use of local energy resources;

3   Great emphasis on quick and efficient technologies through the development of a major body of expertise engaged in technology transfer and commercialization on a day-to-day, full-time and professional basis;

4   Adequate staffing and facilities at the station for marketing and promoting investment related to renewable energy development, including providing support for consumer products development;

5   Safeguards against shoddy and hazardous energy services and products through vigorous institutional arrangements for consumer protection and standards that interface well with the Caribbean marketplace, its consumers and the existing standards institutions in the region;

6   Provisions for on-station equipment manufacture and for on-station commercial production of energy feeds, fertilizers, livestock, biomass and energy/fuels prototype machinery.

Energy Investment and Renewables Policies

By the year 2020, the sugar industry, other rural industries and the residential sectors ought to be able to substitute renewables for between 62% and 98% of petroleum imports under present patterns of energy usage if a vigorous programme is pursued without delay. In fact, with increasing awareness in the region of the characteristics of energy and how to avoid abusing it, patterns of usage are more than likely to be restructured along more economic lines dictated by supply and demand. Consequently, the level of substitution predicted above may well be excessively conservative. The overall picture suggests that if attention is focused on the solution of the fuel imports problem by building up institutional capacity and facilitating the economic structures to deal with it, a 61% substitution of imported fuel by indigenous renewable energies is achievable in one generation.

In 1984 dollars, the potential saving in fuel import costs to this group of countries would be of the order of US$2.4 billion at today's prices per barrel of oil equivalent. The eventual substitution of renewables on such a scale would diversify and decentralize the provision of energy for the countries concerned. Self-sufficiency with respect to this most critical of commodities would be achieved to a very significant degree. Furthermore, instead of trapping capital and displacing workers, the renewables, by their very nature, would provide jobs, promote income distribution and protect national security by dispersing the bulk of our energy resources in such a way as to make them less vulnerable to strikes, sabotage and other forms of disturbance.

By way of illustrating this point about national and economic security, it is only necessary to point out that one sharpshooter armed with a high-powered rifle can completely disrupt the electricity supplies of all of Jamaica or all of the Barbados grid by destroying any two conductors on a suitable section of the high-tension transmission lines. In Trinidad, the opportunities for sabotage are even greater. With renewable sources dispersed among the populations, and more exposed and responsive to the rigours of the market than any monopoly can ever be, greater efficiency and lower vulnerability of energy supplies will be realized.

It must be underscored, though, that in order to realize the promise held out by renewables, it is not sufficient to have between one and 20 professionals per country engaged in energy development and working essentially in isolation. At present, the energy imports problem looms larger in money terms than that of food self-sufficiency throughout the sub-region, yet all but the tiniest countries have over 20 professionals working on various aspects of food production. The major problem facing the Caribbean requires a commensurate solution. Part of that solution lies in comprehensive and concerted efforts to develop renewable sources which are able to sustain economic development, create employment and optimally use each dollar of scarce capital. This is the rationale for investment in renewable energy.

The following is a list of parameters that should be central to the development of renewables in the region:

- The research and development facilities must liaise with energy users, the public utilities and the governments as much as possible.
- Devices, processes and systems promoted or developed should aim to be technically simple and should require a minimum of maintenance by any 'technological priesthood'.

- Emphasis should be placed on people-centred, democratic, decentralised systems of energy production, while not ignoring opportunities to use or continue using more economic centralised systems of energy.
- Aim for systems with low replacement costs.
- Optimize the use of local raw materials and locally made equipment in order to save foreign exchange and promote job creation.
- Always aim to get standard designs and develop equipment with a high proportion of interchangeable parts.
- Design for slow obsolescence and high reliability.
- Design for high volume production to take advantage of the abundance of labour in some countries and of mass production techniques.
- The marketed systems or processes should minimize disruptive interventions in the consumer's way of life and require a minimum of attention.
- The mark-up on each product should be kept to a minimum.
- Vertically integrated, agriculturally-based systems with by-products for food and fertilizer production should be given priority.
- Trivial 'Mickey Mouse' projects should be consciously avoided since energy development is urgent and the devices in use are essential to economic life. They are not toys.
- Opportunities for co-generation should be appreciated and exploited in general practice.
- Whenever possible, let the system be petroleum compatible in the light of the proven versatility of petroleum and high susceptibility of renewable systems to natural catastrophes.
- Explicitly design to promote environmentally benign projects.
- Let activities be related to demand and endeavour to attract capital investment to mass-produced energy devices and systems.
- Encourage utilities to finance householders and other users to implement renewable systems.
- Stress the proper legal protection and exploitation of intellectual property developed by or transferred to the research facilities.
- Encourage technological exchange with both the developing and developed countries.
- Remain financially viable.

REFERENCES

Lovins, A. B. (1977). *Soft Energy Paths: Toward a Durable Peace*. Harper, New York.

Minott, D. A., Hales, A. L., Delisser, R. A., Forrest, D. A., Harrison, V., Herr, C. H., Hinds, A. M., Jarret, M. I., McMorris, V. R., Masters, T., Rose-Green, E. P. & . Silvera, B. C. (1985). *The RRED Station Report: A Technical, Financial and Economic Feasibility Study*. ENERPLAN/CARICOM Secretariat, Kingston.

Minott, D. A. (1983). *Toward Regional Science and Technology Development in CARICOM Territories and Surinam: New and Renewable Energy*. ENERPLAN/CARICOM Secretariat/UNFSTD, Kingston, second edition.

17 Renewable Energy for Rural Development in Mexico

MANUEL MARTINEZ

Energy Requirements and Supply for Rural Development

The government has published estimates of energy requirements by the rural sector ((SEMIP, 1984). The total energy requirement in the form of heat varies from $110x10^{15}$ to 389×10^{15} per year, representing between 4.3% and 15.2% of all the national demand for the year 1982. Electricity requirements varied from 1811 GWh to 3649 GWh per year (between 2.5% and 5% of the net electricity generation). If both types of energy are combined, the rural energy requirements were between 5.2% and 17% of the total energy demand in 1982. These figures were larger than the total energy used by the agricultural sector during that year (3.7%).

Sound data on the supply and demand of energy for the rural sector were first published for the year 1987 (SEMIB, 1988). The per capita daily consumption of energy in rural areas was 11.458 kcal, equivalent to 43% of the national figure. About 15.69 million tons of firewood was consumed per year, equivalent to a daily consumption of 1.77 kg per capita. The firewood was mainly used for cooking, water heating, house heating and as fuel for furnaces. Rural monthly average consumption of LPG was about 2.80 kg per capita, or an annual total of 814 million kg (about 49% of the national average), mainly used for cooking, water and house heating, lighting, refrigeration and transportation.

Petrol consumption in rural areas was 1277 million litres per year, which constitutes a monthly average of 4.39 litres per capita. This represented only 21% of the national average. Petrol is mainly used for transportation, and to some extent for lighting. Rural consumption of diesel was about 648 million litres per year, or 2.35 litres per month per capita on average, which was only 21% of the national average. The main uses were agricultural machinery and transportation; it was also used for water pumping, irrigation and electricity generation.

Rural electricity consumption (by extension of the grid) averaged 10.09 KWh per capita per month and represents only 12.5% of the national average. Electricity was mainly used for lighting. Other applications vary with the economic level: radios, grinders and motors for low incomes and a wide range

219

of domestic devices, pumping and refrigeration for high incomes.

The consumption of kerosene in rural areas was about 179 million litres per year, which represents a monthly average of 0.61 litres per capita, or 20%. The main uses were for lighting and starting wood fires.

Firewood is the most important source of energy in rural areas of Mexico. It is consumed by more than 75% of the population in all the villages. The average consumption per family varies widely from region to region and depends mainly on the size of the village and its accessibility. Villages with large numbers of inhabitants and better communications have a large choice of commercial energy at lower prices. Obviously, firewood consumption also depends on the availability of local resources, climatic variations and income level. The highest family consumption of firewood is about 1300 kg per month and the lowest around 100 kg. This energy source is essentially non-commercial: less than 10% of the firewood consumed is traded.

More than 80% of the rural families use firewood for cooking. They state that food cooked using firewood tastes better. In the great majority of villages, the 'three-stones stove' is still used, because it is the cheapest. Women and children collect firewood and usually no cost is associated with this type of work. In the majority of the Mexican villages, to collect firewood implies travelling between one and seven kilometres, which accounts for one to three hours per day. Ooccasionally carts, sometimes hitched to an animal, are used.

No other new and renewable sources of energy (NRSE) are significantly used in the rural areas of Mexico.

A recent study (Martinez, 1988a) evaluated various electricity supply sources in the present socio-economic conditions of rural Mexico. The main factors considered were social needs, electricity requirements, availability of energy sources and techno-economic viability of different systems. A typical rural village was considered to have 250 inhabitants, 50 households and a community centre. The social needs, electric devices and average energy demands were as estimated. A standard net present value method was used to perform the economic comparison between the various systems studied. The economic scenario was based on goals presented by the government for 1986: annual general inflation rate 45%, annual energy prices increase by 51% and a 1986 energy reference cost of US$4.38 per gigajoule. Accordingly, the annual discount rate of 60% was used.

The alternative power systems considered were: extension of the utility grid, diesel generator, photovoltaic system, biomass system, wind energy conversion system and hydro-electric generator. The main conclusion was that, at present capital costs, the diesel generator was marginally the best option, if a proper scheme of operation and maintenance could be established. For the given techno-economic scenario, biomass, small hydro-electric and diesel systems were better options than an extension of the grid by one kilometre. Photovoltaic systems had to decrease in cost to US$3 per KW to be as competitive as the others.

For the estimated needs and electricity requirements of the proposed typical rural village, the primary energy provisions should be about 2000 KWh per cubic metre of annual irradiation, four cubic metres of appropriate wastes plus 75 litres of warm water, a daily average of 7.5 hours with winds at speeds of 15 metres per second, and waterfalls with a product elevation by flow equal to 5.5. In the Mexican case, with the exception of solar energy, all energy resources requirements are above the national mean values and restrict the implementation of these systems.

Social-Cultural and Environmental Issues

Socio-cultural issues have been neglected in the past. Several projects (such as the implementation of solar cookers by concentration of sunlight) failed because only technical issues were addressed. An educational programme relayed to television sets powered by PV systems was seriously threatened by poor user training. Only in the case of firewood have socio-cultural issues been properly considered (SEMIP, 1988). The amount of firewood used depends on several factors: income level, number of inhabitants, access roads, educational level, weather and vegetation. The largest firewood consumption corresponds to cold climates, small communities and low income households.

In terms of energy demand, rural areas fall into three main categories. The first category is less dependent on firewood, which provides between 36% and 57% of the total energy consumed. Petrol accounts for more than 30%, while diesel and LPG account for 10% each. Electricity has a significant share – more than 4%. The use of kerosene is marginal. The second category is characterized by a greater dependence on firewood (60% to 75% of the total). LPG accounts for 9% to 15%, with a corresponding decrease in the use of petrol and diesel. Electricity accounts for between 2% and 3% and kerosene slightly less. The third category is typical of the less developed rural zones. Firewood accounts for more than 88% of the total. Petrol contributes 4%, LPG between 1% and 4%, electricity and kerosene between 1% and 2% each, and diesel even less.

In the rural areas, the primary concern is socio-economic development and no special consideration is given to environmental impact. Obviously, if there are alternative programmes with different ecological profiles, the one with the least adverse effect will be chosen. No official policies have been published on environmental issues and problems associated with energy production and use in rural areas.

Research and Development in Rural Energy Supplies

There are about 20 active research and development institutions ranging from universities through institutes of technology to national laboratories. The thrust and scope of current programmes is suggested below.

Solar energy

1 *Passive systems*: Research activities focus on the evaluation of new components in dwellings, numerical simulation of heating and cooling of premises, basic research into natural convection and elaboration of standards for official implementation.

2 *Solar thermal systems*: Research covers collectors (flat-plate, evacuated tubes and concentrators), cookstoves, large-size dryers, process heat and distillation, domestic and industrial refrigeration, water pumping, solar ponds and electric power generation.

3 *Photovoltaic systems:* Activities range from basic research to systems implementation. The main solar cells under study are made from silicon (amorphous, poly- and mono-crystalline), gallium arsenide, cadmium telluride and indium phosphide.

Biomass

1 Research activities concern the development of new types of biogas systems; improving the performance of biogas units of the Indian type; and designing large systems for industrial application.

2 Combustion research aimed at improving the performance of stoves.

3 Basic research projects in gasification.

Wind energy

Ongoing research activities include work on wind-generators, basic research and numerical simulation on wind-energy conversion systems, development of systems for installed capacities larger than 15 KW, and studies on their integration with the utility grid.

Hydro energy

For small waterfalls, the priority is the design and manufacture of electric power systems with an installed capacity of up to 40 KW and on the methodology to implement these systems in rural areas. Special efforts are also under way to assess the potential of each resource.

Work has also been done in rural energy planning, in particular the study of integrated systems: their techno-economic feasibility; their impact on specific social and economic aspects of rural communities; the required institutional arrangements; the information flows needed; and the integration of this sector with national goals and programmes.

Finally, it is important to mention the educational efforts carried out at different levels. There are programmes for training, extra-mural courses, B Sc degrees in energy engineering; one-year courses on solar design for specialists; M Sc degrees in energy engineering and solar energy (with solar-thermal energy and photovoltaics as options); and Ph D degrees on related fundamental energy topics.

Energy Investment and Pricing Policies

Energy is of paramount importance in all the economic sectors, regions and main macro-economic parameters. This area contributes about 5% of GNP, more than 50% of national income by exports, more than 30% of total government income and about 30% of total public investment.

The electricity sector has serious financial problems, with a large deficit. The average price of electricity is less than 50% of its average production cost. The tariffs are established according to different users, with larger subsidies for the agricultural consumers (in particular, for maize grinding, flour production and irrigation) and for domestic users, both rural and urban. The average price paid for electricity by the domestic sector is about 3 US cents per KWh, while tariffs for grinding and irrigation are about 2 US cents and for mid-level consumers perhaps 6 US cents. There is no structure relating the price to base or peak load. The local prices of hydrocarbon fuels are also subsidized; they correspond to an estimated cost of about US$6 per barrel of oil. There are especially low prices for LPG, which is used in both the rural and urban household sectors. There are no special policies on investment and pricing for NRSE. Renewables do not enjoy the level of subsidy that is extended to commercial fuels.

Action Proposals for the Promotion of NRSE for Rural Agricultural Development

With respect to energy planning, the following actions are recommended:

1. Establish the producer and the rural community as the fundamental element in the process of rural energy planning for integrated rural development;
2. Foster the utilization of new and renewable sources of energy for rural agricultural development;
3. Develop rural energy planning as an important tool for achieving integrated rural development;
4. Acknowledge the importance of energy in raising the productivity and enhancing the quality of life of rural communities;
5. Accompany any planning process with practical activities;
6. Investigate the rural energy planning process itself; in particular, establish organizational schemes and methodological instruments that are flexible and multi-directional;
7. Incorporate environmental considerations in the energy planning process;
8. Foster the education of human resources in planning and in extension;
9. Establish national programmes, with specific objectives and goals, for

supplying energy to needy rural communities.

Key recommendations on resource assessment include:

1 Identify methodologies for the evaluation of the potential of each energy resource, at regional and local levels;
2 Identify the minimum information needed for planning rural agricultural development;
3 Strengthen the capacity for data gathering;
4 Establish a data bank with the minimum necessary information;
5 Expand the resources data bank according to specific projects to be developed.

The priority in technology demonstration should be to identify mature technologies for integrated energy systems that can satisfy the social requirements of rural communities, and to initiate promising demonstration projects for the utilization of NRSE in integrated rural development. In addition, steps should be taken to implement technically and economically viable demonstration projects for increasing the productivity and enhancing the quality of life of selected rural communities.

The present approach to research and development does not need new themes so much as more resources for ongoing activities and the coordination of existing programmes. Finance should also be sought for the dissemination of information, particularly by NGOs.

It is also important to incorporate NRSE technologies into the existing investment schemes for commercial energies to ensure fair competition. Finally, a methodology for environmental risk analysis in energy projects should be developed, and policies designed to minimize adverse environmental impacts in the energy sector should be formulated and implemented.

References

Martinez, M. (1988a). 'On the electrification of rural Mexico'. *Solar & Wind Technology*, Vol. 5, No. 2, pp. 177–80.

——— (1988b). 'Energy diversification priorities for the Mexican electrical sector'. Vol. 13, No. 10, pp. 787–96.

SEMIP. (1984). 'Demanda de Energeticos Alternos', *Energeticos* (Mexico City), Vol. 1, No. 5 (March–April) pp. 23–30.

——— (1988) *Energia Rural en Mexico*. Government of Mexico, Mexico City.

VI THE SOVIET UNION AND EASTERN EUROPE

18 Applications of New and Renewable Sources of Energy in the Soviet Union and Eastern Europe

Eugenie V. Nadezhdin

The Soviet Union

The efforts of the Soviet Union to intensify agriculture and industrialize animal farming, together with the large-scale use of intensive technologies in the crop production and processing sectors of the nation's agro-industrial complex, have resulted in a considerably higher energy intensity of agricultural output and lower direct labour costs. Agricultural energy consumption has doubled, and the use of electricity has tripled, over the decade 1975–85. The total power output of the agricultural mechanized fleet and energy-generating units (522 million KW in 1984) greatly exceeds the total output of electrical power plants across the entire Soviet Union. Tractors account for 36% of that output, automobiles for 29%, combines for 13%, and electrical engines and units for 22%.

In 1985, agricultural production consumed about 10% of the total end-use of energy resources. The fuel and resource breakdown of the 111 million tons of oil equivalent (mtoe) consumed was as follows: solid fuel, 13 mtoe or 12%; petroleum products, 64 mtoe or 58%; gas, 14 mtoe or 12.5%; electrical power, 14 mtoe or 5%. In 1990, agriculture will consume 130–136 mtoe; by 2000, this will rise to 156–158 mtoe. The annual petroleum demand of the crop production sector constitutes 55 million tons or about a half of energy resources used in agriculture. At present, agriculture consumes more petroleum products than any other economic sector.

Over the next 25 years the USSR's agro-industrial complex will increase its energy consumption by 80%–100%, since projections show that a 1% increase in crop yields requires a 3%–4% increase in energy use. Since the dependence of agriculture, on fuel and energy consumption cannot be decreased, the Soviet Union has come up with a set of measures to make rural production and household energy use more efficient.

The key guideline for developing the national agro-industrial complex provides for the elaboration of resource-saving and waste-free technologies, implying a large-scale use of non-conventional sources of energy and secondary energy resources. The geographically varied agriculture of the Soviet Union is characterized by a large number of users dispersed over a vast territory,

227

the relatively low power demand of many types of production equipment, and numerous rural installations with a decentralized power supply. Therefore, agriculture is the major large-scale user of new and renewable sources of energy (NRSE), particularly in remote areas with a low load density (from 0.1 to 1.8 KW per square kilometre) where existing equipment allows for considerable efficiency through liquid fuel substitution.

The application of new and renewable sources of energy help save organic fuels and – yet more important – improve work and living conditions. Moreover, they have no adverse effects on nature and facilitate the development of remote areas (such as deserts, the extreme north, islands, mountain regions, the tundra, steppes and forest steppes). With the nation's overall environmental degradation, stronger and more organized environmentalist movements, stiffer hygiene rules and safety regulations, and as the majority of the constituent republics strive to make the most of their local energy resources, NRSE applications are becoming more attractive.

Solar energy

The USSR has 335 million hectares of rural land in which climatic conditions allow for solar power applications, with 2000–3000 sunlit hours per year and a total annual solar radiation level of 1100–1850 KWh per square mile. Rural areas favourable for solar power use are inhabited by some 52 million people, producing over 60% of the gross agricultural output and containing virtually all seasonal pastures.

The Soviet government is now testing over 200 decentralized solar power plants based on silicon photovoltaic modules, intended for use in various economic sectors (water elevators, sea and river buoys, radio and TV broadcasting stations, navigational equipment, cathode protection of gas pipelines). For over a decade, photovoltaic systems have demonstrated their capacity for sustained service without degraded output parameters in all the climatic zones. Besides, they are ecologically clean and are simple and convenient to maintain with very low manpower requirements. Other features include the low metal content of their structures and the transportability of low output systems.

In the remote areas of the USSR, where fuel supplies are scarce and difficult, photovoltaic systems are already substituting for petrol-fuelled electricity-generating equipment in some agricultural uses. Such plants will be most widely used in water pumping, irrigation and supplying electric power to isolated users in pasture farming and fruit production. The Soviet-made FEVU-1-20 photovoltaic-powered water pump with a capacity of one cubic metre per hour from a depth of 15 metres makes it possible to save up to 1.8 tons of liquid fuel a year and to ensure an annual cost efficiency level of about 1,200 roubles in pasture farming.

The use of photovoltaic systems to supply electrical power for the production and household needs of shepherd teams will reduce liquid fuel consumption considerably and improve work and living conditions for farmers.

Typically, the users of photovoltaic systems for decentralized power generating will be sparsely populated areas with a low load density (0.1–0.8 KW per square kilometre) but a total livestock population of over 120 million sheep, goats, camels, cattle and horses – such as plains, mountain regions, deserts, semi-deserts, steppes and forest-steppes.

Currently, over 200 million hectares or 65% of all grazing land in the Soviet Union consists of pastures supplied with water from 122,000 man-made sources: pit wells account for 54% of this number, drilled wells for 22.5%, ponds for 22%, and springs for the remaining 1.5%. Photovoltaic water pumps and generating units will be used to secure dependable water supplies and to improve the living standards of shepherd teams. The total generating capacity of photovoltaic power plants to be used in agriculture by the year 2000 is estimated at 500 MW. To make this possible, the state is now concentrating on reducing the unit cost of commercially produced solar cells and initiating mass production of photovoltaic system packages, including solar cells, batteries, electrical energy converters and automatic control units.

Experts estimate that Soviet agriculture uses about 200 million hectocalories per year for thermal processes. Because users are scattered across a large territory, thermal power is generated by low capacity plants burning chiefly light petroleum fuels. Thermal drying of grain, grass, fruit, vegetables, cotton and other produce requires over 75 hectocalories a year. The existing technologies burn from 230 to 300 kg of petroleum products, depending on weather conditions, per ton of dry grass to be processed into grass meal. With an annual grass meal output of 7.5 million tons, the liquid fuel rate is about two million tons.

The use of solar energy for water, space and air heating has the following advantages:

- There are many industrial and household applications at a typical outlet temperature ranging from plus 30°C to plus 65°C, depending on the intensity of solar radiation and the flow rate of the heat-transfer agent;
- Simple design of low temperature solar collectors and their operational accessibility for the personnel of agriculture installations;
- Relatively high coefficient of energy conversion in flat plate collectors, ranging from 0.2 to 0.6.

Water and air heating and heating for agricultural processes are the most feasible and efficient applications of solar energy. As a rule, agriculture uses low temperature heat supplied by solar collectors without concentrates of solar collectors or servo systems. The Soviet Union has developed a number of liquid and air flat-plate collectors based on the use of forged and welded steel components, glass, aluminium, plastic, polymeric films and heat pipes. Liquid heat-transfer collectors are used in solar systems in piggeries, for water heating at summer grounds for horned cattle, in field camps, in solar heat showers, and in household water and space heating systems. Solar air collectors are used for the completion of hay drying as well as for drying products such as grain, grapes, tobacco, melons, vegetables, raw cotton and skins.

The USSR has developed a number of solar energy systems which are now used in agriculture, such as:

- Solar energy units for water heating at cattle summer grounds and mobile milking stations. They have a collector surface of 30 square metres. By 1990, such units will be used at 800 installations.
- Rural household systems for water and space heating and for cooling, with a collector surface of 70 square metres. By 1990, these units will have been installed in 400 houses.
- Solar energy water desalination units with an active surface of 200 square metres, producing 4–5 cubic metres of sweet water daily. Twelve such units are expected to become operational in 1990.
- Photovoltaic electricity and heat supply solar systems for piggeries, with a collector surface of 80 square metres, to be installed on 210 farms.
- Solar energy dryers for grass and hay, with a collector surface of up to 2000 square metres, by 1990.
- Solar energy dryers for fruit, grapes, melons and vegetables, with a collector surface of 120–1000 square metres each, are expected to be used in ten installations by 1990.
- Solar greenhouses with a subsoil heat storage system. By late 1990, their total production space will reach 2.1 hectares.
- Decentralized solar energy systems for sheep-breeding farms in deserts, each with a capacity of 800–1000 sheep: 12 will be installed by late 1990.

Wind Energy

The wind energy sector in the USSR has been developing to serve both decentralized and integrated power networks. Decentralized wind power use is based largely on wind machines with an output range of 0.1–100 KW, intended for independent energy supply. Their applications include water supply, irrigation, water desalination, electrical energy and heat generation. The principal users are agriculture and water affairs (pasture farms, drinking places, irrigation systems, deer-raising farms, fisheries, shepherd camps) as well as mountain and island villages not connected to the central energy network. There are decentralized users in some other economic sectors as well. Integrated wind power use involves wind machines with a capacity of more than 100 KW per unit and provides for interconnected electricity generation in areas with high constant wind speeds in order to save organic fuels.

The basic challenge of decentralized wind energy applications consists in mass producing and packaging reliable wind machines for a wide range of rural users. Two major trends have emerged in the agricultural context. In the first, machines delivering low mechanical and electrical output (up to 5 KW) supply water and electricity to shepherds and deer-breeders. In the second, machines delivering from 10KW to 100 KW supply electrical power to settlements with a population range of 50–1000 inhabitants, located in areas with an annual average wind speed of more than five metres per second.

Pasture lands adjacent to the Caspian Sea, along the Volga River and in the Kazakh republic have been earmarked for the most extensive utilization of wind energy. Over a quarter of all watering sites there are to be equipped with wind-powered water pumps.

The Soviet Union has launched a full-scale production of wind machines with an output range of 1–4 KW and has developed 16 KW wind power units for the decentralized electricity supply of low capacity users. At present, 30 KW, 100 KW, 200–300 KW and 1 MW wind generators are at various stages of development. Today, Soviet agriculture employs over 4000 wind machines with an output range of 1–4 KW. The government programme for NRSE development has a Scheme for Rural Wind Machine Development and Deployment which determines the demand for wind machines designed for pasture water supply and the range of wind machines intended for use in various regions of the nation. By the year 2000, 30,000 wind-powered water pumps will have been made to meet the agricultural demand for such units.

Bio-energy sector

The environmental degradation resulting from large-scale animal and poultry production and the need to manage ever larger amounts of urban sewage and domestic solid waste have brought into focus the recovery problem. In this context, waste-processing bio-energy units have been developed, allowing for a cleaner environment and the production of gaseous and liquid fuels as well as organic and mineral fertilizers. In the USSR, the principal sources of organic waste for such treatment are agriculture (360 million tons, of which 230 million tons is from animal farming and the rest from crop production), forestry and the timber industry (70 million tons), and urban solid and liquid waste (70 million tons). Existing techniques for processing agricultural waste may produce up to 120 billion cubic metres or 100 million toe. However, realistic projections for the coming 15–20 years place annual biogas output at 15–18 billion cubic metres: large animal and poultry farms and cities requiring waste management are the principal production sites.

The annual petroleum consumption of Soviet agriculture is estimated at 60 million tons, including 15 tons used as a boiler-heating fuel. The USSR's high potential for the production of gaseous fuels through bio-conversion is expected to meet the agricultural demand for heat-generating fuels. Twelve pilot commercial bio-energy plants based on the processing of animal and poultry farm waste include the following:

- a unit with an annual capacity range of 2.5–3 million cubic metres of biogas installed at a 24,000-hog farm, the Ogre state-run farm in Latvia;
- a unit with an annual capacity range of 4–4.5 million cubic metres of biogas at an inter-farm pork production complex with 54,000 head of livestock in Parnu, Estonia;
- a unit with an annual capacity range of 8–9 million cubic metres of biogas at a pork production complex (108,000 head of livestock) and a unit with

an annual capacity of 8 million cubic metres of biogas at an animal production complex (10,000 head of livestock) on a state-run farm in Dnepropetrovsk Province named after the 60th anniversary of the Soviet Ukraine.

The Soviet Union is seeking to launch mass production of various bio-energy units and is carrying out a set of research and development programmes to make sophisticated models. In 1990, biomass energy will account for up to 1,672,000 toe, including 290,000 toe of biogas. It has been projected that by the year 2000 the large-scale use of bio-energy units based on waste processing will have created an additional six million toe worth of primary fuel.

Geothermal energy

The USSR's prospected geothermal water resources (temperature range 40–200°C, mineralization up to 50 grams per litre, occuring at a depth of up to 3,500 metres) bring forth about 20 million cubic metres of water daily, equalling – in energy terms – 40–45 million toe a year. Today, approximately 70 million cubic metres or 0.6 million toe are available annually.

So far, the USSR has been using the geothermal waters of Daghestan, Georgia, the Krasnodar and Stavropol regions, the Chechono-Ingush republic and the Kamchatka peninsula. Geothermally heated greenhouses in the Soviet Union have a total space of 100 hectares. The Plodovosch intersectoral enterprise in the Krasnodar region has a certain expertise in integrated geothermal energy applications, having saved 57,320 toe, worth 2 million roubles, through the use of geothermal waters. Geothermal energy is also used in conventional hot-water, warm-air or combined heating systems for animal production farms and residential space in Daghestan, the Krasnodar region and the Kamchatka. A valveless chute system with a long service life, for heating the protected soil for higher vegetable yields, has come into operation in the Ochamcharsky area in the Abkhazian republic.

Geothermal applications in agriculture call for totally new technologies for mineralized water in order to achieve an integrated use of its heat and mineral components for higher crop yields, to protect the equipment from corrosion, and to preclude pollution of the environment. By the year 2000, thermal water output will have reached 320 million cubic metres a year. Thermal water will be made available for use largely through a system that will return spent water to the stratum and ensure the subsoil circulation.

Hydro-power

In the USSR, the application of micro-hydro plants (with output ratings of 100–30,000 KW) is regarded as feasible and cost-efficient for the purpose of loss-free energy supply of small installations on mountain pastures and farms, in forests and on agricultural construction sites, among other potential sites. There are provisional estimates of the small-scale hydro-electric potential of selected regions in the Soviet Union. In particular, the hydro-electric potential of 159 Kazakh rivers is rated at 44.7 billion KWh per year, and that of Kirghiz small rivers at 9 billion KWh per year. Mass production of portable pipe micro-hydros ranging in output from 0.5 to 10 KW has begun, while 10–100KW micro-hydros are being developed.

A micro-hydro system consists of a hydro-power generating unit, a pressure pipe and a connecting cable. It is to be used at a flow drop of two metres and above. The cost range of electrical energy is 3–20 kopeks per KWh, depending on the plant output and the length of operational period. From 1946 to 1952, the construction of low output hydro-electric systems was in full swing and over 6000 of them, with a total output of 500 MW, were built in rural areas over five years. Subsequently, with the development of the energy system, most of them were removed from service or dismantled.

The environmental problems caused by large output hydro-electric systems have led to the rediscovery of the above technologies. A number of standard automated mini-hydro designs with unified building units have been developed in the Soviet Union. Under the national programme for the rehabilitation and construction of small-scale hydro-electric systems, their total output will have reached 3200 MW by the year 2000.

Bulgaria

So far, the development of NRSE in Bulgaria amounts to no more than a few applications of solar and geothermal energy. In the coming 20 years, the share of non-conventional sources of energy in total power consumption will be relatively small. They will account for 600,000 toe in 2010 and for 1.5 million toe in 2020.

In the projected period, solar energy will be used for both low-grade heat and electricity generation. At the present stage, however, only the transformation of solar energy into heat is economically and technologically feasible on a large scale. Water and space heating at residential, industrial and agricultural sites seem to be the principal applications prior to 2010. By this date, various types of solar energy collectors will be in operation, with a total surface of six million square metres; the target for 2020 is over 12 million square metres. These units will save 340,000 toe by 2010, and 600,000–700,000 toe by 2020.

The construction of large solar electric plants is a prospective goal. Experiments in solar electricity generation will be carried out on small pilot plants. A 50 MW solar power plant for commercial use is planned for 2010–2015, and a 100 MW model for 2020. Work to develop and optimize photovoltaic cells is planned for the period prior to 2000 and beyond.

Geothermal resources in Bulgaria have low thermodynamic properties. Low-potential thermal waters with a temperature range of 20°C–100°C prevail, allowing only for heating and hot water supply applications of geothermal energy. The exploitation of the prospected anomalous deposits in the country for electricity generation is not feasible technologically or economically. Eighteen sources of geothermal water are used for greenhouse and household heating applications.

In general, Bulgaria has a low wind energy potential, with an annual average wind speed of less than three metres per second, and wind power cannot make a serious contribution to the country's total energy balance. The existing wind power capability and conditions, however, fully meet the technological and economic demand of a low-capacity wind energy sector.

Biomass applications are currently at the embryonic stage of development. The year 2000 may see the deployment of several pilot biogas recovery stations based on the use of organic animal and poultry farm waste and intended for the supply of energy to large agricultural enterprises and other decentralized users. In future, the development of this sector will be promoted.

Hungary

Non-conventional renewable sources of energy are the only resources other than coal allowing for the expansion of national fuel and power output. The experience of recent years indicates a potential for the development of many renewable sources of energy. According to national projections, in 2010 the NRSE share of total energy will be about 1.2–1.4 mtoe.

Solar power may be used for low-grade heat before the year 2000 and for electricity generation thereafter. By 2010, Hungary is expected to have solar energy collectors with a total surface of 15–18 million square metres. Solar absorption refrigeration may be expected by 2000, first for technological purposes (chiefly in rural areas) and subsequently for residential air conditioning. Large-scale photovoltaic electricity generation is not envisaged prior to 2000. However, direct conversion of solar energy into electricity is planned for decentralized users in intensive solar radiation areas.

Heating applications of geothermal energy are relatively extensive. In the projected period, geothermal energy will account for 1% of the total heat supply. Electricity generating applications of geothermal water are not planned before 2000 because of its low temperature and high mineralization, as well as inadequate technology in that sector.

Hungary has a low wind energy potential. The development of powerful wind machines is not feasible at this stage, though 4 KW wind machines will be developed before 2000 for rural use and to supply energy to low-capacity users outside the national grid. Prior to 2010 and beyond, wind power applications will remain local in scope.

Biomass programmes will aim at recovering energy from animal and crop waste, the production of combustible gas through urban sewage treatment, and the processing of solid domestic waste for the residential and administrative heat supply. The national experience shows a great potential for the development of this sector. Priority attention is therefore being given to the construction of biomass energy recovery systems, mainly based on agricultural waste processing. Programmes of waste treatment, including garbage collection, transportation and incineration, are under way.

Poland

According to national estimates, the use of renewable sources of energy before 2010 will be negligible because of high costs and lack of material. Beyond 2010, however, their intensive development may get under way, with such sources accounting for about 5% of the national energy demand.

Romania

In Romania, solar power is used in residential, municipal and administrative contexts for water and space heating, refrigeration and air-conditioning; the production of hot air, water and steam for commercial applications; the powering of pumps; and electricity generation based on the thermodynamic cycle, in both industrial and agricultural sectors, through direct conversion into electrical energy. The total surface area of solar collectors installed has reached 800,000 square metres. The nation's positive experience of solar heaters means that solar energy applications will be promoted further.

The wind energy sector is regarded as having great potential, with an annual average wind speed of over six miles per second and a total blowing time of 2500 hours per year. Applications include the following: agricultural irrigation and drainage, production of electrical and mechanical output for decentralized users, and electricity generation for the national energy system. In 1988, over 400 wind machines, each of 100 KW capacity, were in decentralized or integrated operation.

Geothermal energy applications include water and space heating and refrigeration in residential and utility contexts, as well as commercial and technological functions that provide for the extraction of all usable components.

Urban and industrial waste will be used to provide residential and commercial heat after the extraction of scrap metals and other secondary materials, and for the recovery of combustible gas intended for heating purposes. Animal and crop production waste will be utilized to recover biogas for use in local electrical power plants and engines of internal combustion, as well as in methanol, synthetic fibre and rubber production. In 1988, there were 97 large biomass energy recovery systems based on animal production waste. In the cities, there are 55 municipal sewage energy recovery systems with reactor capacity ratings of 1500, 3000, 4000 and 5050 cubic metres; 25 additional units of that type are under construction. In the food processing industry, there are three bio-energy units and 35 more are under construction. Individual plants with reactor capacity ratings of 5, 10, 25 and 50 cubic metres are common, totalling 7000. In 1989, 800 biomass energy recovery systems came into operation in the agricultural sector alone. Heat pumps will be used widely for water and space heating.

Renewable sources of energy now substitute for 500,000 tons worth of organic fuels or 0.5% of the total energy demand. The target for 2010 is 4–5%.

Czechoslovakia

Of all non-conventional renewable sources of energy, only wood residues and urban solid waste are in modest use in Czechoslovakia. In future, their applications will be expanded. Solar and geothermal energy, biogas and heat pumping applications are at an experimental stage.

Solar energy collectors will be used for water heating and drying agricultural produce. There are plans to sophisticate solar energy systems and their components, and to conduct fundamental research into semiconductor materials and photovoltaic converters. The question of how to reduce heating needs by introducing better building designs will be studied.

Geothermal energy applications will include water and space heating and water heating for industrial purposes. Heat exchangers and corrosion-free materials will be developed and the question of how to dispose of the used geothermal water will be considered. Research into geothermal energy harnessing is yet to begin. Possible use of great depth heat (up to 3000–6000 metres) is under survey. Given the high cost of sinking such wells, this technique has been made the subject of a feasibility study. In the projected period, there will be no geothermal energy applications for electricity generation.

Biomass, in the form of agricultural and other organic waste, will be digested anaerobically with the release of biogas for various applications. An important goal is to develop the prototypes of the necessary equipment for producing biogas and to launch its mass production.

Wind energy potential is relatively low and cannot contribute significantly to the total energy balance of the country. At present, there are no plans for manufacturing wind machines. By the year 2000, mass production of wind machines with an output range of 10–30 KW may begin and appropriate windmills may well be imported.

CONCLUSION:
Main Report, Policy Conclusions and Recommendations for Future Action

I. Background

1. The United Nations Conference on New and Renewable Sources of Energy was held at Nairobi in August 1981. It adopted the Nairobi Programme of Action for the Development and Utilization of New and Renewable Sources of Energy,[1] with the main objective of promoting concerted action for the development and utilization of new and renewable sources of energy to help meet future energy requirements, especially in developing countries.

2. The Conference identified five broad policy areas for concerted action, with the support of the international community according to national plans and priorities: energy assessment and planning; research, development and demonstration; transfer, adaptation and application of mature technologies; information flows; and education and training.[2]

3. In resolution 36/193, section I, the General Assembly endorsed the Nairobi Programme of Action. By resolution 37/250, section II, the Assembly decided to establish an intergovernmental Committee on the Development and Utilization of New and Renewable Sources of Energy and charged it with responsibility for guiding and monitoring the implementation of the Nairobi Programme of Action. The Committee has held four sessions.

4. At its fourth session, in March 1988, the Committee decided on three themes for detailed consideration at its fifth session, in 1990, one of which related to the contribution of new and renewable sources of energy to integrated rural development.[3] The Committee requested the Secretary-General to prepare a report for consideration by the Committee at its fifth session, based on an in-depth study of the current achievements of States regarding this theme. The Committee invited interested States and organizations to convene technical and scientific meetings related to the theme that would contribute to its in-depth examination.

5. In implementation of the Committee's decision, the United Nations Group of Experts on the Role of New and Renewable Sources of Energy in Integrated Rural Development was convened at Stockholm in January 1990. The meeting of the Group was sponsored by the Swedish Agency for Research Co-operation with Developing Countries (SAREC) and organized in co-operation with the Department of International Economic and Social Affairs of the United Nations Secretariat and the Food and Agriculture Organization of the United Nations (FAO).

6. The following topics were discussed:

237

   (a) Integrated rural development:
      (i)   Definition and goals of integrated rural development;
      (ii) Energy for integrated rural development;
   (b) Energy supply and demand in rural areas:
      (i)   Demand considerations (household, agriculture, rural industry, transport, economic, social, climate, others);
      (ii)   Assessment of energy needs of rural and agricultural activities;
      (iii) Assessment of energy needs for cottage activities, village enterprises and rural industries;
      (iv) Supply considerations (traditional, conventional, new and renewable);
   (c) Energy options and considerations for rural and agricultural development:
      (i)   Technological options: efficient energy use; fuelwood; conventional sources; new and renewable sources;
      (ii)   Socio-economic considerations: energy consumption, distribution and quality of life; socio-cultural issues; participation in the formulation and implementation of plans; women's role in rural development and rural energy development;
      (iii) Environmental issues and impact: environmental problems associated with energy production and use in rural areas; policies and measures designed to minimize adverse environmental impacts of rural energy development programmes;
   (d) Energy investments and pricing policies:
      Energy investment requirements and methods of financing;
      Energy pricing for integrated rural development;
      Role of the local private and public sectors;
      Role of multilateral and bilateral assistance programmes;
   (e) Action to promote renewable energy sources for rural and agricultural development:
      Energy assessment and planning (integration of rural and agricultural energy needs into national energy, rural and agricultural development plans and programmes);
      Technological development (identification of priority research, development and demonstration activities in the light of the present and future international energy scene);
      Institutional aspects;
      Investment aspects;
      Information flows;
      Environmental issues;
   (f) Country or regional experiences.
7. Technical papers were presented by experts from both developed and developing countries, as well as from academic institutions and United Nations bodies.[4]
8. The highlights of the discussions and conclusions of the meeting as agreed to by all the experts participating are set out below (for the list of participants, see the appendix to the present report).

II. Opening Statements

9. In welcoming the participants, the Director-General of SAREC said that allocations

of 47 million Swedish kronor in energy research over the past 15 years had been devoted to renewable energy sources and technologies as well as energy policy and planning. The focus of this support had been Africa south of the Sahara. The latest initiative was the support given to the African Energy Policy Research Network.

10. In opening the meeting, the Under-Secretary of State, Ministry of Foreign Affairs of Sweden, said that in the decade that had elapsed since the adoption of the Nairobi Programme of Action not much progress had been made in the development and utilization of new and renewable sources of energy. In the past few years, however, there had been increasing awareness of the interrelationships of development issues, particularly with regard to poverty in developing countries, energy development and the global environment. At the same time, there was increasing realization that an integrated approach was required in efforts to arrive at solutions of complex problems with global dimensions.

11. He said that the beginning of the 1990s had been accompanied by new hopes for world peace, with prospects for military cutbacks that could result in a sizeable 'peace dividend', thus freeing considerable resources, part of which should be directed towards economic and social development in developing countries.

12. He noted the greatly improved role of the United Nations in political aspects and called for the strengthening of the Organization in the economic and social fields.

13. The Assistant Secretary-General for International Economic and Social Affairs of the United Nations Secretariat also made a statement as summarised in the Preface.

III. Energy Consumption and Supply

14. At the beginning of the last decade of the twentieth century, energy consumption in the rural areas of developing countries continues to be dominated by traditional sources, especially biomass. Consumption of fuelwood has been increasing rapidly because of fast population growth, which has sometimes resulted in the clearing of forests for more food, thus reducing wood supplies. Regional climate change and desertification have compounded the problem.

15. While oil consumption has been limited in the rural areas of the developing countries, higher prices since the early 1970s have contributed to the energy and economic crises, especially if account is taken of higher costs of other agricultural inputs such as fertilizers and pesticides. The more recent economic crisis of deep indebtedness has also accentuated poverty in the developing countries, including rural areas, with consequent repercussions on their energy situation.

16. In these circumstances, biomass fuels are being consumed faster than they are being replenished, foreboding even more serious problems in the future. Efforts to alleviate this situation have concentrated on a variety of measures to promote more efficient use of the limited supply of available energy resources, particularly with regard to household appliances and equipment for irrigation and general farming. For a variety of reasons, including the initial cost and limited social acceptability, experience with technically efficient cook stoves has been disappointing in many developing countries. There have been successes in a few developing countries, however, notably China and India. Similarly, reforestation programmes have generally failed to arrest, let alone reverse, the deteriorating situation.

17. Pressure on the rural biomass supply is further aggravated by the increasing demand

of urban residents for fuelwood. Because of this demand, deforestation has often been more widespread near growing urban centres.

18. Efforts to develop local commercial energy supplies, such as small coal mines and mini hydro plants, have been successful in a few countries with appropriate natural resources and social organizations for the provision of the necessary capital, technology and trained manpower. Small oil and gas fields have, in some cases, made similar contributions. For the majority of the developing countries, however, higher oil import costs have been translated into higher prices for petroleum products, such as kerosene, which are widely used in rural areas. More recent measures to cut or eliminate subsidies for petroleum products have aggravated the situation.

19. The deteriorating position of traditional as well as conventional supplies has led to increasing attention being given to other technologies, such as solar cells and windmills, which promise decentralized and therefore more appropriate rural energy. However, despite significant technological advances with consequent reductions in cost, their application has been experimental and quite limited. High capital requirements will have to be cut substantially before widespread use can be expected.

20. Governments and development agencies have been concerned with the deteriorating environmental conditions related to rural energy supplies, especially as they are expanded in order to promote rural economic development. This concern has been heightened by the potential for global climate change due to the increase of the so-called greenhouse gases, from increased burning of fossil fuels, deforestation and so forth. This concern may lead to increased efforts aimed at the more efficient utilization and increased supply of appropriate rural energy.

21. The task will be enormous since it is estimated that of a total population of 3.6 billion (1985) in the developing world, 60 per cent or 2.2 billion have no access to electricity.

22. In analysing the rural energy situation, it is important to bear in mind that rural areas in the developing countries are highly heterogeneous. Rural people live and work in diverse and widely varying ecological and social settings even within a single country. The rural energy patterns and changes are affected by diverse cultural, social, political and economic contexts. Within each rural community, there will often be diverse or even divergent interests.

23. With a few exceptions (e.g., China), conventional energy sources such as coal, oil and gas are generally not locally available in the rural areas of the developing countries. These areas have also generally not been adequately explored for such resources. The cost of imports are high especially in relation to the very low incomes of rural people. Rural electrification programmes have had limited success because of high costs for interconnections and high capital requirements and operating costs of independent electricity supply systems (e.g., diesel power).

24. Apart from hydraulic energy, which, however, is often classified as a conventional energy source, biomass constitutes the most important renewable energy source. Biomass resources include organic wastes, natural forests and energy crops.

25. Considerable advances have been made in technologies for the development of new and renewable sources of energy and they are now mature enough to be applied in rural areas. These technologies include photovoltaic and wind systems and a

variety of new technologies which convert biomass into secondary energy forms and more efficient energy use through such devices as cookstoves.

26. Energy resource assessments are of particular importance in rural areas for proper planning. In assessing energy sources in rural areas, consideration should be given to all sources, conventional as well as new and renewable. Assessment surveys of rural energy supplies have, however, met with a variety of difficulties, including, in the case of biomass, lack of standardized methodologies and trained personnel as well as unsatisfactory participation of rural energy consumers who often possess the necessary information. Solar and wind energy assessment problems involve information gaps, access and availability of monitoring equipment.

27. There is a need to adequately address the problems of assessment and measurement. Optimal use should be made of the information and know-how normally available within national meteorological services and other relevant institutions. At the same time, an appropriate balance is required between the need for accuracy and comprehensiveness in the collected data and the imperative for action.

28. Knowledge of existing natural forest resources and their productivity under management for sustained yield is generally poor in developing countries. Methods for their management for sustained yield exist in only a few cases. A similar situation applies to the possible production of artificially generated (planted or sown) forest stands, for which there is, to some extent, some knowledge in medium to high productive areas but little information in the low productive, semi-arid areas.

29. Rural energy consumption has been dominated by the household sector and rural energy surveys have tended to ignore other important sectors such as agriculture, local industry and transportation. Many of the surveys undertaken have covered specific geographical areas and time periods, with the result that extrapolations to cover the whole country or forecasts for future demand are often misleading.

30. In order to evaluate rural energy needs properly, it would be necessary to improve survey techniques to include detailed end-use information, which requires the participation of consumers. In this context, energy analysis should also focus on changes that take place over time because of important shifts in patterns of both rural energy requirements and supplies, particularly during periods of abrupt economic change.

IV. Technological Options

31. Over the past two decades, numerous technical options for the generation and distribution of energy for agricultural and rural development have been developed and field tested in a large number of developing countries. The results of many such initiatives have often been below expectations, one of the main reasons being the unexpected complexity of developing, selecting and implementing appropriate options that adequately address the rural energy question.

32. The scarcity and difficulty of obtaining information on the rural energy sector constitute important constraints in the selection and diffusion of appropriate technological options. Much of the available information is geared to the needs of decision makers but not to personnel in the field. Past attempts to collect data on rural energy have often been static in nature and content: the data collected provided

a snapshot of the energy situation but were not able to capture the dynamic and fluid nature of rural energy. Part of the problem is that those active in the field belong to many different disciplines or do not publish or otherwise make available information on their work.

33. Past attempts at addressing the rural energy question tended to focus on specific technologies for generating energy, for example, a micro-hydro plant or a biogas plant. As a result, current understanding of how stand-alone energy technologies perform is not matched by an adequate appreciation of the institutional environment that is necessary for the successful introduction of rural energy technologies.

34. It is necessary to adequately address basic needs in rural areas. In particular, special effort should be directed towards enhancing equity in these areas. The introduction of rural energy technologies is not in itself sufficient to address the question of equity. In certain cases, rural energy technologies may widen income gaps instead of narrowing them.

35. Of increasing concern at the level of research and development is also the gap between developing and developed countries, which is large and growing. Of critical importance in the development and wide-scale dissemination of rural energy technologies is the need to address the requirements of users and ensure their full participation. In this respect, rural energy technologies are no different from the more conventional technologies. In both cases, user needs are paramount and user participation is an essential component of technology development. User needs and participation are now prerequisites for the successful implementation of rural energy technologies. It is important to encourage efficient energy use and local manufacture of such technologies. These questions are discussed below.

Efficient energy use

36. Energy conservation has several intrinsic advantages. First, it does not entail the high investment and costly financial outlay of exploration and energy production. Secondly, it is generally not equipment or machine intensive. Energy conservation is, however, information intensive. It requires an in-depth understanding of current energy use patterns in order to identify the most cost-effective and promising conservation opportunities. It should be noted that the choice of certain construction materials could lead to savings in energy, as could the appropriate design of rural dwellings. The application of conservation technologies has, however, had limited results.

Fuelwood

37. An estimated 2 billion people, many of whom reside in rural areas, depend on fuelwood to meet their cooking and space heating needs. Other rural uses of fuelwood include charcoal production, post-harvest crop processing (e.g., tea drying and curing of tobacco) and brick manufacture. Fuelwood technologies that have been developed to date can be subdivided into three categories: production and supply, conversion and end-use. The research and development work in these categories has focused more on enhancing the efficiency of the three processes mentioned above than on the systematic development of innovations.

Conventional sources

38. Conventional energy sources for rural development include large-scale hydropower, coal and petroleum products such as diesel and kerosene. Being relatively better established, conventional energy technologies do not suffer as much from the shortage of trained manpower for installation, operation and maintenance of associated equipment and the lack of infrastructure. However, conventional energy technologies are heavily dependent on external inputs either in the form of fuel (petroleum) or machinery or spare parts. As a result, these technologies require access to adequate imports. With most of the developing countries facing chronic shortages of foreign exchange, the continuity of service for rural areas by means of conventional energy technologies cannot always be assured.

New and renewable energy sources

39. By the early 1980s, a number of technologies to develop new and renewable sources of energy had demonstrated an unexpected level of success in addressing energy problems faced by agriculture and development initiatives in rural areas. In particular, the following technologies have shown a promising level of performance in rural areas: (i) small hydro plants for shaft power and electricity generation, (ii) wind pumps for water lifting, (iii) biogas plants for cooking and lighting, (iv) photovoltaic units for lighting and refrigeration, (v) solar thermal energy and (vi) improved stoves.

Contribution of agricultural residues

40. Agricultural residues are divided into two broad categories: (i) crop residues including woody residues, crop straws, green crop residues and crop processing residues and (ii) animal residues such as cow dung and poultry and pig manure.

41. Large quantities of residues are produced in the developing countries. The actual quantity produced depends on agricultural practice. The use of the residues depends on bulk and density as well as the cost of the logistics and collection. The main consuming sectors in rural areas are households, agriculture and industry. The extent to which each sector uses agricultural products depends on many factors, including; (i) the agricultural mix - some crops generate residues low in energy value; (ii) agricultural practices – in some countries these involve clearing large areas of forest or woodlands for farming; (iii) the scarcity of other fuels - residues tend to be substituted for wood fuels; (iv) the energy demand pattern - this is influenced by the level of economic development and geography; and (v) competing demands – in most countries residues are used for purposes other than fuel (as fertilizers, for example).

42. It is difficult to estimate the demand for residues in developing countries. First, not enough is known of the nature and patterns of energy demand in many countries. Secondly, the bulk of the energy sources are considered 'non-commercial'; hence data on them are not readily available. There are also major differences in the level of residue use from region to region.

43. It is possible, however, to identify the activities in each sector of the economy for which residues could be used as an energy source. For example, (i) fuel in rural industries for heating, cooking, wood or metal working, forging, smelting, brick-

making, mineral-processing and agro-industry; (ii) fuel in agriculture for planting, pumping, harvesting, drying, parboiling and milling; (iii) fuel in the household sector. For those countries surveyed, the supply of agricultural residues has been found plentiful. Some residues can be converted to appropriate forms, and thus facilitate demand and supply matching. There are, however, constraints to the development and widespread use of agricultural wastes including (i) cost of conversion and end-use technology; (ii) non-availability of suitable technologies; (iii) lack of information on the resource base and socio-cultural inhibitions of the population with regard to some applications; (iv) lack of convenient collection techniques and excessive transportation distances to processing points.

44. A wide range of technologies for particular end-uses in conversion processes are available. The main problems relate to the availability of skills to operate and maintain the hardware and the cost of technology.

45. It would be useful to develop a uniform methodology for assessing the supply potential of agricultural wastes, taking into consideration the issue of accessibility of non-farm residues. In this context, it must be borne in mind that the expected level of accuracy of data depends on the target group envisaged - including policy makers, planners or field project officers.

46. Economic feasibility studies of the various options for the conversion or utilization of agricultural residues are necessary. Technologies best suited for application of agricultural residues should be promoted, through demonstration, provision of credit facilities and extension services. Furthermore, local capabilities for the manufacture of suitable technologies should be promoted and developed.

V. Social, Cultural and Political Aspects

47. The lack of progress in the development and utilization of new and renewable sources of energy in rural areas may in large part be attributed to inadequate knowledge of, or attention being given to, the socio-economic condition of rural people and their political and social organizations and structures.

48. The supply of energy can be a powerful mechanism for change in rural areas; it can make human energy more efficient, thus helping to alleviate poverty. To realize this goal through supplying energy, one must be fully aware of the social, economic and political realities of the lives of rural people. Energy technologies should not reinforce the gap between the haves and the have nots, either within the household or between socio-economic groups. It is most important to recognize the political context in which a change in energy use is to be introduced and how that change can be affected by national, local and household decisions.

49. Some of the improved stove programmes provide examples of failures resulting from lack of attention to the above-mentioned issues. A woman's time is of the utmost value. Women spend more time in agricultural and household activities than do men. Fuelwood collection, cooking and food processing can take an average of four hours a day. If the 'improved' stove demands more wood chopping or is not appropriate for the type of cooking required, if it does not save her time, a woman will not deem the stove more efficient or a value added to her life. Any new energy source and any technology used has to fulfil an obvious need as

perceived by the user, either in time saving, reduction of a health hazard or improved sanitary conditions.

50. Ignorance of the dynamics of the power structures in the household, area or country can often result in rural energy schemes failing from the start. For example, afforestation on common land, although well-intentioned, has sometimes only eliminated a safety net for the very poor who gather wood there. The same holds true for some schemes for the utilization of agricultural residues. In some cases also, programmes launched to create income-generating activities for women have resulted in women doing all the additional work but not gaining control of the resulting income. Energy supply for micro enterprises or cottage industries such as milling, beer-making, food-making, flower and vegetable cultivation is important and benefits women, especially if accompanied by policies for supporting transportation infrastructures to gain access to local markets and providing some credit mechanism targeted for women. More information on the functioning of existing micro enterprises is needed.

51. Men may perceive themselves as losers in such development efforts, at least at the beginning. There is, however, a general feeling that, despite initial resistance, when the benefits become obvious, the men in the community whole-heartedly support energy programmes targeted at women. This may be illustrated by an example from a project in West Asia to introduce biogas digesters into a very poor village. Improved sanitary conditions inside and outside the home were perceived by the men as an added benefit. In many countries the involvement and approval of the men may be needed if projects targeted at women are to succeed.

52. The influence of socio-economic level on the type of energy used is in some cases not so great as assumed in the past. For example, in a community in India, cow dung and fuelwood were used for cooking by all levels of society because this was considered more economical than the switch to more conventional fuels and modern technologies. An increase in surplus cash income for rural populations is, however, a necessary (but not sufficient) condition for the switch to more conventional fuels and modern technologies.

VI. Environmental Aspects

53. Environmental aspects of the supply and use of rural energy can be looked at from two points of view; the first relates to the specific effects on the local environment and the second to the intercountry and global dimensions. On the supply side, environmental concerns relate to deforestation caused in some cases by a rapidly growing population, which needs to add to agricultural output through the clearing of additional land and to provide more fuelwood. Generalizations are not possible because available studies and research deal with specific areas and time periods and quite often lead to inconclusive or contradictory results. Consideration of the relevant environmental costs of conventional energy would generally promote the development of new and renewable sources.

54. Often neglected but requiring much closer attention are environmental effects on the lives of rural people, particularly in the household sector. Women as the main users of energy in the household are the main victims of health hazards such as

smoke and unsanitary conditions. Biogas digesters are a promising example of an environmentally benign energy source for cooking; they can provide fertilizer for increased agricultural production, while reducing diseases caused by organic wastes.

55. Similarly, solar thermal collectors can supply energy in the form of heat or mechanical power while windmills and photovoltaic systems can supply electricity to rural areas. The quality of life in these areas could be improved, household drudgery, particularly for women, could be reduced and higher incomes could be generated through agro-industries and related activities.

56. From a global perspective, there is an interest in promoting more environmentally benign energy technologies in the developing countries, in particular in areas having large rural populations. But these environmental concerns should not detract from efforts to increase energy supplies in rural areas. Economic and social advances in rural areas perhaps lead to more efficient utilization of energy resources, and a shift from traditional to conventional and renewable sources of energy - or rather to a fuel mix that is relatively benign for the environment.

VII. Energy Investments and Pricing

57. Investments in programmes and projects in new and renewable sources of energy had been scaled down even before the collapse in oil prices in the mid-1980s for a variety of reasons, including the apparent high cost of such investments, unduly high expectations of major technological breakthroughs and inadequate commitment on the part of Governments for the development of new and renewable sources of energy.

58. The economic condition of developing countries, especially in Africa and Latin America, deteriorated during the 1980s owing to a variety of factors, including foreign indebtedness and adverse terms of trade. Economic readjustment in many developing countries resulted in lower investments in social programmes with particularly adverse consequences for the poor, especially in rural areas.

59. Lower energy prices led to much lower investments by transnational oil corporations, particularly in energy-deficient developing countries at a time when their energy consumption had resumed an upward path. A resumption of economic growth during the 1990s would result in considerable increases in energy consumption in those countries. The prospect of higher oil prices during the decade would once again result in serious problems for the energy-deficient developing countries, particularly in rural areas, with additional pressure on limited biomass resources, such as fuelwood.

60. Developing countries are expected to experience higher rates of economic growth, industrialization and urbanization. Energy demand in those countries is expected to grow accordingly, with energy conservation and efficiency offering the prospect of partial relief only. This is especially the case with electricity, which requires heavy investments at a time when both multilateral and bilateral financial sources are scaling down their activities.

61. Although as a matter of policy the World Bank continues to support efforts to develop applications of new and renewable sources of energy, its overall involvement, except in the case of fuelwood, has tapered off. This trend mirrors

similar policies in other international financial agencies and bilateral co-operation activities in this area.

62. In the early 1980s, when interest in new and renewable sources of energy was high, developed countries devoted much research and development to these resources as part of their national effort and in relation to bilateral and multilateral assistance programmes.

63. Similarly, a number of private corporations also initiated research and development programmes. Since then, both public and private research and development activities have been scaled down. In many developing countries, research and development programmes, including the establishment of several institutes and research centres, have been undertaken with national financing and/or outside assistance. In most cases, however, projects have not moved beyond the demonstration stage.

64. There have been some notable investments and developments in the field of new and renewable sources of energy – for example, in the rural areas of China and India. In China, government policy that encouraged investment in certain technologies in rural areas has led to widespread application of such technologies, which have played a significant role in helping meet the energy needs of rural areas.

65. In India, a total of 1.2 million biogas plants have been set up, with an estimated saving of 4.24 million tons of firewood equivalent, valued at $US 100 million a year. In addition, the production of 20.4 million tons of enriched manure a year is valued at more than $US 100 million. As a result, total investment in biogas plants is paid back over a period of 2 1/2 years. Similarly, over 6.3 million improved stoves have resulted in a saving of four million tons of firewood equivalent a year, with a monetary benefit of $US 95 million.

66. New environmental concerns, especially climate warming and the contribution of carbon dioxide from fossil fuels, have led to increased interest in the energy situation and prospects of developing countries, including rural areas. This interest is related to deforestation trends and their impact on both the local and the global environment. As a result, several developed countries have expressed interest in increasing their financial assistance for energy development in developing countries, including new and renewable sources of energy in rural areas.

67. A major problem continues to be the urban bias of both national and outside investment sources. This issue is related to political development efforts in rural areas of developing countries, which, with a few exceptions, have not yet led to equitable distribution of income and economic development efforts in those areas. In many cases, conventional energy sources in developed and developing countries have been subsidized for long periods of time. The expansion of rural energy supplies would also require subsidies especially with regard to new energy technologies. However, as an overall policy, end-users would eventually have to finance investments through competitive prices. In some cases, a nominal price at least, would have to be charged as an incentive to users to maintain energy facilities properly.

68. A number of new examples of financing facilities such as revolving funds and energy banking have been introduced to enhance energy investment in rural areas. In India, the application of the concept of energy banking could facilitate the introduction of electricity from wind and photovoltaic farms into existing electricity systems.

69. Investments for the supply and use of rural energy are of course influenced by the nature of the facilities, which are isolated and small, and by the socio-economic conditions of the country concerned, including organizational structures in rural areas such as co-operatives and individual ownership of land. The private sector has sometimes participated successfully in energy investments for rural areas.

VIII. Proposals for Further Action

70. For each theme discussed, the following proposals for action were agreed upon:
    (a) Energy Supply and Demand
       (i) National and regional assessments of available resources of new and renewable energy should be encouraged; they should be carried out using available data, information and knowledge;
       (ii) Development should continue with the aim of providing improved, common and standardized methodologies for surveys on resources, supplies and use of new and renewable sources of energy in rural areas, with emphasis on evaluation of their accuracy in order to provide a better base for planning and the formulation of policies;
       (iii) Multilateral and bilateral assistance agencies should expand their programmes to assist developing countries in carrying out surveys of energy resources and demand and supply prospects with particular reference to rural areas;
       (iv) Inventories should be made of existing natural forests. There is a need to develop management systems and implementation programmes for natural and artificially regenerated forests for sustained yield with the involvement of the local population, and to assess the possible production of these forests; to this end, efforts should be made to integrate woody vegetation into farming for the stabilization of farming systems and for the production of wood and other forest products, parallel with agricultural production;
       (v) Evaluations should be carried out on the availability, distribution and techno-economic feasibility of expanded and more efficient use of agricultural residues for rural energy supplies and related applications, bearing in mind competition with other uses of fertilizers.
    (b) Technological options
       (i) Ways and means should be examined for the transfer to developing countries of technologies developed largely in developed countries and for their application in order to promote national self-reliance and long-term capabilities. Such technologies include:
          a. Small hydro plants for shaft power and electricity generation;
          b. Wind pumps for water lifting;
          c. Biogas plants for cooking and lighting;
          d. Photovoltaic units for lighting and refrigeration;
          e. Solar thermal energy;
          f. Improved stoves;
       (ii) Research and development centres on new and renewable sources of energy in developing countries should be strengthened and further action

should be taken by the United Nations Committee on the Development and Utilization of New and Renewable Sources of Energy to promote the networking of centres on priority technologies at the regional and subregional levels;

(iii) Local manufacturing industries should be promoted to ensure increased utilization of new and renewable energy resources and, in the process, develop local know-how;

(iv) National and regional organizations should assess the availability and distribution of manufacturing industries, resources and technological capabilities for the increased application of such technologies in rural areas. Relevant manufacturing standards and specifications should be developed;

(c) Social, cultural and political aspects

(i) Social, cultural and political aspects of energy development and use with particular reference to the role of women in integrated rural development in developing countries deserve much closer attention and analysis;

(ii) Efforts should be made to channel energy to household activities that generate income;

(iii) An evaluation of the impact of energy in alleviating household and rural drudgery should be undertaken;

(iv) Guidelines should be developed for updating local data through rapid rural appraisals;

(d) Environmental aspects

(i) Assessment should be made of the environmental impact of new and renewable sources of energy, including local, national and global effects with projections incorporating scenarios of their expanded development and utilization;

(ii) When the environmental impact of energy in rural areas is evaluated, note should be taken of the competition and conflict between alternative uses of land; for example, for developing urban conglomerates, for roads and for forestry or agriculture including the competing uses of biomass for industries;

(iii) Environmental costs should be incorporated in the assessment of energy project proposals;

(e) Energy investments and pricing

(i) Information should be exchanged on financial and price incentives and their effects on investments for the development and utilization of new and renewable sources of energy, including research and development, with particular reference to rural areas. Factors having a bearing on national and outside sources of financing in this field should be included;

(ii) New and renewable sources of energy should be incorporated into existing investment, pricing policies and schemes for conventional commercial sources of energy in order to provide them with an opportunity for fair competition;

(iii) When investment analyses for new and renewable sources of energy projects and programmes are undertaken, it must be realized that the development stage is four times as expensive as the scientific discovery stage. More resources should thus be allocated to the development stage;

(iv) Countries should encourage the development of credit and marketing systems specially designed to promote the use of promising technologies;

(v) A balanced system for taxation and customs policies should be developed to correct the wide variations that currently exist for different imported items in the form of finished goods; for example, diesel generators and material for solar water heaters.

71. The following overall suggestions were agreed upon:

(a) Strategies, plans and policies in developing countries should incorporate new and renewable sources of energy as an integral part of overall energy in the context of rural development which, in turn, should be viewed as part of national development. At the same time, rural energy policies and plans should form part of national energy plans which should, in turn, be viewed as an integral part of national development strategies;

(b) Action should be taken to promote the establishment or strengthening of extension programmes for education, generation of awareness, popularization and dissemination of energy technologies in rural areas;

(c) Action should be taken to promote the exchange and enhance the flow of information on energy technologies and related matters, considering the interdisciplinary nature of energy development. In particular, national, regional and international information networks and new and renewable sources of energy for rural areas should be strengthened. In this context, those active in the field are urged to publish or make available information on their experiences;

(d) More effort should be directed towards establishing or strengthening national institutions for policy formulation, planning and implementation of energy development strategies including those for rural areas. This should include training of personnel in various areas of expertise including assessment of energy demand and supply, development, adaptation and transfer as well as identification of appropriate and mature technologies for renewable sources of energy; and construction, installation, repair and maintenance of rural energy technologies. The training of trainers should be emphasized;

(e) Intended users of energy technologies in rural areas should actively participate in the planning, design and implementation of programmes and projects in order to enhance the prospects for success in the introduction and widespread application of such technologies;

(f) Bilateral, regional and international co-operation in new and renewable sources of energy should be promoted through exchange of information and transfer and adaptation of technologies.

NOTES

1. *Report of the United Nations Conference on New and Renewable Sources of Energy, Nairobi, 10-21 August 1981* (United Nations publication, Sales No. E.81.I.24), chap. I, sect. A.
2. *Ibid.*, chap. I, sect. A, para. 26.
3. *Official Records of the General Assembly, Forty-third Session, Supplement No. 36* (A/43/36), annex, resolution 1 (IV).
4. A list of the technical papers presented is available in the files of the United Nations Secretariat.
5. See the report of the Secretary-General on the implementation of resolution 2 (III) of the Committee on the Development and Utilization of New and Renewable Sources of Energy at its third session (A/AC.218/15).

List of Contributors

Michael W. Bassey
Senior Program Officer,
Post Production Systems
International Development Research Centre
(IDRC), P O Box 11007, CD Annex
Dakar, Senegal

M.R. Bhagavan (Co-Chairman of the
Stockholm Meeting)
Head of Section, Natural Sciences,
Technology and Industrialization
Swedish Agency for Research Cooperation
with Developing Countries (SAREC)
P O Box 16140, S-10323, Stockholm

Gustavo Best
Senior Officer, Energy and Environment
Programme
Food and Agriculture Organization of the
United Nations

Maheshwar Dayal
Former Secretary
Department of Non-Conventional Energy
Sources
Government of India, New Delhi

John Diphaha
Head, Botswana Technology Centre (BTC)
Private Bag 0082
Gaborone, Botswana

Hassan Wardi Hassan
Head, Solar Energy Department
Energy Research Council
Khartoum, Sudan

Anhar Hegazi
Director, Technical Affairs
New and Renewable Sources of Energy
Authority
Ministry of Electricity and Energy
Abbasia, 19 Aden Street, El Mohandens
Cairo, Egypt

Stephen Karekezi
African Energy Policy Research Network
(AFREPREN)
P O Box 30979
Nairobi, Kenya

Manuel Martinez
Senior Researcher, Laboratorio de Energía
Solar
Universidad Nacional Autonoma de Mexico
Aparthado Postal No. 34
62580 Temixco, Morelos, Mexico

J. G. M. Massaquoi
Head, Department of Mechanical
Engineering
Fourah Bay College
Freetown, Sierra Leone

Dominic J. Mbewe
Director, Department of Energy
Ministry of Power, Transportation and
Communication
P O Box 50065
Lusaka, Zambia

Dennis Minott
Director, Energy Department
Enerplan Ltd.,
Kingston, Jamaica

Eugenie V. Nadezhdin
Director, State Committee on Science and
Technology of the USSR
Gorky Street 11
Moscow, USSR

Qui Da Xiong
Professor
ITESA/INET
Tsinghua University
P O Box 1021
Beijing, China

Mahmoud A. Saleh
Regional Adviser in Energy
United Nations Economic and Social
Commission for Westerm Asia

B. P. Sepalage
Chief Engineer, Alternative Energy
Development
Ceylon Electricity Board
50 Sir Chittampalam A
Colombo 2, Sri Lanka

C. V. Seshadri
Director, Energy Division
Shri A. M. M. Murugappa Chettiar
Research Centre
Tharamani
Madras 600 113, India

Ernesto N. Terrado
Industry and Energy Department
The World Bank
Washington D.C

Irene Tinker
Professor, Department of City and Regional
Planning, 228 Wurster Hall
University of California
Berkeley, CA 94720, USA

251

List of Other Participants at the Stockholm Meeting, 22–26 January 1990

Participants from Sweden

Bengt Säve-Söderbergh
Under-Secretary of State, Ministry of
Foreign Affairs
Government of Sweden
P O Box 16121
S-103 23 Stockholm

Bo Bengtsson
Director General, Swedish Agency for
Research Cooperation with Developing
Countries (SAREC)
P O Box 16140
S-103 23 Stockholm

Jöran Fries
Professor, International Rural Development
Centre
Swedish University of Agricultural Sciences
P O Box 7005
Uppsala 750 07

Carl-Johan Groth
Head, Multilateral Department
Ministry of Foreign Affairs
P O Box 16121
S-103 23 Stockholm

Anders Hagwall
Head, Energy Section
Swedish International Development
Authority (SIDA)
S-105 25 Stockholm

Lars Kristoferson
Vice Executive Director,
Stockholm Environment Institute (SEI)
P O Box 2142
S-103 14 Stockholm

Marianne Lindström
Conference Secretary, Swedish Agency for
Research Cooperation with Developing
Countries (SAREC)
P O Box 16140
S-103 23 Stockholm

Klas Markensten
Director, Agricultural Division
Swedish International Development
Authority (SIDA)
S-105 25 Stockholm

Maria Nyström
Lund Centre for Habitat Studies,
School of Architecture
Lund University
Solvegatan 24
S-22100 Lund

Ulf Svidén
Head, International Division
Ministry of Environment and Energy
S-103 33 Stockholm

Participants from the United Nations System

Department of International Economic and Social Affairs of the United Nations Secretariat

Göran Ohlin (Representative of the
Secretary-General),
Assistant Secretary-General
Office for Development Research and Policy
Analysis

Shem Arungu Olende (Rapporteur)
Chief
New and Renewable Sources of Energy
Section
Energy and Resources Branch

Office for Development Research and Policy Analysis
Elizabeth Barsk-Rundquist (Technical Secretary)
Associate Economic Affairs Officer
New and Renewable Sources of Energy Section
Energy and Resources Branch
Office for Development Research and Policy Analysis

Charles Constantinou (Co-Chairman of the Stockholm Meeting)
Chief
Energy and Resources Branch
Office for Development Research and Policy Analysis

Centre for Science and Technology for Development of the United Nations Secretariat
Erazm M. Omeljanovsky
Deputy Director

United Nations Centre for Human Settlements (Habitat)
Mario Piche
Chief
Building and Infrastructure Technology Section
Research and Development Division

Economic and Social Commission for Asia and the Pacific (ESCAP)
Gerard Saunier
Senior Adviser

United Nations University (UNU) and Centre for Science and Technology for Development of the United Nations Secretariat
Walter Shearer
Senior Programme Officer
Centre for Science and Technology for Development

UNITAR/ UNDP Centre on Small Energy Resources
Antonio Naviglio
Director

United Nations Educational, Scientific and Cultural Organization (UNESCO)
Boris Berkovski
Director
Energy Programme

World Meteorological Organization (WMO)
L. Olsson
Chief
World Climate Application Programme

United Nations Industrial Development Organization (UNIDO)
Keiki Fujita
Director
Industrial Technology Promotion Division

Index